Scotland After Enlightenment

Image and Tradition in Modern Scottish Culture

Craig Beveridge

and

Ronald Turnbull

Polygon
Edinburgh

©   Craig Beveridge and Ronald Turnbull 1997
First Published by Polygon
22 George Square
Edinburgh EH8 9LF

Printed and bound in Great Britain
by Cromwell Press, Broughton Gifford, Melksham, Wiltshire

ISBN   0 7486 6223 5

Contents

Series Preface

Scotland's history is often presented as punctuated by disasters which overwhelm the nation, break its continuity and produce a fragmented culture. Through the 1980s such conceptions have been challenged by a wide range of critical and analytical works that have shown just how profound the tradition of Scottish culture has been, and how dymanic the debates within it have remained – even in those periods (like the period after 1830) which cultural history usually looks upon as blanks in the nation's achievement.

Too often, in the past, particular ways of seeing Scottish culture came to dominate simply because they went unchallenged – worse, unexamined. The vitality of a culture should be measured by the intensity of debate which it generates about its past, and about its future role in the world, rather than by the security of the ideas on which it rests. It has been one of the signs of the health of Scottish culture in the late 1980s and 1990s that there has been such a vigorous engagement with definitions of the nation. In place of a few standard conceptions of Scotland's identity that had often, in the past, been tokens of thought about the country's culture, a series of debates have been opened up which have led to the re-examination both of the Scottish past and of Scotland's relationship to other cultures.

Determinations was launched in 1988 with Craig Beveridge and Ronald Turnbull's *The Eclipse of Scottish Culture*. We hope that many of the subsequent books in this series have helped bring Scottish cultural history back into focus, and that the series has made its own contribution to the enormous creative achievement of Scottish writing, both creative and analytic, of the past fifteen years. And we trust that a culture which has the confidence to challenge itself about its own identity is a culture which has already moved a long way towards self-determination.

Cairns Craig, General Editor, Determinations

1

Introduction:
Images and Traditions

The essays presented here address a number of issues in history, cultural analysis and philosophy. They are all primarily concerned with Scottish culture, in a broad sense: with interpretations of Scottish history and cultural development, and with contributions by Scottish thinkers to theoretical debate.

In much discussion of Scottish history and culture there operates an assumption (which is no less effective for being seldom stated) that there is a privileged position or vantage point from which uniquely rational and objective observers survey human affairs in a way which is neutral as to ideological and theoretical disputes. Just as sociology can be projected as occupying this Higher Plane, displaying a different order of rational understanding from the traditions which are viewed as merely the subject of its enquiry, so the implicit assumption of many historians is that their discipline affords a similarly elevated view. *They* have objective historical 'explanations' which encompass the whole. *Others* have myths and traditions which – the historians would no doubt agree with David McCrone – are 'meaningful though partial interpretations of social reality and social change'.[1]

In fact of course, the histories considered in the following chapters are constructed, consciously or otherwise, from a particular point of view and for particular purposes. The points of view are varied (though in some respects not very). Among them may be a shocked Twentieth-Century Social Democrat; an Empirical Watcher of the Shipyards; a Post-Marxist Nationalist: by their fruits ye shall know them. None need delude themselves that they stand, at the last, for anything but another tradition. The point was made with some eloquence many years ago by the French historian Lucien Febvre:

> History in the last resort meets the same need as tradition, whether the need is conscious or no. History is a way of organising the past so that it does not weigh too heavily on the shoulders of men . . . It explains facts and so, in order to

explain them, it arranges them in series to which it does not attach equal importance. For history has no choice in the matter, it systematically gathers in, classifies and assembles past facts in accordance with its present needs. It consults death in accordance with the needs of life.[2]

In the second essay we analyse what turns out to be a remarkably uniform set of images of Scotland's recent past which is offered, in purportedly 'general' histories, by leading historians writing for non-specialist readers. The history of modern Scotland, to summarise these representations in vocabulary prominent in such texts themselves, is essentially a story of grimness, poverty, deprivation, darkness, repression, even brutalisation. This discourse, we argue, involves three characteristic reductions. In the first place, attention is centred in these texts on the experience of the poor in industrial towns and cities; other Scottish experience is treated as atypical, and ultimately – the suggestion seems to be – not part of the significant, the 'real' history of the nation. Secondly, and within this first reductive movement, the experience of the industrial working class is approached almost exclusively through such indicators as statistics on housing, health, poverty, and unemployment. The poor are thus seen as passive victims of a cultural/socio-economic system, and little or no attempt is made to depict the different ways in which, as subjects, they responded to their predicament, developed their own cultural expression, and sought fulfilling forms of leisure and recreation. (This is not to overlook the fact that such texts admit, or even stress, widespread flight into drink and primitive forms of religious and political enthusiasm – but this confirms rather than contradicts our thesis.) Thirdly – in what, after all, are presented as, and no doubt taken in good faith by most readers as being, general histories of the nation, and not simply economic or social histories, or histories of the working class – cultural endeavour and achievement are largely ignored, or, in more or less subtle ways, as we indicate, marginalised and sidelined.

Where the only significant facts of a national history are taken to be statistics on the housing conditions, health, financial circumstances etc. of the industrial working class – facts sometimes presented, incidentally, in ways we find scarcely credible, as being of unique, unparalleled awfulness – it is hardly surprising that within the discourse the central question of modern Scottish history should then be, as one naive reviewer quoted on a Smout blurb says, 'why?' How was such failure possible? What tragic flaws in Scottish culture, or what mark of Cain on the Scottish psyche, prevented Scotland achieving minimal levels of civilised life for its inhabitants, and inspired instead a history of misery, of material and spiritual deprivation? It is not hard to see at this point how our standard historiography (whatever the private intentions of the historians concerned) feeds directly into wider political and ideological conflict, or how it forms part, within this wider milieu, of the 'symbolic domination' and 'symbolic violence' (in Bourdieu's terminology) to which Scotland is subjected.

Fortunately, it is now possible to construct more adequate accounts of modern Scotland than the highly selective representation which is conveyed by the standard general histories. As far as the experience of the industrial urban populations is concerned, an important corrective to the dominant images is provided by accounts given in memoirs and oral history collections by those whose history – after all – this is. Here we can see that, in spite of the crude caricatures mongered by historians, 'ordinary' Scottish people, even if exposed to indigence, ill health and hardship, also engaged in recreational activities and pursued various forms of cultural interests. The topic is developed in the third essay. Here, let us mention just one example of such evidence, that offered by R. D. Laing in his autobiography. It might be objected that Laing's case is not 'typical' or 'representative'. This is certainly true at least to the extent that his family were not impoverished slum dwellers. His father was an electrical engineer employed by Glasgow Corporation, and the family were, in sociological terms, upper-working or lower-middle-class. But Laing's Glasgow childhood in the 1930s must have been of a kind shared by many thousands of other Scottish children of the time. His account of his school and family life does not paint over the warts, but it is in general positive and appreciative. Here is an extract:

> I would be back home at four-thirty unless it was an after-noon at the playing field, when it would be later. Then out for a music lesson or out to play. Back by six for tea when my father would have come home, practise before it was too late for the neighbours, maybe a bit of radio, 'The Brains Trust'. . . , 'Henry Hall's Guest Night', Charlie Kunz and Chopin; and then homework, and then bath, bed, prayers and sleep.[3]

If, from some present-day perspectives, this may well appear a mono-chrome and unduly earnest childhood milieu, it is very far from being a world of cultural and spiritual deprivation. However, – to insist – it is a world of experience of 'ordinary' Scottish people which, like many others, is rarely if ever glimpsed in the standard histories, because it does not accord with their governing themes of immiseration and *Kulturlosigkeit*.

As far as the wider cultural arena is concerned, an expanding numb-er of valuable works on the arts, music, the history of ideas, and so on, challenge the judgments routinely offered in the prominent general histories concerning the processes, and interest and value of cultural achievement in the modern and contemporary period. The third essay also considers Scottish art, architecture, design and townscaping – aspects of Scottish life and cultural activity largely passed over by the social historians – and emphasises that, contrary to certain common misconceptions, Scottish middle class interest in and support for artistic endeavour has been significant.

Our fourth chapter revisits a topic in Scottish history which has been central in recent cultural controversy: Jacobitism. The Jacobite movement has often been dismissed by historians as an 'irrelevant', or anachronistic, or even semi-farcical phenomenon; and cultural theorists, especially of the anti-tartanry and 'Scotch Myths' school, have stressed the disastrous influence of the cause and its symbols on later Scottish culture and politics, portraying them as vehicles of escapist sentimentalism, or as constituting a 'deformed' and 'deviant' element of national culture which has undermined 'real' and respectable forms of nationalism. It is time, we want to suggest, to take a more sympathetic view. Drawing on recent, revisionist work in history and cultural analysis, we offer a critique of some of the entrenched positions, and argue that a very different interpretation of Jacobitism and its role in Scottish history and culture can be constructed.

The preponderance, in typical analyses of Jacobitism, of highly negative and censorious assessments is part of a wider phenomenon in Scottish historiography and cultural theory which achieves its apotheosis in historians' treatment of Scottish calvinism. In Chapter 5 we consider the old conundrum which such constructions pose: how could the eighteenth-century Enlightenment have occurred in a backward and bleakly presbyterian land such as Scotland? Here we present a summary of a recent important work which overturns conventional assumptions in this area, and provides a fresh perspective on the intellectual life of the pre-Enlightenment period, which dominant historiography has long caricatured and dismissed as a dark, even barbarous age.

In what way or ways could Scottish history be important for contemporary self-definition? Are Scottish traditions relevant to current ideological movements? These are the questions we approach in the later chapters of the book.

In 'History and Identity' we consider two studies which postulate a 'subversion' of the Scottish past in the consolidation of the Anglo-Scottish union. One, which belongs to what can broadly be called a 'liberal' tradition of historiography, derived from aspects of Enlightenment thought, leads us to the view that this past is unusable, that is, devoid of ideological and intellectual relevance to later history. The other account, written from a radically distinct position, has very different implications. This is one of the most remarkable and important contributions to Scottish historiography to have appeared for many years. Astonishingly, it seems to have been entirely ignored (or overlooked) by the academics and journalists who determine the agenda of cultural debate in Scotland.

Next, in Chapter 7, we turn to general theory, and by means of a discussion of the latest work of Alasdair MacIntyre offer an expansion of the argument, first developed by George Davie, that there is a distinctive movement of Scottish thought in the twentieth century, which is deeply rooted in a calvinist or augustinian anti-modernist outlook. This anti-modernism, as we try to show, is of outstanding relevance to our contemporary predicaments.

Chapter 8 is concerned with education. Here once more MacIntyrean theory is centre-stage: we discuss the affinities between MacIntyre's views and those of John Anderson and George Davie, and offer an account of MacIntyre's position, which – whether or not the reader agrees with its central theses and proposals – must surely be considered one of the most insightful, radical and stimulating contributions to educational thinking to have appeared in recent decades. MacIntyre's work here is of exceptional additional interest in the context of the present volume in highlighting the discourse of 'encyclopedism', and its canonical formulation, the *Encyclopedia Britannica*, that remarkable product of nineteenth-century Scotland, whose ninth edition (1875–1889), which included such contributors as Clerk Maxwell, Robertson Smith and J. G. Frazer, reflects what MacIntyre describes as the second Scottish Enlightenment.

In the final essay we discuss aspects of two recent works about Scotland by Scottish writers: Colin Kirkwood's *Vulgar Eloquence*, and David McCrone's *Understanding Scotland*. These exemplify two prestigious modes of modernist discourse, therapism, and sociology, respectively. Our objective is not to offer a comprehensive review of the texts, but rather to indicate what, from a perspective sympathetic to the augustinian anti-modernism described in previous chapters, appear to be some of the inadequacies and limitations of these discourses.[4]

A volume which covers so many different topics inevitably raises, if only by implication, a further important cultural issue, concerning specialisation and generalism, which has often been at the heart of Scottish cultural debate. For the validity of such a text will be challenged by those who consider that the only serious and worthwhile forms of intellectual debate are those conducted by and among specialists. This and related questions are taken up in some of the essays, but it may be useful to offer a brief preliminary response here. We should note, firstly, that the objection cannot even be made without self-contradiction. For to deny the validity of a discourse which transcends the discourses of particular specialisms already involves a commitment to the view that at least one specialism – transcendent proposition (the denial) is valid. Secondly – to turn to substantive issues – the objection carries a significant implication which, in our opinion, ought to be resisted. The implication is that there is no possible way of systematising or making coherent our views on, for instance, ethics, politics, psychology, education. These are to occupy, so to speak, separate compartments of the mind; we are thus condemned, on this account, to a radical form of personal incoherence. Thirdly, the specialist case reveals a striking complacency about the trend in our society towards an ever more pronounced cultural segregation, of the professional intelligentsia from the rest – who thus seem to be judged fit only for such cultural products as television and journalism.

The Scottish tradition of democratic intellectualism, as we understand it, articulated a belief in the possibility, and the necessity, of communication between the world of learning and a wider reading and thinking public; a belief that philosophy, in a general sense, or the discussion of matters of fundamental human import, cannot, except at great cultural cost, be the preserve of an elite whose members commune only with themselves. (As we shall see, this position has recently been forcefully re-stated in MacIntyre's critique of the contemporary academic order.) The construction and development of forms and forums of debate in the spirit of this tradition is an urgent cultural task.

2

'A World of Deprivation':
Images from the Historians

What impression of Scottish 'civilisation' in the modern age do we get from the most popular general histories of the country? What images are projected as representing modern Scotland's story? And of the wide range of social experience involved, what summation do these works provide? This essay examines the general-history texts most commonly found on the shelves of our bookshops and libraries in an effort to answer these questions.

Even the most cursory examination indicates an almost morbid fascination with urban squalor. The perceived centrality of the history of urban life has not produced the kind of rounded accounts which have been provided by the historians of New York, Chicago, Berlin, or Paris. An almost obsessive concern with poverty, degradation and the constant rehearsal of statistical indicators demonstrating them, largely obscures individual and civic responses to the commercial, technological, religious and socio-political change demanded of Scottish city dwellers since the mid-nineteenth century.

The portrayal of Scottish urban history in T. C. Smout's influential *Century of the Scottish People* is illustrative. His account is developed in a twenty-five page chapter on 'the tenemented city'.[1] This opens with a single page acknowledging architectural achievement over the period. There is no development of the theme. No time spent on what by any standards was a remarkable expression of confidence and style in Victorian and Edwardian Glasgow; on the slow but definite development of Edinburgh's potential as a city, expressing two eras in Scottish social and cultural history, and as an (at least episodic) focus for international culture; on the ambition and pride of smaller burghs in the sandstone Scottish-baronial civic buildings which are again 'emerging' to attention through contemporary restoration programs. The page ends with a quotation from Simone de Beauvoir on the impression she and Sartre gained on a visit in the late 1940s: 'Our hearts sank at the grimness of the towns.'[2] The impression of a few days' holiday (perhaps it was raining) functions to kill stone dead the massive achievements of how many architects, engineers, artists, stonemasons and craftsmen over a hundred years.

Most of the rest of this chapter is devoted to what Smout calls 'the true grimness of the Scottish town'. The environment of working class communities should clearly have a major place in a general history of Scotland since 1830. But the nature of Smout's portrayal of life in 'the tall, grim, blackened tenement blocks' sets the tone, in its impersonal statistical and narrowly materialist approach, for the treatment of Scottish working class life throughout his history. The totality of ordinary life in the period he covers is sharded into fragments which produce no sense of integrated social experience, and constantly betray the historian's distaste. The suggestion seems to be that the poor housing was accepted through a lack of motivation or awareness that anything better could be aspired to. (Later an entire chapter on drink, temperance and recreation will imply a mindless flight from these social problems into one form of excess or its repressive converse).

The failure of the Scots to achieve (and perhaps appreciate) reasonably civilised standards is established by drawing a number of statistical comparisons: 'in 1911 when half the Scots lived in one- or two-roomed houses, the proportion in England and Wales was 7 per cent; in 1951, when a quarter lived in such houses in Scotland, the proportion in the south was 2.6%. . . As late as 1951, again, 15.5% of Scots were still overcrowded at more than two to a room, compared to only 2.1% of English people.'[3]

The last sentence in this quotation which appears near the beginning of the chapter, is actually repeated close to the end, and followed by the observation that 'subsidies worth £80m paid between 1919 and 1952 had not removed the Anglo-Scottish differential in overcrowding.'[4]

There is, in fact, considerably more than an implication that the Scots just didn't appreciate the value of better (English) housing standards and were more than dilatory in 'catching up' (even when 'subsidised'). Explanations for the denser high-tenement housing related to Scottish historical experience or to French influence are dismissed in a sentence. It is suggested that those living 'in a cold dark country' saved a few bawbees in this way. But probably it was sheer lack of appreciation of standards, low expectations and the absence of an attitude of self-help:

> Since the first world war, the Scots do seem to have spent less on housing than the English, and a general survey of the 19th century suggests that the Scots did not put a high premium on trying to secure good housing for themselves. Of course, if a population becomes accustomed to living in small, poor-quality homes . . . it may seem a disproportionate sacrifice

of other goods to spend more on larger homes — though this does not explain why others have been more willing than the Scots to improve their housing expectations from low levels.[5]

Although there is acknowledgment of some Scottish municipal developments and the work of the medical officers of health in Glasgow and Edinburgh, the deleterious contrasts with England predominate. By the 1890s in public health 'Scotland had fallen a long way behind England'. In the 1900s 'overcrowding remained between five and ten times as great in Glasgow as in corresponding English cities'.

The rise of modernising political movements seeking reform is associated with English inspiration. The ILP campaign for good housing 'seems to have been based on an idea of an immigrant English engineer, John Burgess.'[6] The inspiration behind better inter-war housing was related to 'the garden suburbs proposed by Ebeneezer Howard in England in 1898, though the Scottish model had neither proper gardens nor separate front doors.'[7]

At one point Smout quotes the London *Builder* journal of 1861 expressing the view that every visitor to Edinburgh would carry away two impressions: 'a sense of its extraordinary beauty and a horror of its unspeakable filth'.[8] In his treatment of this entire subject, Smout concentrates almost exclusively on the 'unspeakable filth'. There is no attempt to consider what the witnesses he most relies on were about, what their perspective and sensibilities were, what purpose they had in visiting Scotland (for they are very often visitors and almost always observers 'looking in'). No one would wish to be an apologist for poverty, but here there is no attempt to come to terms with the subjectivity of those who experienced these material conditions.

This treatment leads Smout to some astonishingly intemperate statements. Of the earlier period he asserts,

> It must never be forgotten that no other country had housing problems on the scale which Victorian middle-class neglect and self-interest had handed on to twentieth-century Scotland.[9]

Is this really sustainable? How were things at the same period in Naples and Valparaiso and the parts of Dickensian London most comparable with the areas of Scottish urban society on which Smout focuses? What had the American middle class done for those in the slums of tenemented high-rise Chicago in the 1880s? *No* other country?

And of the modern era:

> The Scottish city that we know today with its glass and concrete office blocks, its ring roads, its middle-class suburbs, and its segregated and ill-served council estates of dirty

harled houses and crumbling high-rise blocks . . . sprawls
over bleak and windy wastes . . . It is often ugly, boring and
crime-ridden . . .[10]

In a single sentence, this perspective is extended to cover all
habitations of the ordinary Scots in the period he covers:

The decaying black-houses of the Hebrides, the damp, earth-
floored cottages on a lowland estate, and the open sewers
between the rows of one-roomed brick houses in the rural
coalfields were as characteristic of Scottish working-class
homes as the single-end in the Gorbals.[11]

It is difficult to describe this perspective exactly. It is reminiscent
of nothing so much as the accounts of early English travellers in the
Scotland of the seventeenth and eighteenth centuries. It betrays a particular, defensively hostile subjectivity in the writer, towards a society
in which he feels alien, perhaps superior, but certainly unsympathetic.
There seem also elements of middle class guilt — perhaps why elements of Scottish bourgeois and lower-middle class achievement receive
scant attention. In any case, the result is a crude and undifferentiated
treatment of the society of which he writes.

Though one can take issue with Smout for the imbalance of the
images he presents, it must be acknowledged that he does seek to
focus his work on the Scottish people. William Ferguson[12] presents
a kind of converse perspective which centres on British history but is
expressed, as it were, through facts and events which occur in Scotland.
It is difficult to form any clear picture of the Scots, Highland or Lowland, upper or working class, protestant, catholic or whatever from
a narrative borne along on broad sketches of economic, political or
religious 'movements', with episodic reference to the beliefs or character of individual figures. Occasional passages in which a sense of
the lived experience of particular groups emerge, stand out as excep-
tions.[13] More typically, to take one passage at random, his account
of the period before the First World War presents us with a series of
discrete pieces of information about different social groups: the 'technical' abolition of crofting and setting up of the land court; the young
James Maxton's difficulties in dealing with some Irish nationalists and
militant orangemen who disrupted his meetings; the fact that 'socialist
doctrines were stirring the masses'.[14] The same section has tantalising
references to the numerous Poles and Germans employed in Scottish
mines who were attributed with 'ungovernable tempers' and so blamed
for social unrest. Yet no rounded portraits emerge to mediate or recon-
struct for us something of the coherent historical experience of these
different groups.

Ferguson gives agriculture, religion and politics a reasonable share
of the narrative, yet his view that in the Victorian era 'the dominance

of heavy industry was an established fact, and one which carried social and political, as well as economic implications'[15] summarises the chief impression left by the book. This is unfortunate since he alludes to the potential for a broader view. He makes reference for example, in considering the mid- to late-Victorian period, to the variety of experience which different environments might provide, though this is expressed in very negative terms:

> life was not uniformly grim or so predictably short in the more prosperous districts of the cities and in the smaller less industrialised towns.[16]

The undifferentiated view of life for the urban working class is, as we have seen, not unusual. But neither is there any elaboration on the experience of the middle class in the cities or of any class in the market towns to which he refers.

Later, in considering the social balance in the early twentieth century, he records that by 1911, those gaining employment from the land had dropped to less than one in twenty of the population but warns that the change, though significant, should not be exaggerated:

> The older 'feudal' society was not altogether destroyed. Scotland was still a country characterised by great estates which in many parts held virtually self-contained communities, such as that presided over by the fifth Earl of Rosebery at Dalmeny. The contrast between such a community and that which existed in the stone canyons of Glasgow was startling. Doubtless economic hardship and social grievances existed in these rural enclaves; but they were muted and on the whole the better-run estates upheld an archaic way of life that seems to have satisfied its partakers. Though an undoubted force in Scotland, the strength of this older form of social organisation is difficult to estimate since it consisted of individual units and could not, in the nature of things, present a united front.[17]

This dismissal of most of rural Scotland because it cannot be defined or could not 'present' itself in terms of a socio-economic force is rather typical. The images which predominate in the histories are often the forces which can be seen as 'presenting' in this way – the Clydeside workers, the orangemen, the catholic nationalists. Although it is often labelled as empiricist, this approach to history in fact fails to appreciate and describe the more complex realities of experience where these defy reduction to stereotype. The use of terms like 'archaic' and 'feudal' indicate the poverty of his conception in attempting to summarise Scottish rural experience in the nineteenth century (or failure to develop an appropriate vocabulary for describing the particularity of Scottish experience).

There is almost certainly an entire 'structure of feeling' being ignored here. The numbers of the population fully employed as farmers, farm-labourers, horsemen and the like was no doubt decreasing to the levels Ferguson describes. But this takes no account of those who moved between rural and urban employment, or the vast numbers who must have travelled constantly among farm, village, and small 'market town': between country town and industrial town; between village and city.

In Ferguson's description the different forms of housing available to the unfortunate rural dwellers throughout Scotland were, before 1945 at least, as archaic as the social attitudes their inhabitants are projected as clinging to:

> The grim miners 'raws' have mostly disappeared, the broken-down unhealthy farm cottages are rapidly being replaced by attractive council houses, and in the Highlands and Islands the old traditional hovels are slowly diminishing in number.[18]

It is likely that, were this passage to come to their attention, a considerable number of the people of rural Scotland, Highland and Lowland, would wish to take issue with such an assessment of their own or their forebears' homes.

Finally, it is relevant to notice that in Dr Ferguson's perception, the cultural achievement of Victorian Scotland was largely confined to the sciences. And while the theorist Clerk Maxwell is given recognition, it accords with Ferguson's general interpretation of the period that he should emphasise the implications of the failure to emulate the example of William Thomson, Lord Kelvin who 'acted as bridge between science and industry'.[19] Otherwise,

> Loss of confidence led to a virtual collapse of Scottish culture: literature degenerated into mawkish 'Kailyard' parochialism and painting into uninspired 'ben and glen' romanticism.[20]

Just as the rise of industrialism is seen, in broad terms, as overwhelming Scottish society, so 'the rise of a scientific outlook . . . hastened the decline of a specifically Scottish intellectualism'; indeed 'the decline of a specifically Scottish culture'.[21] This is history written, not of course consciously, but at a very fundamental level, from the perspective of the core societies of the West and their conception of the trajectory of historical development.

In addressing the issue of 'The Scottish Identity' Sydney and Olive Checkland provide an interesting and balanced assessment at least in relation to pre-industrial Scottish experience.[22] Yet in the era which their book largely addresses, the notion that the Scots and their culture passed through what is conceived as a 'corrosive industrialising experience',[23] establishes at some fundamental level the way in which the society is subsequently portrayed. Their sense of its being 'corrosive' must be borne in mind when, amongst the principal themes of the Victorian and Edwardian eras, they conceive

> as the prime mover . . . the industrialising process, impelled
> by the inventors and innovators, operating on the long
> continuities of the Scottish past.[24]

These authors recognise the significance of religious and cultural themes in their history but even in their more balanced perspective of the period, the foreground and the framework are given in chapters on 'entrepreneurs and industries' and 'the urbanisation of Scotland'.

Such an approach might not, at first sight, seem illegitimate. Yet it comes to permit and justify, in the very early stages of the book, both an undifferentiated portrayal of the urban centres themselves and the extension of this characterisation to the society as a whole. The entire social 'mass' is in some sense affected in every part by this 'eating away', corrosion, contortion.

Heavy industry defines social existence outside the home. The tenement contains and constrains all experience outside work:

> The experience of Glasgow's set of satellite towns continued
> to have much in common with their industrial metropolis.
> Heavy industry, iron and steel, textiles and mining set the
> tenor of life. The tenement set the framework of home and
> family.[25]

There is brief recognition that there were country towns but their characters are slightly drawn, impinging little on the main narrative where the most dramatic images somehow focus on those other themes. Middle-size towns like Paisley, Dundee or Kirkaldy are viewed in the same way as Glasgow's satellites:

> . . . each of these places in later Victorian times was unthink-
> able except in terms of its basic industry, and the kind of
> society it generated.[26]

Heavy industry comes to define and characterise the deepest elements of 'the west' – which in practice becomes a proxy for the entire society:

> the dominant ethos of the west derived from heavy industry.
> It was held in its various forms by owners, managers and
> men. This industrial complex was Scotland's chief generator
> of wealth, and of its social problems.[27]

This perspective leads directly to a particular way of seeing any aspects of Scottish cultural expression which cannot be associated with 'the dominant ethos'. Indeed, it comes to justify the assertion of a disjunction between Scottish society of the Victorian and Edwardian age, and its cultural achievement. (This is not entirely unknown as a framework for the treatment of other eras in Scottish history). The

Checklands can treat of Scott and Stevenson, and go on to describe the achievements of the 'Glasgow Boys' and the Scottish colourists, yet imply that they must be considered as phenomena aside or apart from, even alien to, their own society.

As with Scottish writers, so with the Scottish artists of Victoria's reign: from neither would it have been possible to guess that they were formed in a society in which industrialisation was the dominant experience.[28]

This is not only an acutely naive conception of how literature and painting might respond to industrialisation, but also simply ignores the possibility of other sources from which Scottish cultural expression might have sprung.

At least one of these sources would surely have been the experience of rural society, the sea and of a trading economy which was far from entirely based on industrial production. But just as cultural expression is treated very much in relation to the 'process of industrialisation'[29] so the nineteenth century countryside is approached in terms of its 'responses to industrialisation'.[30] Yet there is no sense of the rural pattern of life or experience having a converse influence:

The cities arose from and functioned without the matrix of the countryside where class in some senses had always been strong, and continued to be so. Our agenda, then, is to consider the countryside as the complement of the cities . . .[31]

Rosalind Mitchison made no attempt to recover and describe the response of the Scottish people to the twentieth century economic and environmental conditions described in her *History of Scotland*.[32] Once again, the environment and conditions highlighted are extremely selective, almost archetypal. On the one hand, stands the heavy industry of the Clyde — the illustration heading the chapter on the twentieth century is a stylised 'Clydeside', dark cranes silhouetted against the sky. The emphasis on Clydeside involves a degree of recognition of Scottish achievement in heavy engineering and shipbuilding, but on the other hand, it is, typically, the discussion of material conditions which is given most attention in Mitchison's treatment, and which (almost literally) colours the account. Here, there are litanies of statistics on poor health, low wages, and, inevitably, the 'horrors of Scottish housing'. The evidential base for the assertions she makes about housing deserves some scrutiny. Very broad statements to the effect that over half the Scots lived in one or two room houses around World War One are juxtaposed with specific evidence drawn from a Royal Commission report of 1917 (no assessment is made, of course, of who was on the Royal Commission or what their attitudes to or understanding of working class environments were). Somehow judgments which *may* have legitimacy, by a *single* investigatory body into conditions which *may* have applied to *half* the population in *particular* locations are assumed to have national relevance:

> The 1917 Report is a grisly document. Overcrowding and squalor, though enhanced by the nature of the industrial specialisation of the country, were *general Scottish features*.[33]

For once, the subjectivity of the Scots is actually brought into the discussion. This serves, however, only to articulate what is normally a latent assumption in this history writing — that the only influence of the Scottish people on their history is such as to demonstrate their *passivity* in the face of conditions which more 'developed' nations would consider unacceptable:

> The Commission did not enquire how far overcrowding was produced by *an acceptance of deplorable standards*, and an unwillingness to pay for anything better, but this feature is one of *the main historical problems of Scottish housing* . . . Acquiescence came partly because the structure of Scottish house-building was what the Scots liked: tall tenement blocks, set end on to the street and built of immense solidity with little interest in fresh air.[34] (our italics)

Later the Scots' supposed lack of interest in housing is implicitly identified as the cause of the country's slow recovery from the Depression of the Thirties: 'Scotland's poverty was generating its own continuance'.[35]

Mitchison's earlier account of the latter half of the nineteenth century emphasises similar aspects of urban working class experience,[36] though here there is more about the rural areas, particularly the Highlands. What references there are to the people themselves, to their characteristics and their experience of life, are uniformly disparaging and unsympathetic. While recognising the general truth of their views, Mitchison chooses to emphasise the Royal Commission's judgment that the evidence of its 'peasant witnesses' was 'erroneous as to time, to place, to persons, to extent, and misconstrued as to intention.' We are told that 'observers had commented' on the presence of 'alien agitators' in Highland communities at this time, and it is held to be 'a comment on the traditional submissiveness of the Highlander to civil and religious authority that it needed outside help to make it vocal.'[37]

'The peasants' are portrayed as rather simple, as failing to understand what had happened to them, and so as forming 'myths about the Clearances':

> Long-term sheep farming ran down the fertility of the soil and in the 1870s and 1880s, when the agricultural crisis of the whole country brought catastrophically low prices, first in grain and then in wool, much of the higher pastures cleared of small tenants for sheep farms, could not be let as farms and became deer forest instead. To the land-starved

peasantry it looked as if they had been cleared out for deer: and this idea became one of the standard myths about the Clearances.[38]

They may have missed one or two of the economic nuances, but the poor peasants don't seem to have been too far out in their attribution of the original reason for the availability of these lands.

Most of all the experience of Highland life is portrayed as determined by the fanaticism of religious life. It is asserted that the doctrines of the various dissenting churches and the Free Church came to encapsulate and, as it were, 'mediate' the sensibility and experience of the mass of Highlanders:

> The extreme rigour of these Free Church tenets gave a narrow and joyless quality to life which accentuated social isolation and economic hopelessness.[39]

In the accounts of more recent Scottish social experience, the emphasis on the centrality of heavy industry in the nineteenth and early twentieth centuries has its corollary in a vision of the all-pervading effects of subsequent deindustrialisation.

Christopher Harvie recognised that this reflex was responsible for the dark and negative tone adopted in his revealingly titled *No Gods and Precious Few Heroes*.[40] This is not of course supposed to be an industrial or even economic history. Indeed it was the twentieth century volume in the Edward Arnold 'New History of Scotland' series, to which many looked for new perspectives on the history of the nation at a time when the 1979 Referendum had brought a realisation of the need, precisely, for alternative self-images to those which (many suspected) had contributed to the Scots' rather hesitant 'Yes' vote. Harvie was not to provide them. His standpoint was:

> . . . a sombre critical one. I leave it to the reader to determine whether this pessimism is justified, as it has informed the structure of the book. In my chapter divisions . . . I have necessarily accentuated the theme of Scotland's industrial stagnation and eventual decline from being by any standards a substantial world power in 1914 to its present insecurity and insignificance.[41]

He goes on to draw a rather strained analogy between Scotland and nineteenth-century Sicily, where 'modern industrialisation and class-formation were too much for the ingrained traditions of the country; and qualities of consciousness, however perceptive, were not enough to combat this; the intellectuals solved their problems by moving out.'[42]

Harvie seems to become fatalistic about all aspects of the Scottish experience because he must relate them to industrial decline. At any rate his whole approach is founded on concurrence with 'gloomy' diagnoses of the nature of Scottish civil society, including the failure of Scottish society to sustain credible alternatives to restrictive class loyalties and mediocre personnel, and to a secretive bureaucracy. A structure of distinctive Scots corporations — church, education, law, local and devolved administration — has effectively transformed organic discontent into a sequence of manageable complaints.[43]

Combined with the unstable nationalist factor, this creates a new *anomie*: but its basic cause is not the collapse of preindustrial society, 'as in Durkheim's day', but of *industrial* society. Hence the way is prepared for his focus on the elements of that industrial-social collapse. The historian's whole cast of mind is to approach the subject of Scottish experience as characterised overwhelmingly by the pessimistic, gloomy and negative. He ends his introduction claiming that he wishes to 'tell it like it happened' and not flinch from Thomas Hardy's injunction 'if way to the better there be, it exacts a full look at the worse'. Harvie seeks out 'the worse' and misses out much of what happened, at least in terms of the experience of the people.

A more specialised work, *The Upas Tree*,[44] S. G. Checkland's modern history of Glasgow, produces a more credible picture, differentiated in terms of the experience and response at least of the Glasgow working class (and he does emphasis that proper research has yet to be carried out, so that any judgments must be tentative — not at all the impression given by the general histories).[45]

The engineering industry, which contributed so much to Glasgow's 'impressive well-being and confidence' in the late Victorian and Edwardian years, is conceived in terms of active 'creative' effort rather than solely as a context for exploitation:

> it was not a question of skills and labour being transferred from London or anywhere else, but was a Clydeside creation, arising out of the values, energies and education of the men concerned.

He sees there must be differentiation in the actual experience of, say, the overcrowded central city:

> one of the consequences of the concentration was to make Glaswegians urbanites of a very special kind . . . identifying with their city to a remarkable degree in the European rather than the English manner. Within it, however, there were strong sub-loyalties to the many former villages of which Glasgow was composed: Maryhill, Eglinton, Govan, Gorbals and the rest. Indeed the city seemed to be composed of its many 'Crosses'.[46]

It is recognised, too, that the tenement form of housing should not, in most instances, be equated with debased slum-dwelling and that it often provided 'a closeknit and mutually supportive community'.[47]

The general histories rely heavily on visual imagery, often reinforced by pictorial illustration and actual photographs, in their depiction of Scottish working class social life. Mediated in this way, the high concentration of people in the tenement cities becomes a basis for 'seeing' a grey and drab social context. Some passages at least in Checkland's work act as reminders that a more rounded reconstruction of social life in a particular historical situation might involve a broader attention to other forms of sensory experience. Overcrowding may be oppressive, but it may also mean that people are 'close' as families, 'in touch' as neighbours, and (certainly on the stair-heids) talking and listening to each other:

> the very compression and density of the central part of Glasgow made for a city life that was colourful and lively, instead of, as in so many English cities, dying when the day's business was done, it was a place of human contact.[48]

And beyond their immediate localities, it is likely that the vast majority would have participated in the variety of activities he acknowledges that the city had to offer:

> Men and women of all classes remembered childhood and youth enlivened by a day 'doon the watter', an evening at the music hall, Sunday afternoons listening to brass bands in the parks, rides on trams, inspection of the statues in George Square, shopping in Sauchiehall Street.[49]

Checkland's account engages much more successfully with the full range of historical experience of those with whom he is concerned, very largely because he recognises that people are never defined solely by their immediate conditions, and that they will in most instances respond to them:

> The working man and woman who composed the life of Glasgow in its great heyday had their own ways of looking at life, at humanity and God: it is dangerous and condescending to impart to them simplified views of 'class consciousness'. Their outlook was derived partly from the lives, experiences and perceptions of former generations. The remoter of their forebears had lived their lives in fields and among the hills . . . Like everyone else they were to a degree prisoners of their situation, but they had their own ways of comprehending it and dealing with it that cannot be reduced to any simple position. Some observers have been inclined to regard the power of the city to debase and corrupt as being without limit. Dire though the effects of urban life can be, this view of human degradation is perhaps to ignore the capacity of man and woman to shape their own lives, at least in part and in some degree.[50]

In examining more recent decades, Checkland keeps such principles in mind. There is a recognition, for example, that many of those in the post-war housing schemes resisted the deterioration in their physical environment. Yet even this rests on the assumption, which he makes explicit a little later, that in this period housing was 'the most important single element of the social life of Glasgow'.[51]

He does discuss the interplay of the modern city's culture and politics in a sympathetic and stimulating way – drawing in the work and significance of figures as diverse as Joan Eardley, Edwin Morgan, Billy Connolly, Jimmy Reid and many other poets, novelists and folk singers in the process.

Yet this is all done in the context of an image of the city and its people as subject to the overwhelming presence and influence of 'the upas tree' of the book's title. In far eastern legend, this was a tree which had the power to destroy all other growths over a wide radius. In Checkland's view of things, the heavy industries and their legacy dominated Glasgow society in the same way.

There is much in the book as an 'artifact', in the way it is structured and visually presented, which accords with this notion. The opening passages create a conceptual framework or screen through which the rest of the book is likely to be viewed.

These passages project the mass of urban Scots almost solely in terms of their heavy industrial occupations. Glasgow's engineering industry required craftsmen 'whose pride and personality were built around their skills and their products, who found a fulfilment in their tasks'.[52]

There is a degree of truth in these observations. Yet the exclusive focus on the workers *vis-à-vis* their tasks creates a distinctive image of the life of Glaswegians. In spite of the much more perceptive passages scattered through his book, this is ultimately the image of the urban masses which Checkland projects. This view of things – typified by the assertion that 'output, incomes and jobs are the fundamental elements of the life of a city and its region'[53] – succinctly summarises the approach evident in the more general social histories.

Despite his more sympathetic treatment, Checkland comes to reproduce the same cultural iconography as the other accounts. Glasgow's engineering and shipbuilding created:

> a special image. . .the young artist Muirhead Bone sketched the yards and fitting out basins with their fantastic masses of frames and hulls, the timber scaffolding, the spindly sheer-legs, the smoking chimneys, and the vast engine shops, all stark and grey against what a contemporary called 'the engineering skies of Glasgow'.[54]

Although the work as a whole contains much more diverse elements, this opening chapter creates a context for the rest of the book. This is

reinforced by the use as illustration throughout the book, of the afore-
mentioned Muirhead Bone's pictorial representations of Glaswegians
as overwhelmed by industrial furnaces, shipyards or poverty and etched
in colours varying only from grey to more sombre shades of black.

Ironically, within his own work, Checkland records the impact of
this reductive iconography:

> in the meantime, there is the image held of Glasgow's cul-
> ture in Britain and in Europe . . . People do not expect gentle
> things to come out of Glasgow; there is a feeling that so
> far north, amid the clang and clamour of heavy industry,
> the veneer of civilisation is perilously thin, scarcely able to
> contain the elemental urges beneath.[55]

It is seldom, and then in small measure, that the oral evidence gath-
ered by the likes of Billy Kay erupts into this explanatory frame, to hint
at the richness, diversity, humour and colour behind the monochromal
images. How many black-and-white photographs of 'poverty-stricken
Fife miners 1904' must there be before a real effort is made to recount
and understand the texture of their subject's experience in the million
other moments before and after the shutter moved?

Smout's own most effective and sustained account of a response
from the Scots is contained in his last two chapters on the radical and
socialist traditions. Here he very effectively distills into general historical form the rise and fall of working class resistance; something
of the emotional power of these movements; as well as an analysis of
their origins both in the fervent commitment to freedom and justice
of the old Covenanting tradition and in the ethical expectations and
obligations of the citizen characteristic of the powerful civic-humanist
strain within Scottish culture.

Yet as a description of the Scots' primary response not only to
material deprivation but more generally to the rapid social and technological change of the modern era, it is extremely narrow. This radical
or labourist image of the Scottish people — and this is the *best* they
can be made to appear — is ultimately no more than the correlative,
the Janus-face of the impoverished dweller in the tenement city or
blackened proletarian of shipyard and forge. The best they could attain
is less a response than a political knee-jerk, a reflex appropriate to the
stimulus of their social conditions.

Yet even this narrowly defined political response is portrayed as
ultimately (and especially after 1920) a long-drawn-out failure. In the
last resort, it was for Smout

> . . . the fruits of the collectivist state, of the rule of the expert,
> and of a policy of welfare determined above and afar . . .[56]

which brought about an improvement in the 'quality of life for the
Scottish people' between the 1940s and '70s.

At the end of his work, Smout is left wondering at how little Scotland 'did for its citizens'.[57] It is a view which pervades the book and is, of course, profoundly locatable within the historian's own time and opinions. Whatever the rights and wrongs of this it may be responsible for his inattention and insensitivity to the active subjectivity, in so many directions, of those whose history he seeks to relate. Christopher Harvie is a partial exception to this picture but only insofar as he at least makes reference to some of the elements of experience of the working class which do not relate to their industrial role, poverty or cramped housing; and at least recognises, however briefly, the Scottish middle classes, artists and intellectuals. For the majority of the historians, the working classes represent the totality of Scottish culture in its real significance; the rest of Scottish experience is not *truly* Scottish by virtue of not belonging to the nexus of poverty, passivity and repression that Royal Commissions travel North to find and bewail. Whatever else happened to happen in Scotland is simply marginal to the reality of Scottish experience, not an essential element *of* that experience. And where it gains purchase on the whole of Scottish life, it is almost inevitably revealed to have been stimulated by external (usually English) influences. And even for Harvie, the achievements of Scottish artists, architects, photographers and all the other creative focuses of Scottish life, are presented as continually and necessarily defeated by the underlying philistinism and deprivation of their social and cultural context. A few quotations will illustrate this tendency to negate every positive Scottish achievement by an economistic 'but':

> In the 1890s Charles Rennie Mackintosh had laid down the principles of a modern Scottish architecture . . . But his aims were confounded by the economic decline in Edwardian Scotland.
>
> These collections of the 'Glasgow Boys' and 'Scottish colourists' . . . deserved their high reputation, but the indigenous art . . . patronised was domestic in scale and socially unadventurous. Scottish art may have avoided the worst ramps of the international 'art market' but public art like murals was non-existent and the innovators . . . got out.
>
> Even photography, potentially the most radical art form and one that nineteenth-century Scots had helped create, rarely escaped from the seductions of a photogenic landscape. Fine work was done in Scotland by the Londoner Jim Jarché and the American Paul Strand, but not by the Scots themselves.[58]

Most of the books examined so far would be considered 'well-researched' and 'scholarly' works. They retail many facts, reproduce the tabulated data of more specialised works and manifest thorough knowledge of all the main sources. What is at issue is something less tangible, less easily defined.

There is a fundamental difference of 'attitude' and 'tone' in Sidney Checkland's account of Glasgow since 1945 as told in his individual history of the city, and the general-history projections of modern Scotland's urban story. It is not to do with the facts, figures and general subject matter. Indeed, like the general histories (though more justifiably) *The Upas Tree* focuses on the economic changes which occurred in the field of heavy engineering and shipbuilding as well as the conditions relating to urban life and housing. It is much more a matter of how the writers choose to organise and view the empirical elements available. A different perspective establishes an image very different from Smout's picture of the irremediably bleak and grim Scottish city, without in any way suppressing the negative elements.

> In spite of much continued suffering, and of resentments against planners and bureaucrats, a major improvement in Glasgow life was achieved between 1945 and 1975 . . . No less than 100,000 municipal houses had been built since the War . . . the percentage of households with exclusive use of hot and cold water, a fixed bath and an inside wc, though lower than the steadily rising national average, improved between 1961 and 1971 from 58.9 per cent to 75.2 per cent. The percentage of the population living at more than 1.5 persons per room fell from 46.9 in 1951 to 26 in 1971 . . . The new road system has a drama and a verve of its own, opening up new panoramas of the city from the Clydeside Expressway and elsewhere, making visible the excitement of an industrial landscape and its setting of encircling hills. Though Glasgow still has its decayed and depressing parts, it has been given a new kind of urban image.[59]

A more comprehensive foil in this sense to the general histories considered earlier is provided by G. S. Pryde's *Scotland 1603 to the Present Day*,[60] whose publication in 1962 actually pre-dates all of them. Pryde, who was Professor of Scottish History and Literature at Glasgow, produces a more complex but more balanced, varied picture.

His description of 'The Ascendancy of Heavy Industry' in the nineteenth century is mediated through a knowledge of different topographies and localities and given meaning for us by illustration of its impact on particular social groups. Some distinguishable (even coloured) images both of products and producers emerge. The Paisley shawl

> . . . was woven, of six or seven colours, in an intricate pattern of conventional geometrical designs intermixed perhaps with flowers and leaves, and always with the characteristic 'pine'

motif, which was practically its hallmark. Arduous as was
his toil, and finnicking his product, the Paisley weaver was
a true, creative craftsman, making a brave if futile gesture
of defiance against the all-conquering machine.[61]

Pryde's account of the nineteenth century social scene recognises
the constant threat to urban working class life from poverty, disease
and poor housing but presents a picture containing at least elements
of greater richness and variety:

The two chief cities had their permanent theatres, and the
principal towns were visited from time to time by travelling
companies. Other amenities included tea-gardens, popular concerts, circuses and menageries, and the sports of
the period comprised golf, horse-races, prize-fights, quoits
and cock-fighting . . . Glasgow's great July Fair was the
Mecca for conjurors, showmen, stall-holders and keepers of
shooting ranges.[62]

Scottish urban society was not confined to the industrialised centres
and slums of Glasgow, Edinburgh and Dundee:

While the social problems of Victorian and Edwardian times
were real and pressing, there were forces making for stability and contentment. Life could be particularly agreeable in
those old county-towns which stood apart from the main
currents of industry and offered their inhabitants pleasant residences, good shops and schools, perhaps theatres,
museums and other amenities: such were Dumfries, Ayr,
Stirling, Perth, Inverness and Elgin. Again, with a prosperous
and expanding economy, the greater part of society enjoyed
steady wages and steady prices . . . In supplying the working
classes with cheap groceries and incidentally inducing them
to save, the many local co-operative societies were highly
successful from the 1860s on.[63]

The reduction of the working day from around twelve to around
eight hours and gradual adoption from the 1850s of the Saturday
half-holiday allowed increasing participation in a cultural life which
'was fostered by concerts and plays, by museums, libraries and art
galleries.'[64]

His summation of the history of the visual arts themselves in this
period recognises the conservatism of powerful elements in the RSA,
but also balances the account in relation to innovatory work within
an international perspective:

In Scotland . . . from about 1880 – as in France, with the
impressionists – a violent reaction against 'academic values
and techniques' inspired the younger artists to make bold
experiments and to apply light and colour in a new and lavish

way. For a generation the 'Glasgow School' set the tone of
Scottish painting and brought wide fame to its members . . . :
associated in spirit with their output were the sculptures
of Pittendreigh Macgillivray, while Sir James Guthrie, later
renowned as a portraitist, felt their influence strongly in his
early work.[65]

In treating of the twentieth century Pryde recognises the importance
of heavy industry to Scottish society, the dangers of the industrial structure having 'too many eggs in one basket' and the almost inevitable
consequences once these industries began to decline. But he consistently recognises that the domination of these sectors and the decline
they were to experience should not become a kind of general metaphor
or barometer of social experience, social morale or cultural creativity.
Modernisation may have spelled danger to particular sections of the
Scottish population at particular generational points and in relation
to specific aspects of their experience – supremely of course in their
existence as workers in traditional trades; but the picture of gradual
decline at a macro-economic level too often leads the historians to
marginalise the Scots experience as, say, consumers and participators,
of food, of education, of leisure-time pursuits, of cultural activities,
of travel opportunities.

Pryde again turns to these aspects of life towards the end of his
chapter on the economic troubles of the inter-war period – an era
which seems to be particularly constitutive of the historians' account
of twentieth-century Scotland as a society in terminal collapse:

> The motor-bus, the private car and the bicycle gave all
> ranks of society a mobility unknown to their grandparents,
> bringing the amenities of the town within reach of the
> country-dweller, throwing open the delights of the country-
> side to the townsfolk, and making it possible for all to
> engage in either work or play at some distance from home.
> Shopping excursions and country rambles, tours and pic-
> nics, holidays at the seaside, in the mountains, or abroad,
> came to form part of the pattern of life.[66]

Similarly, his account of changes in rural society in the Victorian and
Edwardian eras and their impact on 'the seasonal cycle of the country-
man's life' is presented in a way which recognises what remained
hard, but also what had improved, what made up its routines, but
also the events which ensured more intense and dramatic social and
leisure experiences.[67] Here, and in his differentiation of the experiences of urban living, Pryde's comparatively early work demonstrates
an openness to the totality of modern Scottish experience which the
general historians of the succeeding twenty-five years were seldom to
emulate.

It should be acknowledged that in the most recent general history of Scotland, Michael Lynch criticises the conception of nineteenth- and early twentieth-century Scottish history as overwhelmingly determined by an undifferentiated industrial experience. His suggestion of the development of a greater attention to 'localism' might be particularly telling if fully followed through. For Lynch there were 'many industrial revolutions' proceeding at different speeds and with their own characteristics:

> Shipbuilding was confined largely to the Clyde, as was the classic complex of heavy industry. There was not one Scottish coal industry, but two . . . Dundee expanded in the nineteenth century, not (like Glasgow) by diversifying out of textile output. Aberdeen, fuelled by a rather different kind of migration from the Irish 'influx' into Dundee, nevertheless experienced similar population growth but its industry moved in a quite different direction. There have also been some who, preferring to show continuity rather than change, have come to suggest that Aberdeen, despite its population growth, did not experience an Industrial Revolution at all.[68]

In Lynch's own coverage of the nineteenth and twentieth centuries, there are only brief glimpses of how a more 'contingent' and localist approach might restore some of the variety, contradiction and colour required to produce a balanced account.[69]

If one tries to imagine the Scots of the modern era from their presentation in the work of contemporary historians, the predominant image is of a bleak, urban dweller whose experience is limited to the struggle for daily existence and whose life is unleavened by any cultural creativity or richness of aesthetic or personal experience. The Scot is under-nourished both physically and spiritually and subject to a culture whose only virtue is a repressive enforcement of public order and private morality. The environment in which the typical Scot lives is cramped, bare and the only escape from it is to an even more cramped and bare pub or a barren church offering a tortuous and warping theology.

Such views have been supported by the literary presentation of generations of writers who have sought in the life of slum dwellers the archetypal image of the Scottish condition, and have approached them half in awe, half in terror, as the very essence of a humanity that has been deprived of everything but a biological definition of being human.

The experience of being Scottish in this presentation is an experience of limitation; a restriction of the choices and opportunities available to equivalent people in other cultural environments. That the Scottish working classes were exploited unmercifully by a system which continually undercut their wages by the importation of workers from other countries, and that the heavy manual labour on which the Scottish economy of the late nineteenth century was built, were dehumanising pressures upon a large number of Scots has been taken to mean that the Scottish working classes were in actuality desensitised and that the whole of Scottish society was defined by that experience.

Entirely lacking in these presentations is the capacity of people to assert their humanity against external pressures, to create and recreate a vital culture encompassing a full range of human potential; and equally lacking is a proper focus on the full range of cultural and intellectual activity which characterised the society as a whole rather than simply that part of it whose experience is assumed to be central. To comprehend the lived experience of the Scots in the past hundred years we have to recover the sense of the society as a whole, the full range of the cultural and human activities which it offered, and the ways in which people of different classes were able both to express and to extend the richness and variety of their experience.

3
Other Modern Scotlands

Certain elements in the Scottish past have suffered particular violence as a consequence of the historical approach described in Chapter 2. Some aspects are particularly distorted, while others, which should be prominent, hardly figure at all. These images require to be restored before the portrayal of Scottish history can be said to have a proper balance.

Professor Smout's dissection of some of the finest achievements of modern Scottish culture from his account of the country's modern history is frankly acknowledged in his introduction:

> I am conscious of much that has been left out that could fairly be considered germane to a larger social history of Scotland. There is little about artistic or intellectual endeavour, though a book could be written about the achievements of the Scots from the *Edinburgh Reviewers* and Thomas Carlyle to the poets of the Scottish Renaissance, from the scientists like Clerk Maxwell and D'Arcy Thompson, to the doctors like Simpson and Lister and the divines like Robertson Smith and David Cairns.[1]

Despite this disclaimer, the fact is that his book *is* taken as a general history. And the notion that a general social history of whatever 'scale' can be written without exploring the relation of the society concerned to its cultural expression is astonishing. Who blew and fashioned and coloured the stained glass? Whose words and tone and linguistic history were the poets of the 'Scottish Renaissance' trying to redefine? Whose deeply held beliefs made Robertson Smith's actions of nation-wide interest and significance? However, Smout had determined to 'show what life was like for most Scottish people'[2] and, evidently, for this objective such questions were irrelevant.

Professor Smout at least acknowledges his focus on 'deprivation'. But as we have seen, most of the general historians follow this approach or, at least, accept that for lengthy stretches of the modern era, Scottish art, architecture and patronage was too stolid, conservative or moribund to sustain much attention.

Patrons and Architects

The Scottish middle class and their local institutions are portrayed as douce, stolid and largely philistine. In architectural terms, for example, their achievement is at most conceived as a predictable mass of suburban housing fanning out from the centres of Edinburgh and Glasgow. Such conformist taste there certainly was, though there is no reason to suppose that it was any more or less conservative than that of the bourgeois of London or Paris. But there was very much more.

Far from ushering in an extended period of cultural darkness, Victoria's accession marked, for the classical architectural tradition,

> the beginning of a new age, for it opened the door to a serious Scottish revival, in town no less than in country . . .[3]

In fact there was an enormous variety of architectural development associated with the height of industrial expansion. In the country towns, the burghers were by no means unadventurous or dull in the visible forms they gave to the development of local government:

> The old town hall of Castle Douglas was given a clock tower of medieval Italian form in the town's vernacular of white granite with red sandstone dressings, presumably before 1862 when a new hall was built on another site. A similar tower at Gatehouse-of-Fleet a few miles away across Kirkcudbrightshire (1871) plays a Montague to its Capulet. More frequently a light admixture of foreign detail enriches the baronial town hall, but hardly weakens the case for seeing it as the continuation of a native type.[4]

There is little justification for portraying the 'physicality' of Scottish society throughout the modern era as limited to, and as defined by, dull grey cityscapes. Architects were introducing new stone materials in many projects, to brighten up the towns.

In Edinburgh architects were using the commissions arising from the schools building programmes, to introduce

> colour with the newly available red and yellow sandstones from outside the city, and liveliness too, with Flemish crowsteps and central lanterns.[5]

A properly rounded account of the history of an intensely commercial society yet one which held learning too in high esteem cannot ignore the expression of these social values in its physical 'urbanity':

> Virtually everything was tried in Glasgow in this great age when architecture was the very coin of commercial prestige, but seldom without a solid backing of scholarship, and never without the desire to spend money in putting on the best possible show on each site. Adaptations of the Italian palace theme were bolder than in Edinburgh and were now

followed, in this city where conformity was not of critical importance, by brilliant improvisations in other styles.[6]

Sir John James Burnet would move from a 'cool, bare classicism', and then once again join in the scholarly free-for-all with the 'astounding red sandstone Charing Cross Mansions, at once huge, intricate and charming . . .'[7]

In Glasgow,

> The dominant late Victorian motifs of gable and corner tower . . . developed as nowhere else, and always with an eye to their culmination on the skyline . . . when Charles Rennie Mackintosh designed the Glasgow Herald tower in Mitchell Street (1893) he was not raising his standard in an architectural desert; carried by a scholarly and adventurous tradition, he was able to go beyond it . . .[8]

Mackintosh emerged from a cultural milieu which was generally responsive to *avant garde* as well as traditional or classical tastes. In the 1870s and 1880s, Glasgow citizens appreciated and patronised the most contemporary European art, certainly as far as painting is concerned:

> Local collectors had been buying important French and Dutch paintings before the work of Millet, Corot or the Maris brothers had even been recognised in the South . . .[9]

Research has recently shown 'the surprising extent to which the enthusiasm for Japaneses art was widespread in Glasgow from the early 1880s onwards.'[10] Such influence stimulated both the Glasgow school of painters and Charles Rennie Mackintosh – as did the extensive interest in Celtic art and symbolism.

As soon as Mackintosh began designing furniture in the mid–1890s individual members of the middle class like William Davidson of Kilmacolm, but also commercial firms like the Glasgow decorators Wells and Guthrie Ltd. commissioned his work. Davidson later gave Mackintosh his first independent commission for a house. He was

> a discerning patron of the arts, and an admirer of Mackintosh's work, so the architect found himself in an ideal situation for exploring his convictions with the full sympathy of his client.[11]

Mackintosh received the same sympathetic freedom from the commercial publisher W. W. Blackie, who commissioned the Hill House at Helensburgh.

Indeed, if all was philistine about the Glasgow middle class, it is difficult to explain the fact that his greatest work, the Glasgow School of Art, was made possible because the Governors decided that new premises were required; launched an appeal in 1895; and by February 1896 had accrued sufficient capital to begin to build.[12] And in the limited competition with twelve other Glasgow architects, a brilliantly individualist effort by a little known architect employing a bold eclecticism of style straddling Scottish domestic and Baronial, English arts and crafts, and Japanese decoration, was chosen.

In the same year, the commissions from Catherine Cranston which allowed him such opportunity for decorative invention were founded on an aspect of middle class social life quintessentially Glaswegian:

> this was a particularly Glaswegian phenomenon of the turn of the century, an enthusiasm for non-alcoholic places of refreshment that combined the facilities of gentlemen's midday clubs with the gentilities of ladies' afternoon tea. In a remarkably short space of time Glasgow became served with a remarkably high standard of public catering.[13]

By his early thirties Mackintosh had been given a senior position in a well-known Glasgow architectural firm; varied commissions from discerning patrons; and generally found both artistic and professional opportunities and significant appreciation within the society around him.

Mackintosh's theoretical and practical commitment to developing an architectural style of and for his own times but drawing inspiration and influence from his own cultural tradition are now clearly established.[14] It is interesting, however, that in his theoretical prospectus read to the Glasgow architectural association in 1891, though he focused on the great-house survivals of the Scottish baronial between the fifteenth and seventeenth centuries he also recognised that the living survivals of that style were chiefly present in Scottish *domestic* architecture. It is the potential for elaborating a social-cultural relation or reflection between artist and environment, cultural expression and society, which is so obviously missing from the general-historical works. Indeed, precisely the opposite is offered: the social and cultural poverty of Scottish domestic architecture.

Mackintosh himself, writing at the height of his architectural achievement, had a quite different view:

> When Burns in his 'Cotter's Saturday Night' after enumerating some of our favourite psalm tunes burst out 'Compared wae they Italian trills are tame', as a piece of musical criticism it may not hold world-wide, yet it is a very sufficient reason and obvious truth to Scotsmen, so in the same manner there are many decorative features in Scotch architecture, which might well be replaced by others of antiquity yet just because we are Scotch and not Greek or Roman we reject. For example, there is the quaint old Scotch gate pillars with the spire resting on three or four stone bullets . . . and very many other features which give

a historical character to the building they adorn . . . In fact
I think we should be a little less cosmopolitan and rather
more national in our architecture . . .[15]

It is unfortunate that the general histories have not afforded Mackintosh himself the historical relationship and context he recognised as so necessary for the understanding of buildings. A more sophisticated approach might have considered not only the relationship of his semi-rural houses like Kilmacolm and the Hill House to Scottish baronial and rural domestic architecture, but in addition the association of his urban work with that *bete noir* of the general histories, the Scottish tenement. Of Scotland Street school:

. . . it could fairly be said that the construction of the walls,
the framing around the window openings, the forms of the
roofs, and the building materials are all in accord with those
of the tenement buildings which had become, notoriously,
the main building fabric of the city during the nineteenth
century.[16]

Yet Mackintosh's relation to Scottish domestic architecture was well-established before most of the general histories of Scotland written in the last quarter century were published. In *The Architecture of Scotland* (1966), J. G. Dunbar observed that

. . . the most significant developments in late Victorian country house design were initiated by a small group of architects
who sought in different ways to re-interpret the domestic
rather than the castellated architecture of the post-medieval
period in the modern idiom.[17]

It is relevant to note that for Dunbar, Mackintosh was only one of a number of innovative Scottish architects working in even this quite specific field of endeavour.

One of the characteristics of the historiography discussed in Chapter 2 is that Scottish culture is largely treated in terms of one or two heroic figures, whose prominence is used, or so it seems, to heighten the darkness around them. Mackintosh is one of the figures highlighted in this way. His remarkable works deserve their appreciation. But where he is mentioned at all, it is as an isolated genius labouring alone to create innovative and original architectural or artistic images.

In practice Mackintosh had a number of near contemporaries who sought with considerable success to address a similar architectural challenge: James Maclaren, with his farm buildings and cottages on the Glenlyon estate; his associates Dunn and Watson with further work elsewhere in Perthshire; Thomas MacLaren, with his domestic buildings in Doune, and many others.[18]

Perhaps the most gifted was Robert Lorimer, whose work extended from small houses and cottages erected in Colinton and other

Edinburgh suburbs to medium-sized houses in Argyle, a hotel for fisher-
men in Shetland, and larger country houses which displayed a more
overtly romantic and 'distinctively Scottish' style which admirably rec-
onciled the demands of contempory planning with the employment
of local materials and customary methods of construction.[19] Lorimer,
like Mackintosh, not only found inspiration in Scottish domestic and
rural architecture, but sympathetic patrons among both the rural and
urban middle class. His first restoration was of the sixteenth-century
Earlshall tower house in Fife for R. W. Mackenzie, whose father was a
Perth lawyer and who himself became first a lawyer and then partner
in a bleaching firm.

> He was generally interested in fabrics, and particularly tap-
> estries. . . If Lorimer was already designing embroideries to
> be executed by his relatives, Mackenzie also made designs
> for woven linen tea towels based on patterns of rooks and
> rookeries derived from those at Earlshall. He ran garden
> fêtes at Earlshall and had pottery fairings with the same
> motif made by the Wemyss pottery which also used other
> designs by him.[20]

Lorimer was also much patronised by less flamboyant elements
of the Scottish middle class and designed a considerable number of
domestic houses for them in a variety of Edinburgh suburbs. Some
have features which reflect aspects of the work of James Maclaren
and even Mackintosh. They constitute 'ordinary' suburban housing,
but Lorimer sought original features or perspectives where he could:

> In the case of the modest suburban house it is quite unnec-
> essary to plump it down – foursquare to the winds – and
> right in the centre of the plot of ground.[21]

There is no lack of imagination, colour and style in these suburban
dwellings, which present a quite distinctive character in comparison
with similar English buildings. Lorimer was perfectly aware of this
himself and though a devotee of the Arts and Crafts movement in the
South, he found little of interest in such English architecture:

> He found all too many English buildings too 'pretty', and
> when he visited Cambridge he complained of the 'beastly
> prettyness of all the best modern work . . . How sick one
> gets of these cuspings and crestings and stuff.'[22]

Lorimer's own background, relatives, acquaintanceship and patronage indicate a middling class oriented towards Scottish tradition;
a mixture of rural and urban life; and often to a variety of artistic
pursuits – an entire milieu profoundly different from the unbending,
dark-suited figures which emerge from the general histories. It might
be objected that prominent architects and artists would know the
more divergent colourful souls. Yet there were a great many architects,

artists and craftsmen working on projects of this kind throughout Scotland. Lorimer himself saw his suburban works, as much as his country houses

> as a collective effort of craftsmen and artists, of cabinetmakers, tapestry weavers, copper beaters, wrought iron workers, stained glass artists, joiners, masons and carvers.[23]

Not a Clydeside welder in view. These other skilled workers and craft-artists have left us many fine works to enjoy – works which are enjoyed and visited in increasing numbers by the Scottish people. Yet their traces in the general histories of Scotland are slight, thinly drawn or missing entirely.

A broader conception of what is significant in presenting Scottish history – a perspective encompassing more than the inner city slums – would not permit such a limited socio-economic or geographic picture to emerge.

Colourists

The images produced by Scotland's visual artists seldom colour the general historians' account of the past century and a half. Perhaps this is for the reason implied in Sidney Checkland's use of the Muirhead Bone illustrations in *The Upas Tree*: because the artists did not dutifully reflect or at least complement those dark hued 'realities' with which the historians seem to imbue the entire picture. It is an omission which excludes much light.

Certainly, before the middle of the nineteenth century David Wilkie had adopted 'a tenebrous later manner' and other early Victorian Scottish painters had come to share his view that 'as richness is the object to be aimed at in all systems of colouring, a dark brown may be a useful colour'.[24] Well-known figures, like John Thompson and Horatio McCulloch, displayed a mundane use of colour, usually expressed in monochromatic green or brown. And landscapists like Sam Bough and Alexander Fraser were timid in their use of colour.

Yet it seems to have been precisely at this point, when industrialisation was at its height, that painters like William Dyce, David Scott, and crucially Robert Scott Lauder began a 'colourist' revolt (stimulated by visits to Europe) which has continued to be expressed and renewed in a variety of schools within Scottish art to the present day.

Even in the 1830s, Thomas Duncan's work looked forward to Scott Lauder, and further, 'to the more robust use of colour and well-nourished pigment which became a hallmark of later Scottish painting'.[25] While the later works of John Phillip 'are astonishingly bold, in their use of powerful colour and handling'. But it was through the 1850s and 1860s that Scott Lauder's pupils from the Trustees Academy in Edinburgh developed – Pettie and MacTaggart particularly – into 'powerful colourists'.[26]

Although MacTaggart eschewed urban realism and so omitted the images of the industrialised cities, he nevertheless developed an impressionism (apparently quite independently of French impressionism) which, despite its subject matter, was 'rooted in realism' and devoted to an ideal of truth to appearances, that is, the appearances revealed by light – to MacTaggart 'the most beautiful thing in the world'.[27]

(Impressionism in France could equally be seen as an evasion of the industrialisation of French society but no one would make that simplistic comparison between social experience and artistic representation.)

Less than a generation later the diverse painters of the Glasgow school brought a further rebellion against the academic painting rooted in the RSA and achieved for Scottish painting 'its return to the expressive qualities of colour and the vigorous handling of paint.'[28] Its adherents found inspiration and a shared perception in both the artistic traditions and the social experience of many societies from Europe to North Africa, the Near East and Japan, without in any way neglecting Scottish social subject matter or landscape. Even those somewhat detached from the mainstream of the movement helped to maintain its celebration of the potentialities of colour and light: the Spanish watercolours of the Angus painter, Arthur Melville

> reach a synthesis of expression hitherto unattempted. Sun-
> light, vivid colour, are blended with suggestive movement.
> Not only is there strength and freedom but also a new power,
> a new statement of reserve, in the handling of light and
> shadow. No pictures have ever been more purely expressive
> of light.[29]

While a contemporary painter like J. Q. Pringle, who was not in fact closely associated with the Glasgow Boys or the wider 'school' associated with them,

> created works of consistent quality that can be astonishingly
> original in technique and both dreamily poetic and pain-
> stakingly observant. His colour is jewel-like and his paintings
> show the most fastidious execution, and a personal form
> of the *pointillisme* of the Neo-Impressionists, whose work
> Pringle almost certainly never saw.[30]

From 1890, the young Scottish artists who were living in London and 'recognised Walt Whitman as their poet, Wagner as their musician'[31] set up in opposition to the royal academy and were instrumental in introducing the most contemporary French painting to the English capital.

In 1891 the 'Scottish Impressionists' were enthusiastically received at the annual exhibition at Munich, then one of the chief art centres in Europe. The gold medals went to Arthur Melville and William Orchardson. The Glasgow School were represented by Walton, Patterson, Hornell and Henry.

The Edinburgh establishment, especially the RSA was conservative and resistant but an independent 'Society of Scottish Painters' was established by the Glasgow School and Melville:

> An exhibition was held that summer (1894) at the Fine Art Galleries in George Street. Sculpture by Rodin and race-course scenes by Degas were shown. Crawhall, Melville, Henry, Hornell and many other Glasgow men were well represented.[32]

Glasgow School painters were very positively received in a major exhibition in 1895 at St Louis in the USA, a 'Scottish art exhibition' at Munich again and later at Frankfurt. The spring of 1897 saw a major exhibition of the Glasgow School, as well as German artists, at St Petersburg.

Arthur Melville's story may also be instructive, in that, although he was opposed by the conservatives of the Edinburgh art world it does appear from his biography that, although a fairly *avant garde* painter, he had a good deal of support and commissions from the Scottish middle class.[33]

The general historians' insinuation that cultural activity either did not exist among the Scottish middle classes or was confined to po-faced disapproval of anything too distant from the Monarch of the Glen is challenged by William Hardy's description of the Aberdeen collector Forbes White:

> He was a polymath of advanced tastes with particular enthusiasm for the Dutch Impressionists and the Barbizon School, and a broad cosmopolitan outlook. Typical of his interests was how he would delight in recounting how on a business journey by coach from Stettin to Danzig he talked Latin for hours with a Polish professor of mathematics. He founded the Homeric club of Dundee and in 1889 gave a lecture there on the newly discovered Tanagra figurines. He was in addition a pioneer photographer, and knowledgeable enough about Rembrandt and Velasquez to write *Encyclopaedia Britannica* articles on them. A wide circle of artists visited his house as their friend and patron, including the Scots, Arthur Melville, Hugh Cameron, Orchardson and Daniel Cottier (whose firm in 1863 installed nineteen

stained glass windows of Cottier's design in Seaton cottage, White's retreat on the Don) as well as George Paul Chalmers and George Reid.[34]

In addition to White, a number of other collectors and dealers in Scotland, particularly in Glasgow, kept in close touch with European movements and helped provide the stimulus for the young Glasgow School of painters.

Less then a generation later, the four Scottish colourists and painters associated with them, reaffirmed the preoccupation of the Scottish visual arts with imagery characterised by new approaches to the manipulation of colour and light. As young men they collectively spent much time abroad, particularly in France, and criticised Scottish life as philistine and lacking in colour. Here, the historians we have criticised might claim justification of their portrayal of Scottish society. Yet the colourists would have been first to admit that they received much of their initial stimulation from the Glasgow School painters and Arthur Melville while the comparison they were making – with Paris in the first decade of the twentieth century – was one which few if any European cultures could have borne. With the benefit of hindsight, emphasis might reasonably be placed on the fact that the Scottish culture of the period had itself produced the colourists – a movement which in the view of a recent English historian of art displayed

> a greater understanding and far more knowledge of the lat-
> est movements in painting in the years before the outbreak
> of war in 1914 than its counterpart in England[35]

– in the same period as it produced in Edinburgh Stanley Cursitter's experimental work ('easily the most Futurist British painting from that early date'[36]), and in Dundee, George Dutch Davidson's paintings which closely parallel (without having been influenced by) the vision of Eduard Munch.

In practice, Cadell, Peploe and Hunter returned to engage with their own society before 1914, and even Fergusson, the most francophile of them all, discovered 'a new delight in the Scottish scene' during the war while painting in the Highlands which heralded his development into landscape painting. Indeed, all of the colourists were to find their own delight in the Scottish landscape at different points:

> The second *Loch Lomond* series painted at the very end of
> Hunter's life includes some of his finest paintings, one of
> which elicited from Peploe the compliment 'that is Hunter
> at his best and it is as fine as any Matisse'.[37]

While for Cadell:

> the white sand and bright green stretches of water character-
> istic of the east shore of Iona in certain weather conditions

provided a pretext for the bold colour schemes of the earlier Iona pictures, as the vermilions of Collioure had for Matisse.[38]

Whatever their views as young painters in Paris rebelling against the RSA and the Edinburgh establishment, the vibrancy and colour and light in the works of the colourists was founded from the first on the culture of their own country (particularly the Glasgow School and Melville) and expressed at the last in reinterpretation and re-expression stimulated by its landscape.

Since the 1920s Scottish painting has produced radicals like William McCance and William Johnstone, who, like their mutual friend Hugh MacDiarmid, criticised the prevailing Scottish tradition and proposed new directions to bring back a coherence and synthesis to modern art.

Yet McCance continued to an extent the colourist impetus into the era of expressionism and, on returning to Scotland, Johnstone found in the National Museum of Antiquities in Edinburgh, a celtic and Pictish symbolism with which to stimulate his work.

The highly colourist work of Alan Davie and Eduardo Paolozzi was very different from the mainstream, but it is difficult to understand William Hardie's logic in concluding that

the international orientation of the abstract expressionism of Davie and the idiosyncratic pop art of Paolozzi (both of whom have long been resident outside Scotland) make a national label difficult to apply to their work.[39]

There was an 'international orientation' to many of the painters making up different Scottish schools (and residence abroad). This must have been true of many artistic traditions in the modern age. No other culture would regard the criteria of international acceptance and residence abroad as basis for exclusion from the national artistic tradition.

Joan Eardley's 'compassionate studies of Gorbals street children, and, later, her elemental and expressionistic paintings of the wild and exposed east coast at Caterline are essentially the work of a traditionalist and show the rich impasto and exuberant handling which had been a feature of Scottish painting since McTaggart.'[40]

The mainstream has been dominated by the Edinburgh School, including D. M. Sutherland, Sir W. G. Gillies, Sir William McTaggart, David Foggie and Ann Redpath:

francophile, colourful, serious and civilised, these prolific artists stamped contemporary Scottish painting with an image which refuses to fade even today.[41]

It is not an image which emerges with any prominence, either from the accounts (where these exist) of cultural development in the general histories of modern Scotland, or, consequently, as an element in the picture as a whole.

Towns

A one-dimensional view of the Scottish urban setting has obscured (save, to an extent, in G. S. Pryde) a more balanced treatment, even celebration, of the sheer variety of man-made environments within the Scottish townscape. Much less has there been any attempt to explore the dynamic historical relationships between such environments and the architectural taste, technical feasibility and social history of succeeding periods.

It is not that specialist works were unavailable as the basis for this kind of effort. In his *Scottish Townscape* (1975) (proof read, incidentally, by Smout, though evidently without impact), Colin McWilliam points the way describing, for example, in a fine historical sweep over the Victorian commercial environment how different social groups and activities interacted with the shops, arcades, offices, pubs and railway stations of the era.[42] Not just by deploying considerably more historical perspective and understanding than the professional historians, but also by relating his account to his readers' present experience in a way they largely fail to do, McWilliam presents a much less dull and grim, yet more credible, picture. In making a typical connection to the present, he reminds his readers that the many Victorian shops they can still find surviving preserve in their ornamental carving, mahogany-stained fittings and varied shop-signs residual evidence

> of the intricate fabric of Victorian life that filled and overflowed from these shops so that, for example, it was quite usual for every square foot of a commercial frontage to be covered with painted advertisements. With houses it is the same. Their plate glass windows were not made to look out so blankly as they do today, for in their time they were three parts filled with curtains and blinds and of course with potted plants.

And while he acknowledges that many will have turned to pubs to escape poor housing, the postmen who have used the Guildford Arms in Edinburgh since Edwardian times drank in an 'immensely lofty' establishment under 'a Jacobean ceiling that would not shame a baronial castle'.[43]

From the general histories, little sense of the visual and spatial distinctiveness of the Scottish townscape or cityscape emerges. The small and middling-size towns of Scotland are hardly separable, for those who know them, from their main parks almost all of which were established over the last century and a half. This would have changed the characteristic environment of these towns quite substantially from one of a comparatively closely-packed main street and adjoining roads, surrounded by countryside to a much more varied townscape in which the open country met stone walls interspersed with trees and parkland, harling and suburban greenery in a much more complex composition. In Crieff there is the 'Macrosty', in Falkirk, the Dollar Park, in Dunfermline, Pittencrieff. The resources would come sometimes from a local patron, sometimes from the municipal authorities.

The experience of the towndwellers must have changed accordingly. Their reactions were probably very varied: the local entrepreneur may have kept many of the locals on low wages to ultimately fund his public benefaction. But many no doubt were glad to have a public 'estate' as grand as the local landowners' policies. We do not know. The general historians do not 'see' any of this, have not researched it, and cannot tell us.

Such initiatives were not confined to the commercially successful entrepreneurs of Victorian Glasgow or their lesser cousins in the market towns of the shires. The baillies of Leith, that 'crawl of cockroaches' in Hugh Macdiarmid's poem 'A Hosting of Heroes' had, for sixty or seventy years before he wrote, been pursuing both slum clearance and environmental improvement schemes:

> Along with slum clearance, ideas of the value of fresh air and exercise began to influence the magistrates, and towards the end of the nineteenth century concern was expressed that the town should acquire parks and open spaces for recreation. This was the thought behind the levelling of the Links as part of the Improvement Scheme in the 1880s. Within a few years other parks were negotiated for . . . in 1907 the Town Council acquired land at Craigentinny and invited Ben Sayers, one of the great golfing exponents of the day, to lay out a nine hole course there.[44]

Similarly the fine stone mills of Galashiels, Selkirk or Alva help to give these towns an unmistakable character and image which many people recognise and find attractive today. Distillery architecture contributes a distinctive man-made aspect to the dramatic landscapes of Speyside or Islay. New middle class opportunities and fashions at the turn of the century established those prominent survivals in many country towns, the great 'hydropathic' hotels of

> the era including magnificently-sited French chateau Atholl Hydro at Pitlochry . . . within whose lavishly equipped basement exercise rooms the curious visitor could until recently sample Edwardian bicycling-machines and plunge-baths.[45]

Equally, the streets of the Tobacco Lords' detached Palladian mansions, and the quite specific form of 'the Glasgow square' render that city quite distinct from Edinburgh, Dundee (or London). Almost nothing emerges of twentieth-century Glasgow's 'Atlantic orientation' and panache. This had social and economic foundations and implications, but it has been strikingly reflected in the city's spatial and architectural character for over a hundred years. Even the later nineteenth century had seen development extend the Merchant City 'into an open-ended street grid more like America than Britain.'[46]

Before the First World War, and especially in the twenties and thirties, this was further emphasised in the response to American classical architectural style:

> this is most noticeable in its commercial heartland where, between the wars, architects like James Miller designed many offices modelled on buildings in New York and Chicago.[47]

There was an equally positive response to the Art Deco style of the thirties, finding its apotheosis in the Glasgow Empire exhibition of 1938 (though it might be observed that in addition to an openness to Atlantic *avant garde* the city was here also returning to seeds sown locally by Mackintosh, some of whose facades – the Willow Tea Rooms for example – had pointed to the thirties decades in advance).

But failure to acknowledge the creativity, variety and indeed colour of the cityscape even in the heart of commercial development and at the height of industrialisation has permitted the projection of a monotony which did not exist.

The heavy engineering industry itself produced striking architectural works including

> William Spence's immense Randolph and Elder Engineering Works, Tradeston (1858–60), whose monumental egyptianstyle facade enclosed an iron and timber framework supporting gantry-cranes and galleried floors.[48]

And among the trading centres of the Clyde:

> By the mid-century, Alexander Kirkland's footbridge crossed the river in a graceful suspended sweep. Later came further architectural splendours – Clarke and Bell's Fish Market facade (1873) in the east, and, over two decades, Burnet's domed buildings for the Clyde Navigation Trust (1883–1905). . . [49]

From a perspective different from that in too many general histories of the period, the tenemented development of central Glasgow cannot be exclusively associated with blackened and broken down slum imagery:

> the later 19th century was characterised by the rebuilding of the central street – higher and higher after the introduction of the lift – clad in rippling red machine-cut sandstone from the new Dumfriesshire quarries and enhanced by wondrous

figure sculpture. These technical changes provided perfect conditions within which the Glasgow Style in architecture and decoration could flourish.[50]

Some tenements are dark, dirty and bare. But few who know Glasgow will be ignorant of the many tenement buildings with stair walls half-covered in dark rich woods or fine glazed tiles, with landing, front-door and flat windows decorated with finely etched or intensely coloured glass.

Of course, these tenements were largely built for the artisan and middle classes. And the Victorian mansions, the splendours of nineteenth century commercial architecture, and the banks of the twenties and thirties may have been built for the better-off sections of the society. But these facts should not lead to their exclusion from the history of the Scottish people.

There are many elements in addition to those discussed here which have fashioned the Scottish cities and towns of the past hundred to one hundred and fifty years: in all their variety these townscapes are immediately identifiable and closely associated with a variety of topographies and localities in the experience of most Scots, whether by connection or as visitors – an often intimate and immediate aspect of their relation to their own history. Their impress, and that of the varied social experiences they represent, is ill-defined in the histories of modern Scotland.

Workers

There is no reason why in writing the history of a people or even a 'class', the aim should be to produce a generalised set of images abstracted from the range of experiences and responses available. This almost inevitably results in a reductive distortion. In practice, there are a whole series of differentiated, yet within themselves, quite coherent elements in any social history – elements cohering on the basis of a whole variety of principles: geographic community, language, class and politics, ethnic background, sport, leisure skills, music and song, clubs and societies. What brings a specificity and humanity to any social history, in this perspective, is unlikely to be discovered by dwelling predominantly on what might be termed the 'economistic factors' directly related to work, lack of it, or the industrial-urban environment.

A history which extended to those other elements would discover a more differentiated, multifaceted, multicoloured image of the Scottish working class than an approach which establishes early and at length an economistic stereotype, then in a way almost determined by the logic of the approach, dismisses the remaining range of social experience as of insignificant and peripheral influence. If there were serious 'breid and butter problems', the logic seems to go, there must have been little else.

Tom Weir was brought up in Springburn, deep in the 'tenement city' of Glasgow. But this did not describe the parameters either of his physical or of his imaginative experience:

> On a clear day I could see unknown peaks of the Highlands from my home in the highest part of industrial Glasgow. Against the clear blue sky to the North, Ben Lomond sparkling white, filled me with longing to climb it. Sometimes, west beyond the city, the jagged crests of the Arran hills would appear tantalisingly.[51]

It was easy for him to get out of the city, to know at first hand walks along the Kelvin or in Cadder woods,

> . . . green places rich in birds, where I saw my first redpolls, corn buntings and greater spotted woodpeckers.[52]

Though Weir was to become a far travelled writer and broadcaster, many of his social peers and contemporaries in the Glasgow of the 1930s shared his pleasure in the readily accessible green and wild places a little to the north. Indeed, it was *precisely* during the times when the life of the urban working class is portrayed as constrained and adumbrated by the dark and silent cranes of the Clyde, that many simultaneously grasped the opportunity to break out into a landscape rich in diversity, depth of colour and sheer exhilarating space. As Weir himself recalled,

> . . . it was these bad times which sparked off the outdoor revolution in which I was caught up. Thousands of Glaswegians were off on the bike every weekend, and I was one of them, lighting fires and drumming up on Loch Lomondside or somewhere in the Trossachs.[53]

Many did not even go so far. It is still possible to see the remnants of the holiday huts which so many working class Glaswegians built and maintained so carefully between Milngavie and the Campsies.

Near this area too, was the famous 'Craigallian Fire':

> . . . a bonfire on the slopes above the loch where weekenders and unemployed made their rendezvous, ate, gossiped, and sang. There are many splendid tales. . . of men who, unable to afford sleeping bags, slept in brown paper or under the Glasgow Herald . . . of epic journeys by lorry or motorbike to tackle desperate climbs with primitive equipment. For these folk there will always be a certain magic in the Craigallian area . . .[54]

Even within and around the cities themselves the undifferentiated grey image of the tenement city cannot really be sustained yet this is the impression the reader is invited to form from the way in which the relevant sections in the general histories tend to be structured. Indeed, oral historical evidence suggests that many people spent only a proportion of their lives in the Glasgow tenement communities. These 'outdwellers' might have been brought up in rural towns or villages (some outlying parts of the city itself were largely rural of course) and then turn to urban living; subsequently they might return to such roots. Alternatively native city-dwellers might move out.

Those brought up in villages on the edge of the city at the beginning of this century recalled it as a rural experience:

> It was right country in Uddingston then. We had a grand garden wi' chrysanthemums and wi' roses growin' up the wall. And we'd a kind of ramblin' fruit orchard for gooseberries and blackcurrants, plums . . . aye and strawberries . . . and there was an apple-tree by the kitchen door. My mother made a lot of preserves and jam.
>
> I left all that when I got wed to Davie and came to live in a tenement. My, some change! But it was my own wee place and I loved it . . . and I knew I was well off by some, at having an outside toilet that was *ours alone* . . .
>
> My wife's family lived in a white but'n'ben cottage at the Mearns. There was other low white-washed houses there and milk floats came in from the farms to the Mearns Cross. Now its a big-big shopping centre and a garage out there.[55]

Such people are unlikely to have brought, or encouraged attitudes of resentment or resignation to the tenement stairs. They remind us that those who can be homogenised by history in socio-economic terms, in reality will have responded to the tenements and tenement society in many different ways, will have 'seen' it in many different lights.

But most of those whose parents, grandparents or greatgrandparents lived in Scottish tenements in Glasgow or elsewhere, will be likely to recognise the set of attitudes suggested by these recollections as more characteristic than the broken spirit of the slum dwellers.

There certainly was great poverty, and personal recollections are subject to rose-tinting, but there is no doubting the fact that there was variety in the experience of the tenement dwellers –

> D'you mind gasogenes? Upstairs had one when I was wee and I thought they must be quite rich. It was a syphon kind of thing in a wire-mesh casing and their papa made soda water in it on Sundays (though mind he was a kirk elder). Then he put in Rose's Lime or lemon juice. That was it ready and he used to say, if you were there, 'come on and get a drink of gasogene, Hen'.[56]

All of this occurred of course in one of those two-roomed Glasgow houses where for T. C. Smout social life was impossible. Indeed Smout would deny that even the most basic and domestic forces of cultural accumulation were available to the majority of the Scots:

> As long as three-quarters of the population lived in houses of three rooms or less, and three fifths in houses of one or two rooms, as was the case before the First World War, there was little space for the accumulation of carpets, furniture, knicknacks and all the paraphernalia of the middle class.[57]

Apart from the fact that the other 'one quarter' of the population would have totalled around one million souls, who can hardly be edited out of this society's history without seriously distorting the account, it is obvious that the smaller households of the working class could not afford or accommodate the belongings of the middle class. But it is also quite wrong to imply that the ordinary Glaswegian in Edwardian times, had no carpets or ornaments. In a typical tenement Room and Kitchen

> . . . the furnishing about 1910 in most homes was horse-hair upholstery and Spanish mahogany with maybe a good table at the window with a chenille cover to save it from sunlight and hullarackit children.
>
> 'I mind yon horse-hair that prickled your bottom, and that you pulled out the wee wiry curls from. My auntie has green velvet on hers but it was rough and sore, no' like a dress. . . oh aye, and we had an aspidistra on a green wally pedestal and veloury curtains hangin' from rings and a pole.'[58]

Smout asserts that ordinary working class experience was not like the more comfortable middle class experience (which we can see) but then spends most of his time describing *the worst aspects* of suburban slum life.

It often seems that his picture of the 'tenement city' is overlaid by his perception (presumably more first-hand, if fleeting) of the post-war council housing estates and high-rise blocks. This substantially distorts the older urban experience:

> Such peripheral housing schemes were . . . a kind of parody of the traditional tenement life of Glasgow: they consisted of tenements indeed, but they were far removed from the urban context in which that mode of life had developed, and incapable of generating their own community life.[59]

Equally:

> The old tenement life was no true antecedent to life in high-rise flats: the tenements had been on a human scale, easy to walk into and about, capable of engendering communities.[60]

The very widespread critical reaction to the clearance of 'good' tenemented districts (as opposed to slums) attested to the positive feelings many had for their experience in these communities. Conditions were created which often produced a close-knit communal experience amongst those of quite different social and material background.

Professor Smout devotes only a few pages to the vast subject of personal or organised working-class activity outside work. This may say much about the historian's perception of those whose story he claims to recount. A subsection on 'Recreation' is appended as a kind of afterthought to a chapter devoted mainly to 'Drink and Temperance'.

There is a brief acknowledgement of the city's efforts

> ... by establishing municipal parks, opening existing gardens to the public, endowing museums and building art galleries. Thus in Edinburgh in 1862, the Trades Council gathered over ten thousand signatures in a petition to open the Botanic Gardens to the public on Sundays after church, and the authorities in Glasgow, apart from constructing the Kelvingrove Galleries, ran the People's Palace on Glasgow Green as a museum and conservatory for the East End, and erected the elegant glass and iron bubble of the Kibble Palace in the botanic gardens at the West End. The public libraries ... were intended for the same purpose.[61]

However, by the manner in which Smout structures his account, all of this comes to be portrayed as an effort (which largely failed) to reform an ignorant, exhausted, ghetto-bound working class. The quality of life of a few improved.

> ... but in Glasgow most of the parks were too far from the most overcrowded areas, the libraries had comparatively little attraction for an undereducated working population that was also exhausted by long physical labour, and the art galleries and museums appealed to a very limited number ... working class or otherwise.[62]

In fact, a different structuring of this account might see these developments in a continuum that would lead eventually to the 'outdoor revolution' of the 1930s and the large number of amateur naturalists, historians, geographers and geologists, who picked up their knowledge, not necessarily at school, which many would indeed have left early, but through self-teaching assisted by libraries, labour colleges or WEA classes.

More specifically, the notion that the city parks were too far away from the workers is clearly preposterous, particularly in view of the vast numbers who took to cycling from the 1880s to the 1930s. As Tom Weir recalled his situation in Springburn:

> We were poor in the thirties, but Glasgow was rich in green space, before it was swallowed up in housing schemes. In these days there was plenty to explore on your doorstep and when motor cars were scarce, cycling was a pleasure.[63]

And while 'long physical labour' as it might have existed in the mid-nineteenth century would have constrained activity outside work, by the 1930s many would defy an only slightly less exhausting working week to enjoy the wilderness areas of the north and west. Weir and his friend left Glasgow at 8.30 on a Saturday evening after a tiring day at work, to travel north by night for a day in the mountains.

There is here a rich and complex dimension of Scottish social history to be explored. It relates to experiences enjoyed by large numbers of ordinary Scots from a variety of classes. The activities which brought these experiences have contributed to an image important to and valued by subsequent generations, an enduring image. The popularity of Weir's books and television programmes, if nothing else, would attest to this.

It has a variety of aspects. It has to do, certainly, with making the life of the industrial workers richer than it often was or is in the modern era. With maintaining a relationship with rural experience and reconnecting with wilderness. But more generally it has to do with asserting the right to skills and knowledge not necessarily *related to work*, in fact precisely valued because *not* related to work: photography, map-reading, mountaineering, geology, ornithology, historical geography, natural history of all kinds, often fishing, sometimes sailing, astronomy, sometimes writing.

This, in some cases, quite heroic reaction, rebellion, of industrial man, is a fascinating matter but is almost completely obscured by the traditional histories' portrait of the passive, broken, welfare supported tenement (=slum) dweller. Rather than explore this rich social response to the material conditions of these times, Smout makes the briefest of references to the development of 'hiking' and 'mountaineering' in the 1930s. (There is none at all in Mitchison, Harvie.) And though he utilises (most unusually) a quotation from Billy Kay's oral transcriptions, it is one carefully selected to re-emphasise his earlier theme of the 'grimness' which characterised the life of the Scots:

> You have to understand what Scotland was like in those days. It was a grim place. . . It really was grim. And you were a youngster in this and you accepted this, you had been brought up to this, this was normal this grimness, then suddenly to find this escape route, this climbing thing, and it absolutely bowled you over . . . It was an explosion, it was a wonderful thing.[64]

It is worth reproducing this comment in full for it is in more than one respect, a revealing quotation for Smout to have seized on. The historian is able to adopt the speaker's logical mistake. The implication can be left to emerge that the subject himself, 'you', and 'the climbing thing', even the mountains themselves, are not also Scotland. This accords perfectly with the historian's selective view.

As we have seen, while he never romanticises urban working class life, Tom Weir's account of this whole movement is quite different. He and his friend are working class youths from Springburn and Dennistoun; they don't want to pursue the lives they might be expected to follow – but the way to an alternative is not an escape from but is directly through, and made available to them by, Glasgow and Scotland.

The city is close to some of Scotland's wild places; they can see them in Springburn; they give them inspiration; Glasgow provides a preparation in its parks and peripheral lochs. The public bus and train timetables, the boats from the Clyde are available to give them access to almost all parts of the mainland and islands. Their own spirit (as that of tens of thousands of others) takes them there despite long hours of physical work. They are able to travel light in their long treks in the North because 'you were made very welcome at any croft-house' (a much corroborated observation). Weir's friend sang 'Scots airs or Gaelic songs' because the city had developed a diverse popular culture. Both would see the places they visited in the context of literature and would subsequently write about and publish their experiences at least partly because they had been stimulated to do so by attending the WEA class on 'The Art of Writing' at Glasgow University.

Smout claims that his book will relate 'what life was like for most Scottish people', but he equates this directly and almost exclusively with 'a world of deprivation and social division'. The history of development in the quality of the Scottish people's experience, the history of this society, *is* the history of welfare (which only significantly improved by the 1950s). Whatever does not accord with this perspective is obscured or appears too fleetingly to modify the general impression. Weir's 'outdoor men' standing by the Craigallian fire in the warm colours of a Strathblane evening or high on the northern hills burnished by a Hebridean sunset don't accord with the grey grimness at all: in the histories of the modern Scots their image flickers briefly and is gone.

The assumption behind much of the writing about the Scottish working classes is that description of the supposedly objective conditions of their material lives and environment is also, and necessarily, a description of their subjectivity. This is a view supported rather than contested by the Left, whose deterministic conception of the relation between material and spiritual conditions encourages the belief that people can be no other and no better than the conditions which they are provided with or which they endure. The implication which is made consistently by the historians is that to describe in economistic terms the deprivation of people's physical existences is, *pari passu*, to describe the poverty of their spiritual existence.

Thus the emblematic reference to the classic slum with its grotesque physical deprivation becomes synonymous with the moral and intellectual condition of all tenement dwellers in Scotland's major cities. The worst of physical conditions is made to stand emblem for the totality of the physical and social environment, and that emblem is taken in turn to represent the spiritual condition of the whole society.

The argument against this position is twofold: first, the conditions of tenement dwellers were not, in general, the conditions described and accounted by the historians – precisely because these were the conditions commented upon at the time as the worst of their time; after all, much of the tenement dwelling of modern Scotland was built in the nineteenth century precisely to replace what were seen to be poor housing conditions; and secondly, the conditions, however unacceptable to us in retrospect, did not determine the consciousness of the people in such a way that their minds and spirits were as narrow as their box beds.

The continuous refrain of these historians is that Scotland suffered some ultimate and unique blight upon its social and cultural experience: this is patently false, both in terms of the commonality of the experience of industrialism in other areas of the world at the same time and in later developments in other continents, and also in terms of the ability of human beings, in Scotland as elsewhere, to fight back and assert themselves against their conditions.

4

Jacobitism in Historiography and Cultural Theory

The deployment of a limited set of theories in Scottish historiography and cultural analysis has been the subject of recent critique. In some areas of inquiry this constricting discourse, with its relentless emphasis on negativities, has been effectively challenged, and new patterns of historical and cultural interpretation have emerged. It is unlikely, for instance, that after the work of Alexander Broadie and David Allan any serious historian would now feel able to depict the Enlightenment in Scotland, in the manner of what Allan could still in 1993 call 'the prevailing model', as a semi-miraculous phenomenon which arose in a backward land with little history of intellectual endeavour and achievement;[1] and William Donaldson has done much to undermine an established assumption that Scottish popular culture in the Victorian period can be adequately defined in terms of kailyardism.[2] Nevertheless, in many areas little has yet been done to question the dominant paradigms; and this is true of a central episode in modern Scottish history which plays a major role both in contemporary cultural debate and in different forms of folk and popular culture.

No longer shadow has been cast by dominant historiography and cultural theory, perhaps, than that which darkens the phenomenon of Jacobitism. On this subject commentary has made familiar a series of damning judgments: about the nature of Jacobitism in its historical context, about the role played by the movement and its symbols in the consciousness of later generations, and about the legitimacy and appropriateness of the use of such symbols to mark Scottish identities and aspirations. Although the familiar positions are deeply entrenched, and so unlikely to be easily overturned, many of the common, dismissive evaluations of Jacobitism are in fact, at the very least, open to question; and it is possible to construct a quite different 'way of seeing' the Jacobite movement and its place in Scottish culture.

It will be useful, first of all, to review some of the conventional perceptions, indicate something of their intellectual background, and draw out certain of the main claims they involve.

1

The Jacobite cause and its symbols, tartan in particular, have been placed at the centre of contemporary Scottish cultural debate by what can be called Scotch Myths theory. This was developed in the 1970s and early 1980s in influential texts by Tom Nairn, Colin McArthur, Lindsay Paterson and others,[3] and also given prominence by the Grigors' 'Scotch Myths' exhibition of 1981. The main argument put forward by such contributions was that Scots have connived at the manufacture and peddling of clownish, contorted versions of their history and culture, for reasons of economic gain and British-imperial participation, and as a way of evading the harsh realities of the Scottish condition. This prolonged and shameful undertaking, it was suggested, has led Scots actually to accept a kind of dream history of their nation, one principally peopled by the subjects of romantic myth. Instead of a serious, realistic history, Scots have embraced a mad circus-show within which caper Robert the Bruce, William Wallace, Mary Queen of Scots – and, of course, worst of all, bedecked in tartan, Bonnie Prince Charlie and the Jacobites. In the symbols of the '45 the Scotch Myths school see the most potent and noxious ingredients of the cooked-up history and identity Scots have come to believe is authentically theirs.

Aspects of this theory have been criticised, by Paul Scott among others,[4] but its central argument is widely accepted, and often simply assumed to be true. To take an illustration from current cultural commentary, Colin Kirkwood presupposes that many Scots cling to a mythical, 'Highlandist' version of national history when he considers it necessary to insist:

> At the heart of the Scottish experience is not the romance
> of ghosts, castles and tartans, but uprooting, loss [etc,
> etc].[5]

The reader might fairly naturally infer from this that the Jacobite movement itself belongs to that romance, a narrative which does not form part of the significant, the 'real' history and experience of the Scottish people. And in fact the author depicts the '45 as a kind of madcap scheme for which in recent years the exploits of Ally's Army provide a parallel.

In any case, such dismissal or erasure of the Jacobite movement, a denial of its historical significance, is characteristic of Scotch Myths theory. Whatever the weight of Jacobitism and its symbols in later dream-and-fantasy history, it was in real historical terms an irrelevance, an irrational attempt to defy the logic of history, or even a form of lunatic outburst. Such assessments may in part be motivated by the theory's own logic and aesthetic: what better or more fitting, after all, than an irrelevant and semi-farcical episode to provide later generations with the stuff of false consciousness? But however this may be, Scotch Myths theory did not originate such interpretations of the place of Jacobitism in its historical context.

The Scotch Myths and anti-tartanry polemicists were able to build on what, only a few years ago, appeared to be an impregnable historiographical structure, a liberal-marxist consensus of ideas which dominated approaches to history in the British universities of the 1960s and 1970s. The great themes of modern British history, as this tradition defined them, were the spread and impact of industrialisation; the growth of urban society; the breakdown of established social relations; the emergence of the bourgeoisie; the development of class consciousness and class struggle; the decline of religion and spread of secular modes of thought; the extension of popular representation and participation in politics. In the intellectual climate where these interests prevailed, Jacobitism appeared to be an irrelevance unworthy of detailed treatment.

It could not be easily grafted onto a story of class dialectic, and its association with divine-right theory, nationalism, religion, tribalism – all phenomena already obsolescent, and destined to disappear completely as the logic of history unfolded – could permit it no place in annals of forward-looking revolution and progress. The accepted view was summed up in E. P. Thompson's judgment that Jacobitism represented a 'nostalgic and anachronistic' movement;[6] and such a backward-looking cause, it was assumed, could hardly have been a powerful ideological force or a significant vehicle for popular disaffection.

In the specifically Scottish context, an extremely influential historical account of the Jacobite movement was supplied by Tom Nairn in his 1975 essay, 'Old and New Scottish Nationalism'. Jacobitism, in this marxist analysis, represented a 'backward', 'pre-feudal', Highland Scotland ranged against the 'advanced', 'bourgeois' Scottish Lowlands and England. In 1745 the 'backwoods' army of Jacobites marched on London 'bearing with it the menace of restored absolute monarchy'. That this motley crew got so far as Derby was 'incredible'. However, the forces of backwardness 'had literally no chance'. And after the '45, 'the Gaeltacht was to be allowed no further opportunity of disrupting civilised progress . . . its old social structure and culture were pulverised . . .'[7]

This is a simple, clear and coherent interpretation; the problem is that, as should become evident in the course of our discussion, almost none of its elements resists critical examination. In his more recent work, however, despite relying on aspects of new, revisionist histories, Nairn recapitulates this reading of Jacobitism as a reactionary force attempting to hold back the tides of the 'developmental process'. Post–1688 Britain's predicament, he writes in *The Enchanted Glass*, permitted 'no developmental escape either backwards (with Jacobitism) or forwards (with Republicanism and industrialism)'.[8]

But, in fairness to Nairn, it must be said that Scottish academic historians, even if they provide more nuanced historical accounts, rarely make available to their readers a substantially different perspective. Here too there is a tendency to depict Jacobitism as a kind of oddity, a hiccup in the inevitable process of Scottish integration into the Hanoverian state. The notion that it was somehow an evanescent, insubstantial phenomenon is conveyed by a central and typical theme, that of its abrupt disappearance from real history after the '45. Bruce Lenman, for instance, perhaps the most highly-respected Scottish student of Jacobitism, writes in his general history that

> The defeat of the Jacobite Army commanded by Prince Charles Edward Stuart at the battle of Culloden . . . finally laid to rest an issue in Scottish politics which most Scotsmen as late as 1744 assumed had been settled 30 years previously.[9]

The '45 was the last gasp of a cause already long obsolete, 1746 marks the disappearance of Jacobitism from *Realgeschichte*; and a line is drawn. Here Lenman is echoing a view to be found in the earlier major histories of the period. In William Ferguson's judgment,

> By mid-century the Union had become accepted in Scotland as one of the facts of life. One reason was that it seemed finally to be conferring the long-awaited economic benefits; another was that the last stronghold of anti-union feeling, the Jacobite movement, had been destroyed. The extinction of Jacobitism was a direct consequence of the conflict with Spain which was absorbed in the great European war of the Austrian succession.[10]

Henceforth, the cause was available only as a vehicle for nostalgia. For G. S. Pryde,

> By mid-century, Jacobitism was a mere sentiment, a far-off memory, the theme of many a plaintive song.[11]

Pryde here touches on the second major theme to be found in standard historiographical treatments, one which has provided Scotch Myths theory with a main supporting structure. This concerns the process by which the Jacobite movement and its associated Highland culture, their role in real history abruptly terminated, would be re-appropriated by future generations of Scots: Bonnie Prince Charlie, tartan, kilts and bagpipes would come to inform a popular nostalgic cult, or, in the more extreme version of the argument, a surrogate, fantasy identity inimical both to genuine nationalism and to the formation of a progressive social consciousness.

Two particular stages in this process are highlighted in Lenman's portrayal of the era after 1745. The first is the irruption of James MacPherson into the polite culture of the 1760s. MacPherson claimed to have discovered long-lost texts depicting the history of Highland Gaelic civilisation. The works are now considered largely his own creation, but certain luminaries of Enlightenment Scotland were prepared to give him the benefit of the doubt, and promoted a new image of the Highlander as a species of noble savage. Thus, having dismissed Jacobitism from 'real' history, Lenman almost immediately provides us with an illustration of Lowland Scotland swallowing and regurgitating myths of a dead Highland culture.

Secondly, in common with most modern histories, Lenman's account stresses the romantic and antiquarian impulses, often particularly identified with the work of Walter Scott, which emerged in early nineteenth-century Scotland. This development, which of course produced many Jacobite-related novels, poems and songs, is seen as part of the response of the landed class to the threat posed to its ascendancy by the new reform movements. George IV's visit to Scotland in 1823,

> in many ways was the final celebration by a virile but doomed provincial ascendancy of their extraordinary neo-feudal romantic self-justification, so compellingly limned by the brush of Raeburn in his Highland portraits, and so persuasively preached by Scott in his numerous novels.[12]

Lenman does refer to some other aspects of the aftermath of the '45 – the forfeiture and then regaining of the estates of the landed rebels, for instance – but these tend to be included insofar as they illustrate or elaborate the main thrust of Lenman's history: the development of the system of patronage which cohered and regulated the British political system of the 18th and early 19th centuries.

The historical account exemplified here informs the thought of many Scottish writers and intellectuals; and it is central to the highly influential cultural theory developed by Nairn, recently described by χ David McCrone as 'the most powerful and dominant analysis of Scottish culture', and as 'the most perceptive and critical account we have'.[13] On Nairn's view, a 'pulverised' Highland culture and dead rebel cause were transformed by the mid-nineteenth century into a mythic, romantic and empty Highlandism, a distorted legend and symbolism which Scots idiotically took to be essential to their national identity.

All over Europe new nationalist movements invented or purloined histories and symbols, with small regard for historical logic or decency. However, in Scotland this borrowing – from which the very name, and so many of the icons of 'tartanry' are derived – was one not in the name of 'nationalism' but in order to enrich a sub-nationalist culture. The latter's characteristic thirst for harmless sentiments and sub-romantic imagery found perfect objects in the debris of a ruined, alien society. On a higher plane, from *Waverley* onwards the emphatic, undeniably 'historic' quality of a deceased culture provided writers with a perfect avenue for that kind of retrospective, once-upon-a-time national feeling which had become mandatory. Once the Stuarts were back in Italy for good, the '45 could become everyone's favourite tale: Prince Tearlach's ultimate dynastic inheritance was that boundless realm of shortcake tins, plaid socks, kilted statuettes and whisky labels that stretches from Tannochbrae to Tokyo.[14]

The similarity of this cultural borrowing to processes in other societies masks, then, for Nairn, the essential difference. Jacobitism and its highlandist symbols, the icons of a cause irrevocably lost, could not inform a genuine romanticism, that is, a forward-looking cultural-political movement intent on national liberation and progress. They served, not to re-animate Scottish life, but to cast over it a dead hand; in turning to this aspect of their past, the Scots embarked not on romanticism but cultural necrophilism.

The work of historians and culture critics on Jacobitism presents us, then, with a number of intertwined and partially overlapping ideas. Some of the more central points we go on to discuss can be summarised here in crude form. Firstly, as prominent in the anti-tartanry polemic, there is the notion that tartan is inauthentic in a variety of senses: it is implied that tartan is not an 'organic' Scottish product at all, and argued that its adoption as a symbol of Scotland reflected the cynical hypocrisy of the elites and the feeble-mindedness of the masses. Secondly, we have a cluster of views about Jacobitism in its historical context: it is claimed, or implied, that the movement was anachronistic, 'irrational', inimical to progress, even farcical, and that it naturally lacked substantial support. A third set of ideas concerns the movement's 'inevitable' defeat, and includes the theory that the later nostalgic espousal of the cause planted bacilli of defeatism in the national psyche. A further argument is that after the '45 Highland culture was extinguished, overwhelmed by modernity, and so as it were made itself available as the subject of myth. Finally, and related to all these points, it is maintained that Jacobitism's claim to express Scottish aspirations was illegitimate in historical context, and that Jacobitism subsequently provided the late eighteenth, the nineteenth and the twentieth centuries with antique, sub-romantic symbols as a substitute for mature political and cultural formations.

2

What, then, of the supposedly mythic nature of tartan itself, and the charge, pressed by anti-tartanry theorists, that it is an inappropriate symbol of Scottishness?

The adoption of tartan imagery is frequently regarded as an even more lunatic feature of Scottish culture than the survival of a certain popular sympathy for the Jacobite cause. On the one hand, it is implied that tartan and Highland dress were little more than fashion creations, concocted only a generation or so before the '45. And, independently of the question of tartan's authenticity, it is argued that there was something deeply perverse about the adoption by Romantic and popular Scotland of the mantle, or plaid, of a backward-looking movement and a dead socio-cultural system – especially as tartan took on new associations of militarism and chauvinism due to its use in Scottish regimental uniform.

In 1983 there appeared an essay, since much cited, which has been widely taken as providing powerful new support for the anti-tartanry case. Far from being an authentic or organic product of Scotland, so the essay argues, tartan is in fact a kind of hoax, the work of conmen who successfully duped the Scots into believing it was a native and ancient sartorial style. The essay, by Hugh Trevor-Roper, no doubt occasioned some rejoicing in Scotch Myths circles. Certainly, as McCrone observes, 'few left-liberal Scottish intellectuals' would care to challenge its main drift.[15]

The article was published in *The Invention of Tradition*, the Hobsbawm and Ranger collection which helped to bring this concept into vogue. There is, of course, nothing original or startling about the bare notion that 'traditions' like tartan or kilt-wearing were invented: all forms of culture, by definition, are human inventions. But Hobsbawm and Trevor-Roper of course use the idea of an invented tradition in a special, non-pleonastic sense. First of all, such traditions owe their existence to the deeds of unscrupulous agents, bent on financial gain or social manipulation. (The *motif* of manipulation and social control is especially dear, as might be expected, to Professor Hobsbawm, who underlines that invented traditions 'inculcate certain values and norms'.) Secondly, as this would imply, such inventions are foisted on a gullible mass of consumers. And third, they lay claim

to a historical longevity, invoked to endow them with the authority of
ancient and hallowed custom, which is in fact, if not entirely spurious,
'largely factitious'.[16]

'The Highland Tradition of Scotland', Trevor-Roper's title
announces, will now be exposed as a fraud in precisely this sense.
Gratified to have found a new vent for his notoriously strong feelings about Scotland, Trevor-Roper launches his attack without further
ado. Kilts, tartans and bagpipes, the 'distinctive national apparatus'
of Scots, he declares at the outset, are not as commonly supposed of
'great antiquity', but 'in fact largely modern'.[17] The knock-out blow
to popular delusions on this matter is delivered a few pages later: the
kilt as it is now generally worn was invented, around 1730, by one
Thomas Rawlinson, an English entrepreneur domiciled near Inverness.
The 'invention' consisted of separating the skirt from the plaid, thus
making it a distinct garment: this was more suitable working dress for
Rawlinson's employees than the older, cumbersome fashion. Trevor-
Roper then makes much of the activities of William Wilson and
Son, a Bannockburn firm of kilt-makers, and the Highland Society of
London – the inventors, he claims, of differentiated clan tartans – in
exploiting the taste for tartan kilts in the early nineteenth-century. The
essay's central theme of fraudulence is sustained by accounts of the
careers of James MacPherson and the self-styled Sobieski Stuarts, who,
like MacPherson, claimed to have discovered a long-lost manuscript,
the *Vestiarium Scoticum*. (It is sadly ironic that Trevor-Roper's own
lasting fame is likely to be that of a victim of historical hoaxsters in
a more recent invented-manuscript affair.)

But none of this demonstrates the truth of the grand initial assertion, nor, more particularly, shows that tartan was an 'invention'.
All the essay establishes in fact is that the plaid and trews evolved
over two or three centuries to give way to the modern kilt when
statutory and military force combined to this end after the '45.
Trevor-Roper himself says that as early as the sixteenth-century 'both
plaid and trews were probably of tartan'.[18] The Highland Companies, disbanded in 1717, had been termed The Black Watch because
of their dark green tartan.[19] And tartan was used by the Gaelic
Jacobite poets to provide a badge and iconographic contrast to the
Hanoverians:

> O hi ri ri he is coming
> O hi ri ri our exiled king
> Let us take our arms and clothing
> And the flowing tartan plaid . . .
> Pity him who on that day
> Wears the ugly coat of red

> His black hat, bordered and cockaded
> Split like a cabbage round his ears![20]

This did no violence to the reality of 'what happened'. As the rebel army reached Manchester at the end of 1745, an observer noted: 'They do not appear to be such terrible fellows as has been represented . . . The guards and officers are all in a Highland dress, a long sword, and stuck with pistols.'[21]

The severity, thoroughness and extended duration of the campaign to eradicate Highland dress after 1746 would also indicate that it was no transient fashion of the aristocratic occupiers of Holyrood in 1745. Moreover, as Trevor-Roper recounts, parliamentarians considered banning distinctive Highland costume after the rising of 1715; if anything like the strong version of the thesis he attempts to insinuate were indeed true, the British parliament would have been considering the prohibition of something which had not yet been conceived – an exaggeration, surely, of the behavioural possibilities of even that institution.

Tartan was not, then, an 'invention'; nor was its association as dress and symbol with Jacobitism manufactured. We come later to the question of the appropriateness of the movement and its symbols as vehicles for later Scottish national expression, but a final point should be made at this stage, on Trevor-Roper's argument, which is also relevant to the wider issue. Even if it could be established that tartan dress was an eighteenth-century or later 'invention', nothing whatever follows about the meaning or meanings associated with tartan by its past and present users. Its meaning could not be frozen, as Trevor-Roper seems to imagine, in the intentions of William Wilson and Son, or in the 'values and norms' an elite might have wished to 'inculcate' in other social groups through its deployment; nor can meanings be dictated from above in the way suggested by Trevor-Roper's wild claim about an 'imposition' of the Highland tradition on 'the whole Scottish nation',[22] for people do not, so to speak, ingest meanings whole, or mechanically register and reproduce them.

The argument made familiar by Scotch Myths theory according to which tartan expresses a series of undesirable emotions and attitudes – from militarism and xenophobia to a maudlin patriot sentiment which contrasts with real nationalist intention – is a hypothesis which, to our knowledge, has never actually been tested by any kind of investigation among those to whom the theorists confidently attribute such attitudes, and whose autonomy and capacity for interpretation they thereby overlook and deny.[23] What *is* known is that tartan is now used as a symbol of Scottishness by people whose commitment to genuine forms of political and cultural nationalism is not in question. If it is undoubtedly true that establishment groups and commercial forces have attempted to appropriate this powerful semiotic system and shape its meanings to their own ends, it is equally indisputable that tartan has been invested with many other meanings, and that it can and does function as an iconography of opposition to Scotland's current political status.

3

We have already referred to the perception of the Jacobite movement as a nostalgic anachronism, an irrational cause seeking to impede progress, the work of social elements dilatory in leaving the historical stage at a time when the logic of history was ushering in a new, modern world. And this naturally suggests that Jacobitism was a fleeting, superficial phenomenon which exercised slight purchase on social and political reality. The risings of 1715 and 1745 appear as colourful yet bizarre events, alien and ultimately irrelevant – even 'meaningless' – irruptions into the normality and inevitability of historical development.[24] Such views can then shade off into a perception of Jacobitism as really a kind of joke or farce, or a cause which was, in any or all of the word's senses, mad.

In the heyday of liberal-marxist approaches to British history, it would have been almost impossible to secure a serious hearing for any alternative interpretation. The focus of such historiography on precursors or origins of later and contemporary developments and concerns, its concern with 'underlying forces' and relative neglect of 'superstructure' – whether, for instance, high political debate, or the world of popular belief – effectively banished Jacobitism to reservations deemed unworthy of serious historical discussion. However, thanks to more recent analyses, it is now possible to appreciate some of the general weaknesses of this tradition and question many of its particular theses, including those which concern Jacobitism.

A new generation of historians has challenged the view that suppport for the movement was insubstantial, or evanescent, or confined to the Scottish Highlands. Even in England, the cause was sustained over several generations by an army of ideologues, polemicists, newspapermen and pamphleteers. There was still a market for their ideas after the '45. 'The Rehearsal', journal of the leading Jacobite campaigner Charles Leslie, was reprinted in a six-volume collected edition in 1750; and Jacobite opinion continued to be served by the 'London Evening Post', 'The Mitre and Crown' (1748–50), and 'The True Briton' (1751–53), as well as periodicals outside London.

Support was motivated in different ways. Some acted out of principle and intellectual conviction, others from personal ambition and opportunism. The Stuart dynasty exerted a powerful charisma. The cause was also, in an age before mass political parties provided channels for the expression of popular opinion, a vehicle for discontent with the existing corrupt regime. Nor should we discount, in attempting to comprehend a world still deeply religious, the fact that divine right was taken to entail the sacred nature of allegiance to the rightful monarch, an allegiance which 'could not be easily dispensed with, any more than could a religious faith or an obligation of personal honour'.[25]

Whatever our contemporary perceptions, Jacobitism was certainly never regarded as a joke by the new regime. There was a sustained campaign to stem Jacobite propaganda and stifle pro-Jacobite sympathy and support. 'The State Papers Domestic for the reigns of the first two Georges are littered with prosecutions of Jacobite publicists', one historian writes, and adds: 'a story of ideological resilience in adversity which has yet to be fully investigated.'[26] Jacobitism was even less of a laughing matter for those whose pro-Stuart commitments brought them before the courts. Looking back from 1745, a Macgregor chief portrayed the anti-Jacobite terror:

> The many sanguinary penal laws since the Revolution, whereby the crime of Jacobitism is rendered more horribly dreadful in its consequences than murder, witchcraft or even open deism or atheism . . . has brought such a habit and spirit of dissimulation on them, that a Jacobite can never be discovered by his words. It must be his actions that decypher him.[27]

Many of the movement's leading figures, like the Irishman Leslie, were forced into exile. They were fortunate. For others, the cost of commitment to Jacobitism was imprisonment, flogging or hanging.

The idea that Jacobitism represented beliefs and values which were incompatible with progress and modernity has a long history. It was expressed, for instance, in that famous work of nineteenth-century historiography, Henry Buckle's *History of Civilisation in England*. In his usual uncompromising style, Buckle averred that

> It is . . . difficult to conceive the full amount of the impetus given to English civilisation by the expulsion of the House of Stuart.

1688 marked a grand turning-point, when 'ancient supersitions' and 'the old theological spirit' were sloughed off, and the 'real interests of the nation began to be perceived.' In consequence, 'as the eighteenth century advanced, the great movement of liberation proceeded'.[28] This kind of Whig perspective is now fossilised in a journalistic or commonsensical understanding of the course of modern British history – in structures, that is to say, which are highly resistant to criticism. Within this mythology, the 'Glorious Revolution' and the ultimate slaying of the Jacobite ogre in 1746 were episodes in the process of gradual evolution, under relatively benign and enlightened governance, by which Britain became a modern, industrialised and democratic society.

It is certainly true that Jacobitism did not stand for democracy, or social levelling, or for what other things the term 'progress' in its sociopolitical sense normally implies. But no significant contemporary force in British politics did. What is more, the older view that the 1688 settlement was informed by a libertarian political philosophy, or at least expressed some tendency towards democratisation, is now generally regarded as mistaken. 'The overwhelmingly conservative bias' of pre–1688 Whig ideology, writes H. T. Dickinson, was subsequently 'confirmed and consolidated'.[29] The Revolution was not intended to and did not involve any compromise of absolute state power or any extension of popular rights, representation or participation: the settlement was designed solely to ensure that the elites represented in parliament shared absolute and unconditional sovereignty with the monarch.

Within Whig and popular understanding the negative meaning of Jacobitism is partially defined by a contrast with the order which overcame it. Critical perspectives on the latter therefore provide us with an alternative way of interrogating received conceptions of Jacobitism; and here we are indebted above all to a theorist whose views on specifically Scottish history and culture we can rarely accept.

The most celebrated attack on the Hanoverian system, the Whig version of modern British history and the English and Great-British chauvinism this underpins is Tom Nairn's *The Enchanted Glass*. A proper treatment of Nairn's argument is beyond the scope of this essay, and we here offer the briefest summary. Nairn argues, essentially, that the 1688 settlement froze England in a state of 'chronic pre-modernity'. The Revolution was not the origin of a process which would culminate in democracy and modernity. On the contrary, it secured the hegemony (later extended over Scotland) of a clique which would throttle authentic industrialisation, thwart the emergence of a meritocratic society, preserve a culture of authority, hierarchy and deference, and successfully perpetuate the reality of closed-elite rule behind democratic trimmings. Nairn's startling indictment merits quotation:

> England permanently kept its structure of oligarchy: that is, it remained what we see at the end of the twentieth century, approaching the three-hundredth-anniversay of William's invasion – an aristocratic, family-based elite uniting land-ownership with large-scale commerce and managing 'its' society as a co-optive estate.[30]

This kind of radical critique of Hanoverianism allows us to question a further conventional thesis about Jacobitism's role in history. The deposition of the Stuarts inaugurated not, as rosy Whig and popular versions of history would have it, a movement towards democracy, but rather the establishment of a permanent patrician oligarchy.

4

Jacobitism was a reactionary, irrational cause; it commanded little substantial support, and was doomed to failure; the '45 was a late 'flash in the pan' of a movement out of its time, a final idiosyncratic flourish of almost medieval tribal militarism; and the outmoded cultural and social world Jacobitism did represent vanished after 1746, a sudden disappearance which confirms the movement's shadowy and anachronistic character.

As deployed by some writers, this circle of ideas carries the implication that the Jacobite episode demonstrated an inclination among many Scots to embrace lost causes and to indulge a taste for glorious defeats. The clans never stood a chance anyway, and the subsequent popular appeal of Jacobite 'myths' should be read as confirmation of the existence of some such national disorder of defeatism. In reality, the notion that the '45 was an inevitable defeat and came to constitute a kind of defeatist paradigm imbuing subsequent national culture and character is sustained neither by history nor legend.

To commence with the latter. A complex set of mythic undercurrents shape the way in which Jacobitism was and is perceived by Scots. Its legendary associations, which originate within Gaelic culture, are not of ultimate defeat, but of the restoration of Scotland as a Celtic civilisation. Jacobite Gaelic poets like MacMaighstair Alastair 'found a way to fuse together . . . [a] vision of the Stewarts, of Gaeldom, and of an ideal Scotland'.[31] This was bound up with age-old images (often shared with the Irish) such as that of Fionn and the Fianna, asleep under the Grampians, who would one day awake and save Scotland. The Stuarts certainly encouraged such associations.

It seems certain that the 'translation' of these ideas into Scottish culture as a whole was greatly assisted by James MacPherson. In this perspective, he deserves a rather different reputation from that provided by the dominant historiographical tradition. For Bruce Lenman (here betraying a number of interesting assumptions),

> Nothing better demonstrates the disintegration of social and moral structures in the Highlands than the career of James 'Fingal' MacPherson, as impudent and brazen a liar as the Celtic Twilight ever sent to plague the Anglo-Saxon world

before the rise of David Lloyd George in the twentieth century.[32]

An alternative estimation would be that MacPherson contributed in an important way to a defence both of the Gaeltacht and of Scottish identity as a whole in the latter half of the eighteenth century.

> The English propaganda image of the Highlander as child-eating savage and lawless bandit was turned on its head by the Jacobite vision of the Highlander as patriot, who alone clung to the heroic standards of the Scotland of Bruce and Wallace. This Jacobite propaganda image blossomed spectactularly among the camouflaged Jacobitism of MacPherson's Ossian poems ... It was Jacobite ideology alone which maintained a coherent framework in which to define the identity of Scotland and the Scots in an era of national and cultural flux.[33]

There can be little doubt that a continuing defiance and sense of hope were sustained in Scottish culture as a whole by the powerful tradition of Jacobite song. These are clearly recognisable in songs which have been retained as part of popular culture up to the present time: just as the 'loyal Macdonalds' will 'awaken', so the waiting leader will 'come back again', and 'Scotland will rise'.

Many of these songs are sung and played within the canon of popular Scottish culture typically denigrated as 'tartanry' or 'highlandism'. What the analyses of Scottish culture which rely on these concepts fail to acknowledge is that many of the images and popular-cultural products they have subsumed as mindless kitsch have in reality operated upon and within a variety of media, ideologies and social formations to help sustain a defiant Scottish identity.

A number of the points made in this essay draw on the evidence and interpretations contained in Murray Pittock's recent book, *The Invention of Scotland*. The title is perhaps unfortunate, as it suggests a product in the Hobsbawm-Trevor-Roper line, and the dustjacket design raises fears of another contribution to Scotch Myths analysis, but in fact the book provides a fresh and fascinating set of insights into the influence of Jacobite ideology and symbols upon Scottish culture up to the present.

We might summarise the characteristics of the positive, libertarian 'post-Jacobite' ideology which developed from the eighteenth-century, through the central figure of James Hogg, to the work of cultural nationalists of the twentieth century in the following terms. It is founded on a conception of Scottish history as a struggle for freedom and for the liberty of the oppressed, a fight viewed in long historical perspective, with Wallace and Bruce invoked as actors in the drama. The Jacobite propaganda image of the Highlander as loyal patriot (as contrasted with Whig history's murderous thief or Scott's anarchic, doomed hero) was extended to cover, by association, the industrial-urban Scots of the nineteenth and twentieth centuries. In this conception, the '45 was not the end, as Scott desperately wrote it up to be, this was not Scotland's destiny, and the risings would continue in the form new ages would give them.

Many of the elements of the assertive and revivalist Jacobite-nationalist ideology associated with Hogg are to be found within those strands of Scottish popular culture damned as 'tartanry' by the Scotch Mythers.

> It's the wild song of freedom I am hearing once again,
> It's the skirl of the pipers and the feet of marching men
> As in days long forgotten, from the city and the glen,
> It's the wild song of freedom I can hear once again.
>
> It sounds over moorland, over heather, over hill;
> The streets of the cities echo loudly to the thrill,
> It calls, Caledonia!, will you waken now as then,
> It's the wild song of freedom I can hear once again.
>
> Will the past be forgotten, will a nation now forget?
> Are the children of Wallace and of Bruce still sleeping yet?
> Will the glory of history be written all in vain?
> It's the wild song of freedom that's upon us once again.
>
> Will you march with the dreamers to your country's destiny?
> So our children tomorrow will be proud of us today?
> Will we forward together from the city and the glen?
> It's the wild song of freedom that's upon us once again![34]

This is a song by the popular 'tartan' entertainer, Andy Stewart, recorded in 1975 (in the era, of course, of another rising). Many other productions of popular 'tartanry' carry forward the post-Jacobite nationalist ideas Pittock describes, even if only in the form of recordings of the old Jacobite songs. In some recent popular musical work, such as *The Cheviot, the Stag, and the Black, Black Oil*, there is an updated use of Jacobite ideology and image. But the Scottish audiences could not have responded so strongly and with such recognition to this work as they did had the music and the political-cultural messages it carried not been mediated and transmitted through so many popular-cultural forms.

But to return, so to speak, to history, and the rising of 1745, we would now like to discuss some culturally influential conceptions of 'what happened', and also highlight some rather neglected aspects of the revolt and its aftermath.

As we remarked earlier, there is still a tendency to trivialise or even ridicule the '45 and see it as a semi-farcical venture, an Ally's-Army-like pantomime, or a primitive, poorly-organised and amateurishly-executed exploit, the image conjured by Nairn's reference to an army from the 'backwoods'. As a new generation of historians now recognise, such depictions bear little relation to historical realities. The rising was not a farce, but, in Jeremy Black's words, 'the greatest crisis that affected the eighteenth-century British state';[35] and the campaign was not a botched and bungled affair, but, according to McLynn, 'an outstanding military exploit'.[36] Among the older works, Ferguson's history, though less confidently assertive than this, also warns against any trivialisation of the rising:

> Charles Edward refused to accept revised French policy and determined to raise a rebellion on his own initiative. He gambled on forcing France to help, and lost, but nonetheless it would be rash to dismiss the '45 as Celtic moonshine, a mere 'romantic but mad fling for a throne'. It had no such appearance in 1745, not to the government, to the rebels, to the general public, nor especially perhaps to those who had to pay Jacobite cess. A makeshift army which marched and counter-marched over most of Scotland and much of England, which sometimes evaded and sometimes defeated superior government forces, which levied money and commanded purveys can hardly be dismissed as a harmless joke.[37]

Lord George Murray's decision to retreat from Derby (against Charles Edward's own wishes) did not reflect cowardice or defeatist panic, but sound military strategy. Michael Lynch writes: 'The decision was undoubtedly the correct one from the viewpoint of the military textbook and the alternative still greatly depended on putting blind faith in a French invasion.'[38] Again, the defeat at Culloden on 16 April, 1746 was not the annihilating blow of popular belief and even some serious works of commentary. The Jacobites were heavily outnumbered, and 1,000 of the 6,000-strong force were lost, but, to quote Lynch once more, 'only three-fifths of the Prince's army had been in the field and the immediate reaction of his commanders was that the battle had not been decisive . . . Murray expected to do better in a return contest with Cumberland, and Lochiel was even as late as mid-May planning a summer campaign'.[39]

After the engagement the rebels regrouped at Ruthven. A message from Charles disbanded them – he had received exaggerated accounts of the losses at Culloden – but it is tempting to speculate on how

Murray's plan for a guerrilla campaign in the central and western Highlands would have gone, particularly in view of the reception the Prince got as a fugitive. Eric Linklater portrays Charles as developing at this stage into a figure of real character, almost a patriotic guerrilla leader. He began to present

> . . . the picture of a man who, having been brought up in the tame luxury of an exiled court, had learnt to live like an outlaw, a partisan, a folk-hero; and perhaps a better portrait than pretty pictures of him in Highland finery.[40]

Here Linklater is repeating an element in the propaganda of Jacobitism itself, developed in the years after the '45:

> By the early 1750s, Charles Edward had established a unique iconographical place for himself. His images were more human, more active and less authoritarian than those of his father. They mingled Republican classicism with tinges of romanticism to create the concept of a bold and virtuous 'patriot' prince.[41]

Indeed, in more general terms, Jacobitism was able both to articulate traditional ideologies oppositional to the British state and to form what might now be seen as surprising alliances with new, more radical ideas. In this perspective, far from being an inevitably doomed medieval throwback, the movement showed considerable potential for development and 'modernisation'.

In the received account of the long-term development of Scottish culture, the defeat of Jacobitism involved the collapse, destruction, pulverisation or extinction of Highland Gaelic culture and society, which thus made itself available as a source of myth; and, as we have seen, the idea of the 'death' of Jacobitism and Highland culture is crucial to the tropes of Scotch Myths and Nairnite analyses. But how credible is the notion of the abrupt demise of Jacobitism, and of a sudden fall of a curtain across Highland Gaelic history and culture?

There were around 650,000 people living in the Highlands and islands in the mid-eighteenth century, perhaps half of the total national population. At first sight, it is difficult to believe that, as Lenman maintains, most of them gave up the cause after 1714, or that they disregarded the clan system after 1750. In fact, as regards the clan system, Lenman seems almost to contradict his own assertion. He goes on to explain the development of the 'patronage system' through which Scotland was governed by Westminster via a Scottish 'Man of Business' – the first of these being Archibald Campbell, Earl of Islay on behalf of the Duke of Argyle. Yet the powerbase of both was their location at the centre of the networks of influence, allegiance and obligation that was Clan Campbell. And as soon as Islay took over from

Duke John in 1743, we are told he threw into reverse the Duke's offensive against the Clan Campbell tacksmen, which had been designed to squeeze them out as 'useless mouths'.

There is also a striking dearth, in the main historical accounts, of any attention to the subjectivity of the Jacobite experience for the thousands who were 'out', and for their families, and descendants. Gaelic culture was above all an oral one. Experiences of this kind would be vividly recounted, passed down, probable embellished. Walter Scott heard directly from veterans of the campaign (and Ferguson confirms that, as far as historical veracity is concerned, there is little romantic about *Waverley*). The '45 must have been an intensely experienced event for the Scottish participants – who were not only Gaels, as the Jacobite army recruited extensively in certain Lowland areas. This would apply also to those who were not directly involved in the campaign. The Jacobite and Hanoverian armies had criss-crossed Scotland. After Culloden, Cumberland's troops cut a swathe of destruction up and down the Great Glen, while the Royal Navy harried along the west coast. Despite these measures, in 1750 intelligence reports to Hanoverian commanders suggested that the Highlands were as rebellious as ever.[42] Jacobitism and the aftermath of the '45 must have been much more than the stuff of 'sentimental memory' for many Scottish people long after 1750.

5

The most important and most debilitating postulate of Nairnism and Scotch Myths theory concerns the supposedly illegitimate and distorted process through which Jacobitism and its symbols came to articulate developing nationalist aspirations. A cooked-up series of associations, it is suggested, were utilised in conjunction with memories of the Jacobites and the old Highland culture to create a malformed ideology – a 'sub-nationalism', in Nairn's famous expression. Tartan and so on are here depicted as tools of an elite of rich unionist landowners, the peers and politicans in Dundas's pocket, returned Scotch nabobs and the black-coated burghers of the lowlands, hypocritically responding to Scott's romantic pickling of a dead culture and cause.

However, in its historical context, Jacobitism was clearly associated with Scottish national consciousness, and with Scottish nationalism, both by opponents and supporters. Lenman observes that 'anything which made the Highlands different was regarded as a seedbed of Jacobitism'.[43] This led to the proscription of tartan, Gaelic and the rest.

On that day of high drama in September, 1745 when Charles entered Edinburgh, Hepburn of Keith, who 'made his reputation as an unregenerate opponent of the Act of Union', played out a symbolic tableau on the steps of Holyrood:

> He ostentatiously went ahead of the prince in a gallery touch meant to convey to the crowd both that Scotland took precedence over the House of Stuart and that to oppose union with England was logically to be Jacobite. It had always been the principal aim of Charles's propaganda to equate Scottish nationalism with Jacobitism.[44]

This was certainly a view shared, and reinforced by the occupying English forces. The racialist attitudes of the English officer corps are brought out by Prebble's account of the aftermath of Culloden. In Aberdeen, 'English officers argued that since all rebels were Scots (or appeared to be) then all Scots might well be rebels'. And in Stirling, the officers 'made plain their opinion that there was no difference between a decent Lowland tradesman and a thieving MacGregor'.[45] Charles Edward's most recent and most thorough biographer relates the severity of the Hanoverians' conduct to this racial animus.

> The Hanoverian officers in general betrayed a frightening, sickening callousness in pursuit of their aims ... They regarded the Scots in general as an inferior race, and the Highlanders in particular as benighted savages.[46]

There is no question that the Scottish Jacobites looked on a Stuart restoration as a means of achieving complete independence for Scotland – as the Irish Jacobites did for Ireland. The issue was high on the agenda of the Scottish rebels: 'Prosperity to Scotland and No Union' was the legend engraved on their swords.

But, it is often argued, Jacobitism did not represent all of Scotland, and moreover was doubtfully a vehicle for real national interests, since it was anachronistic and backward-looking. This argument invokes old historiographical notions which, if still unchallenged at the level of popular belief, are no longer widely accepted by historians. On the supposed 'anachronism' of the movement enough has already been said. But what of Jacobitism's geographical and social bases? Did not Jacobitism represent only the Highlands and more conservative elements of Scottish society?

What Jonathan Clark calls the 'reductionist picture' offered by historians such as Insh (and which we met earlier in the form of Nairn's account) of 'the risings as a conservative, localist Highland reaction against the encroachment of a modernising, materialistic commercial nexus' has been replaced by a view of the Highland aristocracy who took arms in the '15 as 'conspicuously anglicised and indeed rather cosmopolitan, pursuing a realistic political option for reasons of hard advantage as well as of credible ideological commitment – reasons which they shared with their counterparts in the Lowlands'.[47] On the '45, Lynch writes:

> If there was a clash within the '45 between a supposedly backward-looking Highland society and a 'progressive', capitalist Lowland economy, it was not a clear-cut one. Cameron of Lochiel, who fought for Charles, was as much a representative of a new capitalist attitude to Highland estate management as was the house of Argyll, ever the mainstay of support for the Hanoverian regime.[48]

It is of course true that there were many Scots on both sides, and that opposition was conspicuous, for instance, in the Kirk, among lawyers, in larger Lowland towns, and in the south-west, but the older stereotype of Jacobite support as mainly limited to the Highlands, or especially to the Catholic clans, has not survived more recent historical investigation. Many clans, both Protestant and Catholic, both in 1715 and 1745, remained neutral or gave only limited and qualified support;[49] and recent analysis of the muster roll of the 'Highland' army actually demonstrates a near-equal balance between rebels of Highland and Lowland origin.

We turn now to the later history of Jacobitism in Scottish culture, and to the Scotch Myths view that it became an element in a 'deformed' culture, or 'sub-culture'. What is missed by historians like Lenman and commentators like Nairn and George Rosie who rely on received historical accounts is the fact of tension, ambivalence and contradiction within the cultural dynamic. Pittock's recent work draws attention to the very different, almost antagonistic representations of the Jacobite issue within the early nineteenth century Romantic movement, and particularly within the works of Hogg and Scott. Whereas the use of elements of Scottish Jacobite history in Scott 'intensified their romance while depoliticising them', Hogg's songs

> stood in the Jacobite tradition of the literature of liberty, which articulated Scottish history as a struggle for freedom against a powerful neighbour. Darien, Glencoe, Bruce, Wallace and Culloden are premises of one common grief, which views 1745 not as an obsolescent dynastic struggle, but the time when 'Scotland for freedom last stood . . .' This is a very different reading from Scott's view of Jacobitism as a fading glory, the sunset of old Scottish honour . . . The songs . . . suggested that the British government and the British state had neither legitimacy nor integrity . . . Moreover, at a time when the divisions of Scottish society were being emphasised with a view to demonstrating how the union had reconciled them, the Jacobite vision of unity and

identity was an uncomfortable reminder of other versions
of history . . . Much of the Jacobite material Hogg collected
made only too plain the correspondence between Jacobitism
and nationalism.[50]

Burns indeed provides something of a 'type' or personification of the
fairly complex and ambivalent *mentalité* required to contain a strong
sense of Scottish identity, a desire to see Scottish sovereignty restored,
a use of Jacobite symbols to articulate these, and the requirement to
live within the increasing reality of the union (and, in Burns' own case,
take employment from its government).

But there was a great deal of this kind of ambivalence around. For
different reasons at different times many groups and sectors of Lowland
society were suspicious of or hostile to the Union in the eighteenth-
century, and Lenman records the widespread 'sense of loss' in relation
to Scottish identity which afflicted intellectual circles in the early
nineteenth century. That a society in this predicament adopts certain
conspicuous symbols does not show the inception of a socio-cultural
malaise. From a different perspective, it is the symbolic articulacy
of Jacobitism which has secured a continuing codified defiance, and
has lent itself so successfully to the expression of popular nationalist
dissent.

> Symbolic gestures such as wearing the tartan and giving
> the toast over the water, to say nothing of white roses and
> whistled airs, had long been the day-to-day discourse of
> Jacobitism. The methods of expression adopted by Scottish
> nationalism in the latter part of the nineteenth century owed
> much to the deliberate manner in which earlier national-
> ists had made themselves plain through symbols, codes and
> tokens . . . Symbolic politics was nothing new, but its capac-
> ity, then as now, to stir Scottish sentiment did and does
> emphasise how long-standing a means of patriotic expres-
> sion it has been. The political language of traditional symbols
> was one which had endured as an encoded record of anti-
> Union sympathies in the eighteenth century. It continued as
> a patriotic language into the nineteenth and twentieth . . . It
> was owing to the traditionalist approach of Jacobite nation-
> alism that the icons of Scottish history were of such symbolic
> importance.[51]

It is scarcely necessary to add that the cultural consequences of this
process include, besides tartan knick-knacks, some wonderful prose,
poetry and song, evocative of loyalty, adventure, idealism, of sorrow
and loss, but also of hope, defiance, and rebellion. Even where these
symbols were associated with the nineteenth-century resurgence of
national feeling in ways recalled by the tartan toy-soldiers available

in Tokyo, there is no justification for viewing military-related expressions of national consciousness in a previous (very military) age as evidence of cultural deformation, socio-political neurosis, 'deviance', or mass lunacy.

> The Black Watch (the 42nd Regiment of Foot) fought heroically throughout the Napoleonic Wars ... savagely pounded by Marshal Ney's *curassiers* at the battle of Quatre Bras two days before, [they] did not bear a prominent role at Waterloo, but they lined the hedges through which the Scots Greys galloped in a famous and destructive charge, encouraged as they went by the shouts of the Black Watch, 'Scotland forever!'[52]

These were not toy soldiers – nor were those, perhaps wearing the same tartan, who fought in later, possibly more 'ideologically sound' wars. The subjectivity of all these men, the ways in which they and others perceived the 'Highlandist' dress and music associated with the regiments, are complex social and cultural issues. It is arrogant nonsense to presume otherwise.

6

In the dedication of his general textbook, where he makes explicit some of the historiographical influences on his work, Bruce Lenman places Scotland as one province within the 'Atlantic Community' of the eighteenth century. In this connection, he draws an interesting contrast between Scotland and the American colonies. 'I do think,' he writes, 'that in an era of supreme crisis for the British Atlantic Community, such as the period covered in this book, there is a case for looking at the most deferential of the British provinces, as well as at the troublemakers.'[53] The most deferential of the British provinces? It seems odd that a country which has for decades been subjected to terror and repression, and then finally been battered into submission, and which has military roads, new forts and occupation forces everywhere, should be described as deferential. A different perspective on Scottish history would emphasise the rebelliousness of a 'province' which becomes the focus of a remarkable series of attempts to overthrow the Hanoverian state. These efforts were in the end to fail, unlike the American revolt a generation later; but it should be remembered that the Americans were trying to hive off from the system – and not, like the Jacobites, intent on destroying and replacing it.

Of course Jacobitism was, in historians' terms, a failure. Paradoxically, in wider perspective it has proved successful, indeed indestructible, in a way it could never have been had any of the various eighteenth-century rebellions triumphed. Nairn and the other Scotch Mythers are right at least in this: the realm of 'Prince Tearlach' was not expunged from history after 1746. In the survival of Jacobitism was sustained a powerful expression of Scottish identity, a symbol of ideals and aspirations which though once defeated, cannot be forgotten or erased, and which constitute the paradigm for an ever-possible Rising.

5

Calvinist Enlightenment

1

That thanks to the ideas of figures such as David Hume, Adam Smith and Adam Ferguson Scotland should have been a, if not *the* main centre of the eighteenth-century Enlightenment has seemed to many historians a mystery. According to a familiar and widely shared historical perspective, with the Reformation Scotland had made its own the intellectual rigidity and dour dogmatism of Calvin; seventeenth-century intellectual life was consequently characterised by philistinism, bigotry, and futile theological disputes. And this cultural darkness, surely, is an unlikely background to the dazzling intellectual feats of Hume and Smith.

Historians have tried to solve this puzzle, or at least reduce the mystery, in a number of ways. Some see the Scottish Enlightenment as in reality a phenomenon which involved no more than a handful of exceptional individuals, who had managed to emancipate themselves from an impoverished cultural heritage, and stood in splendid isolation from their benighted compatriots. One particular recent formulation of this view is worth quoting because it reveals more general, anglocentric assumptions about Scotland which many historians share, but rarely express in quite so direct a fashion:

> Such Enlightenment as existed in eighteenth-century Scot-
> land was confined to a tiny minority who lived surrounded
> by a narrow-minded nationalism and bigoted puritanism
> which have survived in part down to our own day.[1]

That the Enlightenment had little connection with indigenous Scottish (calvinist) culture is a view on which there has long been general agreement. And since the native soil cannot account for Scotland's apparently sudden intellectual flowering, historians have sought the seeds of Enlightenment in external influences. In this regard, the Union of 1707 is often credited with an 'opening-up' of Scotland to English and other foreign cultures, a process – so the argument runs – which permitted some Scots at least to escape from the suffocating religious spirit and stultifying theological preoccupations of traditional local culture. After the Union, we are informed by Neil McCallum, the 'winds of Augustan England blew northwards', helping 'to liberate the Scot from the shackles of his theology'.[2] The importation of English manners, customs and interests, of club-and-journal Addisonian 'politeness', and of 'whole systems of foreign knowledge', on such a view, provides us with the key to an understanding of Scotland's enlightened age.[3]

Whatever the particular emphasis, there is then an established historiographical assumption that Enlightenment thought was in central and crucial ways discontinuous with earlier Scottish culture. It involved, to quote the especially forthright formulation of an American scholar, a 'revolutionary rift' with local intellectual traditions.[4]

The familiarity of this position has all but obscured its overwhelming implausibility. In other spheres, historians have taught us to be extremely wary of tales about abrupt 'revolutions' and total transformations, and draw attention to the ways in which, often contrary to appearances and to the rhetoric of would-be revolutionaries, cultural formations display deep and enduring continuities. It is also difficult to credit that people are able, in the manner received accounts postulate and require, to 'liberate' themselves from the social, cultural and intellectual milieux in which they grow. This is to put the objection to the voluntarism inscribed in the established view in common-sense terms; it would now be possible to state it in a more rigorous way by using the social theory being developed by Pierre Bourdieu, with its stress on the crucial explanatory value of the 'habitus', the internalised, enduring system of codes and dispositions the person acquires from the social and cultural environment.[5]

But if what we refer to as the received view is so implausible, we then have to explain why it has achieved such currency. In part, this reflects the success of the eighteenth-century 'enlightened' thinkers' own propaganda and self-justification. Accusations of poor scholarship and 'superstition' were directed at their predecessors in order to advertise the value and originality of their own work. A second factor is the assumption of Whig and marxist historiography that religion in general is a principle incompatible with 'rational' belief and intellectual progress. The notion of a sharp break between religious culture and rational and 'enlightened' thought is naturally congenial to historians working in these traditions. Finally, – though to make this point will inevitably provoke charges of 'narrow-minded nationalism' – much influential Scottish historiography has been written by individuals whose own habitus involves a certain English superiorism and ingrained condescension towards what is native and particular in Scotland. It is hardly surprising that historians disposed to regard

England as the *fons et origo* of civilisation should discount indigenous culture ('bigoted puritanism', etc) in tracing the origins of the
Scottish Enlightenment. Of course, not all recent historians have been
content to dismiss pre-Enlightenment Scotland as a culture of religious dogmatism and intellectual narrowness – or, in Tom Nairn's
phrase, 'theological squalor' – which a more civilised age conveniently
left behind. Anand Chitnis, for instance, has pointed to continuities
between seventeenth-century theological interest in social change and
the inquiry of the Enlightenment. At the same time, philosophers such
as George Davie and Alasdair MacIntyre have drawn attention to the
ways in which some of the central ideas of thinkers like Smith and
Hume can be seen as secular expressions of fundamental calvinist doctrines. Smith's insistence on the unintended consequences of human
actions, for example, with its implication that society cannot be ordered
according to a rational plan, is clearly harmonious with the calvinist
emphasis on the limitations of human reason; in the case of Hume,
this anti-rationalism is expressed in the view that reason is powerless
to control the 'passions'.

But now the balance of forces in this debate has been dramatically
altered with the publication of David Allan's *Virtue, Learning and
the Scottish Enlightenment*. This is the most detailed and substantial
attempt so far to connect the Enlightenment to indigenous traditions
of intellectual culture, and thus the most ambitious available challenge
to the established readings. It will no doubt be the subject of specialist
debate for some years to come; but since its argument bears on general perceptions of Scottish culture, it is a text which is of more than
purely scholarly interest. It may be worthwhile, therefore, to offer a
brief summary in an attempt to highlight the main features of Allan's
analysis.

2

Allan's objective, in his own words, is to place Enlightenment thought
'in a distinctively Scottish intellectual context'.[6] In order to carry
out this task, he sets out to demonstrate certain continuities between
Enlightenment inquiry and its local predecessors. He does this by
concentrating on a relatively unexplored area of Scottish intellectual
history, historiography.

By the eighteenth century Scots could look back on a long and fecund
national tradition of historical inquiry, represented by such famous
works as those of Hector Boece, John Mair and George Buchanan, as
well as a host of texts by now obscure or forgotten figures. In the period

from the Reformation to the Enlightenment, interest in history was a prime intellectual concern because of the influence of both Humanism and calvinism. Each granted the study of history a privileged status. In Humanist discourse, history was regarded as providing vicarious human experience. It was thus a special and indispensable source of wisdom and aid to the understanding of human affairs. The early-seventeenth-century historian John Spotswood voiced this conception in the following way: 'There is not amongst men a greater help for the attaining unto wisdom, then is the reading of History.' For 'it teacheth us at other mens cost . . . in a few hours reading, a man may gather moe Instructions out of the same, then twenty men living successively one after another, can possibly learn by their own experience'.[7] This justification of historical study would often be repeated, sometimes in almost the same words, at the height of the Enlightenment.[8]

But history provided more, the calvinist tradition urged, than simply accumulated human experience. God acts through history, so that historical record is second only to Scripture itself as a revelation of divine will. Moreover, since events represent the fulfilment of biblical prophecy, careful historical study furnishes us with a means of discerning what may or will happen in the future. It is a measure of the importance the presbyterian intellectuals assigned to history that they saw in the preservation of historical records itself a special act of providence designed to facilitate human instruction.[9]

The particular amalgamation of calvinism and Humanism which evolved in Scotland laid great stress on the moral and edificatory function of historical study and writing. History provides inspiring examples of noble conduct, and so serves to inculcate the virtues. Writing in 1701, Robert Fleming commented that history supplies 'the best examples that can be, to be imitated by us, and an account of the worst also, that we may avoid such pernicious courses'.[10] A few decades earlier, Drummond of Hawthornden observed that it is 'a great spur to virtue to look back on the worth of our line',[11] while the declared aim of Robert Johnson's *Historie of Scotland* (1646) was to bring 'readers minds to embrace vertue, honesty and wisdome'.[12]

Behind such formulations lay a rejection of 'scholasticism' and the ideal of pure learning or learning as an end-in-itself. Renaissance and Reformation thought had converged to establish a scholarly consensus that knowledge must have a practical orientation and be put to use in the exercise of one's calling. As this would imply, while the Scottish historians of the pre-Enlightenment age acknowledged the need for truthfulness and accuracy in their narratives, they did not see themselves as scholars in the sense of the putatively impartial and disinterested investigators of the modern liberal academy. Rather, as Allan shows, in believing that historical writing had above all a moral and edificatory function, they conceived their role on the model of the orator and the preacher, social agents whose function it was to instruct and improve the community.

> The historian was to be the fount of advice and a credible instructor of his audience. So he would have to adopt the persona of the orator and the preacher, a role which . . . had familiar and highly sympathetic resonances both within humanist social thought and in the Calvinist vision of the moral community.[13]

Their identification with the rhetorician's role is reflected, Allan goes on, in the way they tended to elevate the significance of *eloquentia* in crucial historical episodes, and to impute outstanding oratorial skills to the heroes of their narratives.

But who, then, as preachers and orators, were these historians primarily addressing? Both calvinist and Humanist thought postulated that a community would possess a defined group whose members exercised social leadership and provided political government: it was assumed also that these social leaders were 'the elements upon which the moral health and direction of the community would depend'.[14] This might be a Christian monarch, court and aristocracy; or a body like the city fathers of republican calvinist Geneva.

> Active and exemplary groups of this kind . . . were the natural audience for the oratory of an intensely edificatory medium. They were the group through whom the humanist author or Calvinist preacher . . . might best hope to influence the moral condition of Scottish society.[15]

But there was, in the special circumstances of this society, a problem inherent in the project. The Scottish predicament involved, after 1603, an absent king and court; and scholarly circles could not perceive in the existing, self-seeking Scottish nobility a suitable group to exercise social and moral leadership. To intellectuals steeped in Humanist and calvinist modes of thought, inherited rank alone could not be a sufficient qualification for leadership. The Scottish aristocracy in the main lacked the virtuousness, learning and true nobility required to lead the nation. The solution the historians adopted, Allan argues, was to attempt through their writing to create a new hegemonic elite capable of guiding and improving Scotland.

In order to grasp the drift of Allan's broader argument, we have to examine in a little more detail the nature of the moral and instructive purposes scholarly eloquence was designed to serve, and the kind of virtue it was to inculcate. Here we come to one of the most arresting parts of the book, where Allan takes issue with a perspective on Scottish calvinist culture which Weberian analyses have made familiar. Allan shows that the presbyterian intellectuals of the Reformation-to

Enlightenment period did not propagate an individualistic or wholly or predominantly spiritual and private morality. The virtue which the historians sought through their work to encourage and diffuse had both a private and a public aspect. Certainly, virtue was taken to involve self-restraint, sobriety, piety and personal righteousness; but it equally implied a concern for and activity directed toward the pursuit of the public good.

One of the texts Allan uses to illustrate his thesis at this point is the radical Covenanter Alexander Shields' *Hind Let Loose* (1687), which reveals, in Allan's words, 'the continuing humanist public obsessions of the authentic Calvinist mind'.[16] 'Discovering a Gallant greatness and generosity of a Publick Spirit, having their designs and desires not limited to their own interests, even Spiritual', Shields wrote, believers should work for 'Christs's Publick Glory, the Churches publick good, the Saints publick Comfort, having a publick concern for all Christs Interests, Publick Sympathie for all Christs Friends, and a Publick declared Opposition to all Christs Enemies.' With reference to enemies of the public welfare, Shields wrote that those 'that make a prey of the Common-wealth, are not joined to us by any civil bond or tye of humanity, but should be accounted the most Capital enemies of God and of all men'.[17]

There was, Allan comments, a widespread and 'deeply rooted sense drawn from Calvinism and Humanism that a concern for the moral and spiritual state of the public community was . . . essential to the proper discharge of an individual's godly responsibilities.'[18] And this conviction, again, was reflected in the historians' attitudes to their subjects. Thus Robert Sibbald, for instance, condemned the ancient Britons for 'minding only what was necessary for their private subsistence', and for being 'little concerned for the Publick Good'.[19]

One final aspect of Allan's treatment of pre-Enlightenment thought must be mentioned. If scholars aspired to be credible and useful counsellors to an actual or potential social leadership, or, in other terms, to be able to provide guidance on how such leaders could shape events, they would have to claim some understanding of the mechanisms of historical change. They were thus forced to confront issues of historical causality. They were in any case conscious that the historian's role was to provide explanation as well as narrative. John Spotswood wrote: '. . . take away from the story the causes whereupon, the manner how, and the purpose whereof things were done, that which remaineth is more like a Fable than a History . . . giving little or no instruction at all'.[20] It was the historian's obligation, indeed, to uncover 'the secretest Causes and Beginnings of great Changes or Revolutions', observed Gilbert Burnet, 'this being the chief Instruction that men receive from History'.[21]

However, in attempting to provide accounts of causality in history, Scotland's pre-Enlightenment intellectuals found that they had opened a Pandora's box of intractable questions. For both Humanist and calvinist discourses contained unresolved tensions concerning the possiblity of human freedom and the efficacy of human agency. Calvinism, of course, posited a providential determination of history, which on any strict interpretation appeared to leave no room for human choice, let alone human control over events. The Humanist tradition allowed for the freedom of human intention and the ability to shape history; but it also stressed the restricted capacity of human beings to control history in the face of an unpredictable world where chance or 'fortune' seemed a vastly greater force than human will and plan. The historians, as Allan shows, were deeply aware of these dilemmas; and the tension between 'a social theory of leadership' and a 'determinist causality' was, he writes, 'at the very heart of Scottish scholarship by the early eighteenth century'.[22] Some generations later, the same tension would mark the inquiry of the Enlightenment.

From the perspective gained by this study of what he calls 'early modern scholarship' (1550–1740), Allan now examines the historiography of the Enlightenment period (1740–1800) with the intention of identifying areas of similarity and continuity.

The notion that Enlightenment thought involved a sharp break with local antecedent culture was first propagated by certain Enlightenment thinkers themselves. Previous historical writing, according to Adam Ferguson, was a collection of 'fictions'; now scholars proceeded, or so at least some wished to claim, in the empirical manner which had brought such great successes in natural science, establishing historical truths, in George Turnbull's words, 'from Facts ascertained by observation, and not from abstract, imaginary Theories and Hypotheses'.[23] But if such scholars sought to add prestige to their own work by linking it to natural science through descriptions of their method which invoked concepts like 'experience' and 'observation', in fact, Allan maintains, historical writing continued to proceed along established and familiar lines and displayed no substantial methodological changes. That this indeed was the case is strongly suggested by the fact that many Enlightenment-period historians deliberately and happily placed their work in a national tradition of historical study, and saw themselves as the heirs of Buchanan, Spotswood, Calderwood, et al.[24]

But the crux of Allan's argument lies elsewhere. It concerns the ways in which the scholars of the Enlightenment conceived the significance of learning and historical study, and the nature of their own role as social actors. For here, Allan contends, 'all the historians of enlightened Scotland . . . retained a clear Calvinist and Humanist sense of their traditional obligations',[25] and shared an 'essentially Calvinist and humanist view of their work'.[26]

Like their local predecessors, the intellectuals of the Enlightenment too considered that history's primary function was to provide moral edification, or, as William Duff's 1749 *History of Scotland* put it, in a reference back to Burnet, 'to make men wiser and better'.[27] For David Hume, the value of history consists in its being an 'antidote against superstition', and 'the most effective remedy against vice and disorders of any kind'.[28] Conceiving history in this deeply moralistic way was, we can say, an aspect of the habitus of the Enlightenment thinkers. As Allan comments,

> The compulsion to present history in this deeply conventional way, indeed to regard departure from traditional intentions as the most reprehensible of scholarly sins, was evidently overwhelming to the Scottish historian in an enlightened age. The authors of the Enlightenment were, after all, still in so many respects using a language first found among Scotland's post Renaissance scholars . . . it defined, directed and defended the tradition of scholarship that had been passed on to the Enlightenment. Its continuing acceptance and relevance actually limited . . . the scope for questioning the *raison d'être* of their own scholarly activities.[29]

History remained, then, essentially a didactic, moralistic medium, the vehicle, in Robert Heron's words, 'of a profusion of instructing, persuading, enlightening, elevating knowledge'.[30] And indeed learning in general continued to be valued only in so far as it went beyond idle speculation and proved 'useful' in the sense of fostering private and public virtue. This conception presupposed both a somewhat pessimistic view of man's natural condition, and the idea that the cultivation of the reasoning faculty through learning was essential to the self-control virtue implied. Vice was linked to ignorance: without learning, men would remain in or revert to a state of lethargy, selfishness, indolence, intemperance and a host of other vices, corruptions and disorders. So strong and constant is this theme that, as Allan suggests,

> many major texts of the Scottish Enlightenment might in one sense be considered as extended Calvinist essays on the unruly passions of man. At any rate, it seems quite clear that the historians of the eighteenth century sought no less than their Scottish predecessors to identify and stigmatise the fatal consequences of luxury and ignorance. They attempted at the same time to portray learning and the applications of reason as the soundest bulwark against their corrosive influence.[31]

As this clearly implies, the Enlightenment scholars did not see themselves as morally neutral or impartial investigators of human affairs. Whatever the degree of truth in the familiar thesis that they can be seen as precursors or originators of 'social science', it is certainly not the case that they undertood themselves to be 'sociologists' or 'economists' in the modern sense of these expressions. They are perhaps best described as civic moralists, intellectuals whose prime interest and concern, like that of their predecessors, was the promotion of private and public improvement, of the virtuous person and the virtuous polity. In other words, they were still more preachers and orators than 'scientists' – and it is hardly incidental that so many of them, like Ferguson, Blair and Robertson, were in fact ministers of the Kirk.

'Enlightened scholarship', Allan writes, 'expressed on many occasions its Ciceronian desire to speak directly and effectively to an attentive social leadership'.[32] William Duff, for example, declared that the purpose of his scholarship was

> to prepare, form, and furnish the Minds of young Gentlemen of Figure and Distinction, to give them lively Ideas of high Life, to fix generous Principles of True Morals, of Government and Conduct in the different Spheres of publick Life, instructing by Examples of past Ages how to act in like Circumstances in the different Stations and Offices of Trust and Power.[33]

Immersed like their predecessors in the role of educating (and now also, Allan suggests, actually supplying) a virtuous social leadership, they too were fascinated by the power of oratory (for good or ill) and by the figure of the orator, as the well-known works of Hugh Blair and George Campbell testify. Here Allan draws out another arresting parallel between the Enlightenment and its predecessor culture. The Enlightenment scholars too underlined in their narratives the special power of oratory in shaping the course of history: Knox, for example, had led the Reformation by deploying 'all the thunder of his eloquence against idolatry', while Andrew Fletcher's fame was in part due to 'the fire of his ancient eloquence'.[34] Moreover, it is only in the light of this preoccupation with figures who were able to provide leadership through their learning and rhetorical skill, Allan suggests, that the Ossian phenomenon can be properly understood:[35] the civic moralists of the Enlightenment in a sense aspired to be the Ossians of their age.

But if the claim to provide social leadership was to be made good, it was necessary to show that rational virtue was indeed capable of altering the flow of historical events. Here, inevitably, the Enlightenment scholars had to grapple with the same conundrums concerning freedom and determinism which had been raised in pre-Enlightenment Scottish thought.

If Hume was able to discern among the causes of historical change at least 'a small ingredient of wisdom and foresight',[36] it was determinism or anti-rationalism which seemed to gain the upper hand in these debates, as Smith and others emphasised the unintended and unpredictable outcomes which attend all human action. This doctrine of unintention, Allen comments, 'brought to secular maturity the deeply familiar separation of human decision and consequent effect which had been implicit in orthodox Calvinist and Stoic discussions of causality offered by previous Scottish historians . . . '[37]

In their interest in history as a unique educational medium; in their deeply moralistic conception of their role as intellectuals; in their objective of creating or supplying a learned leadership for the improvement of society; in their wrestling with issues of historical causality; – in these and other ways, Allan shows, the scholars of the Scottish Enlightenment were following conventional patterns of Scottish intellectual culture. The achievement of this compelling and innovative study, then, is to anchor – 'at last,' as the author says – the Scottish Enlightenment in its native local environment.

3

Historians have been responsible for creating a vision of the Enlightenment as a golden age of Scottish culture which contrasts with the mediocrity, backwardness or gloom of national culture in the centuries before and since. Such a perspective, dutifully relayed to a wide audience by journalists and *littérateurs*, has only recently begun to be challenged in a serious way. Thanks to Alexander Broadie, we now know that there was a thriving and sophisticated Scottish philosophical culture in the early sixteenth century. Allan's work makes plain the inadequacy of the old view of seventeenth-century Scotland as a realm of intellectual darkness which was left behind by a later, cultured age.

Unfortunately, in the final section of his book, when he turns to the nineteenth century, Allan fails to offer the kind of fresh, revisionist perspective on this period the reader might well expect. Indeed, quoting judgments of Tom Nairn and Michael Fry with approval, he actually underlines some of the cliches about nineteenth-century Scottish culture – a world dominated by tartan trumpery and kailyard kitsch – which have long served as substitutes for serious investigation and analysis.

'Scotland was apparently reduced by the middle of the nineteenth century to the sort of yellowing provincialism associated with the virtual absence of cultural innovation,' he writes, and goes on to ask: 'Why . . . had an extraordinary culture of endeavour and intellectual attainment faded away so rapidly and apparently so completely?'[38]

How are we to account for the 'seeming demise'[39] and 'apparent waning'[40] of Scottish culture? The qualifiers here, it turns out, represent more than academic bet-hedging. For, he goes on to say, 'the view that by the 1830s Scotland had simply sunk back into her customary intellectual moribundity may well need to be treated with at least equal suspicion' (as, that is, 'the hoary myth that the Enlightenment condensed, as it were, out of nothing.'[41]) However, Allan's criticism of the kind of view expressed in Nairn's remark about the 'disintegration of a great national culture' never rises above the tentative and half-hearted. It was certainly not sufficiently forceful to prevent one reviewer – Angus Calder – from speaking of the 'withering' of Scottish intellectual culture after 1800.[42]

Before the end of the century which began with the 'demise', 'disentegration' or 'withering' of this culture, and saw Scotland sink into the mindlessness of tartanry and kailyardism, another generation of Scottish calvinists had re-ordered intellectual discourses in ways arguably as profound and influential as the achievements of the previous century. William Robertson-Smith would pioneer the sociology of religion; J. G. Frazer's work would establish anthropology; James Clerk Maxwell – now in Scotland inexplicably forgotten – would revolutionise physics. The story of what MacIntyre has termed this second Scottish Enlightenment, as of so many more areas of nineteenth-century Scottish culture, remains to be written.

6
History and Identity

1

Dean Ramsay's *Reminiscences of Scottish Life and Character* was one of the most successful works of Victorian Scotland, running by the 1870s into more than twenty editions. What lends it interest today is above all the valedictory register indicated by its title. Ramsay was convinced that he was recording the details of a cultural life which, if not already dead except in contemporary memory, was rapidly to vanish forever. The 'lingering traces of our past individuality' were 'fast fading from our view'. Ramsay remarked in his conclusion that 'I seem to linger over these Reminiscences as if unwilling to part for ever with the remnants of our past national social history'. As far as this observer was concerned, Scotland had now 'lost her individuality', and the Scots were 'destined soon to lose all indications of a national existence'.[1]

Ramsay was not the first and by no means the last commentator to write Scotland's obituary; and two generations or so after he wrote it was still possible to believe the Scottish identity was disappearing. 'Scott saw Scottish manners inevitably melting into those of England', Edwin Muir stated, adding that 'Scottish manners have melted still more since he wrote . . . '[2]

Ramsay and Muir were in their different ways deeply patriotic observers. The passing away of Scottish culture was for Ramsay a reason for mourning and regret, while Muir could say in the work quoted that 'it is of living importance to Scotland that it should maintain and be able to assert its identity'. Our present-day obituarists in political and cultural debate are a very different breed. They tend to pronounce the erasure from history of a distinct Scottish identity, and its assimilation to an English, Anglo-American or international cultural order with barely concealed glee.

They would perhaps be more circumspect if they were aware of the long pedigree of their funeral orations. In fact, of course, assurances about the death of distinctive Scottish identity and descriptions of Scotland as a glorified UK region (or inglorious minor county) reflect political zealotry rather than serious analysis. And in their anxiety to deflate Scottish cultural and political pretensions, the obituarists typically lapse into self-contradiction, asserting that there is no Scottish cultural identity, and then cataloging essential characteristics of Scottish culture (division, bigotry, philistinism, etc.) which invalidate any kind of nationalist project. To hold that Scottish identity is such that it is best left to fester battened below hatches at least amounts to a coherent view; but it can hardly be combined with the idea that Scottish identity does not exist.

More than a century after Ramsay penned his reminiscences, the culture he took to be dying before his eyes would generate a mass political movement which challenges British-state control of Scotland. Scottish identity would remain a subject of investigation and controversy. Whatever it is, whatever transformations it has undergone, and however it is to be evaluated, Scottishness, perhaps against the odds, is still very much with us.

2

The movement for Scottish political and constitutional self-determination which has evolved over the past two decades or so interlocks with a cultural process: self-determination in the alternative sense of self-definition. Attempts to define and explain contemporary Scottish identity – from both nationalist and anti-nationalist positions – have become a familiar feature of our cultural commentary and debate.

One model has achieved a sort of dominance in these discussions. Based on an analysis of Scottish historical development, and a conception of a natural or logical pattern of historical evolution, this presents Scottish identity as highly unusual and 'deformed'. Stress is laid here on the failure to mobilise national identity in the kind of struggle for cultural emancipation and political independence which was so typical of other small European nations in the nineteenth and early-twentieth centuries. Since much mobilisation did not occur on any large scale here until the 1970s, and remains incomplete, Scotland is seen as suffering from retarded cultural-political development. This retardation is linked causally to the special circumstances of Scotland's incorporation after 1707 into a plurinational state. This created a dual or split self in which a local or peculiarly Scottish identity is counterbalanced or overlaid by identification with the state nationality. The latter became the essential focus of political and ideological allegiance; the former, thus deprived of serious projects and concerns, was reduced to a site of nostalgia and sentimentality (neutered couthiness, celebrations of tartanry, and so on).

Those who accept one or another version of this account – which is most powerfully expressed in the work of Tom Nairn – are naturally inclined to take a dim view of indigenous cultural traditions. The Scottish past here appears to be devoid of inspirational value, incapable of informing any meaningful contemporary political or ideological project; but at the same time it is regrettably and remarkably rich in reactionary, self-limiting and stultifying symbols (the menagerie of Covenanters, Jacobites, Scottish sodgers, Orangemen, and other nightmarish shades). What the model can then sanction is wholesale rejection of the Scottish past, a great 'nay' to everything, and ideological *Flucht nach vorn.*

The theme of splits and divisions remains prominent in the arguments which drone on interminably in letters to the press and contributions in the personal-impression and anecdote genres of commentary. 'Divided Scotland' – Highlands and Lowlands, Protestants and Catholics, tribalism, sectarianism, etc – has proved a handy device for those wishing to jeer at Scottish aspirations. It is almost invariably present in established rituals of native self-debasement, and in metrocentric accounts of Scotland as a country of dreadful night. This superannuated apparatus is regularly resprayed and trundled on stage, wheezing but still serviceable, as in a major recent *Guardian* feature on Scottish identity where Scottish culture is portrayed as little more than a patchwork of senseless, parochial antagonisms fuelled by primitive spite and venom.[3]

A newer and refreshingly sanguine conception of contemporary identity has emerged which challenges aspects of these established models. Here too Scottish identity is seen as unusual and split or fragmented; but the notions of developmental retardation, cultural deformation and neurosis, and atavistic rivalry are discarded. 'It is silly to see ourselves as laggard and inefficient compared to other European countries,' writes Angus Calder. 'We have a unique history.' Once we abandon the now dated thesis that there is some normal, natural, logical or ideal pattern of historical development, it makes no sense to see Scotland as deviant, and there is no need to 'measure our own culture against another and find it wanting.' We should not then be concerned if in comparison with others Scottish culture looks 'confused and incomplete.' This culture does not flow in a single channel: 'It is made of bits and pieces, striking and distinct in themselves . . . ' Where others see divisiveness and paralysing absence of unity, for Calder cultural fragmentation represents a rich pluralism: 'We should cherish and enjoy our mongrel culture . . .'[4]

This 'bits and pieces' account of Scottishness recalls the 'pick'n'mix' model of Scottish identity proposed by David McCrone. McCrone depicts Scottish identity-fragmentation as a precocious case of a spreading phenomenon of postmodernity, which is replacing the older reality and ideal of unitary, homogenous national culture and identity.[5]

A different angle is provided by the Welsh writer John Osmond in *The Divided Kingdom*, which is a pioneering and still valuable survey of ideas on the various British or UK identities. Osmond largely follows a Nairnite, tartanry-and-kailyard, 'deformation' account of local Scottish identity. But at the same time he points to the existence of an alternative sense of Scottishness. This is informed by memory of national and popular struggle for liberty, a tradition of popular-sovereignty ideas, and 'a republican sense of "the people"' (as contrasted with the peculiar, classist English notion of 'the public').[6] Osmond suggests that this provides a more promising basis for a contemporary democratic politics than the dominant English or Anglo-British identity, which is bound to the anti-popular totems of Crown and Parliament.

These different readings of Scottish identity raise a number of interesting and important issues, some of which are addressed in other chapters of this book. Here we will concentrate on ways of interpreting and evaluating the cultural identity which preceded the creation of Anglo-Britishness. Our discussion is based on two substantial recent studies in this area. Each, inevitably, articulates a particular ideological stance: to adapt Thomas Nagel's famous phrase, there are no views from nowhere. One operates within a familiar and customary problematic, the discourse of historians, sociologists and political theorists (together with a journalistic appanage) whose fundamental commitments are to one or another form of liberal modernism. The other is derived from a quite different theoretical agenda; and it therefore affords a new perspective in the debate.

3

The nature of 'British' identity, and its historical genesis and development, are increasingly subjects of scholarly investigation. Linda Colley's work is a prominent example of current inquiry in this strangely neglected field. In *Britons: Forging the Nation*, Colley argues that a British patriotism was fashioned in the eighteenth and early-nineteenth centuries out of such materials as Protestantism and virulent anti-Catholicism, Gallophobia, militarism (fuelled by military success) and a popular cult of monarchy. The process was assisted, she believes, by exposure, in war and conquest, to other peoples and cultures, contact which served to diminish consciousness of differences between the Scots and the English.[7]

Such analyses, however instructive, leave unanswered what, from a Scottish perspective, appear to be two crucial questions. Why is Britishness so overwhelmingly sensed and defined in terms of *English* history, myths, manners, codes and institutions (the Magna Carta, the mother of parliaments, pragmatism, fair play, etc, etc)? And secondly, why has this Anglo-British identity for so long been so dominant in the terrain of politics over an older, organic Scottish national identity?

Two obvious but unsatisfactory explanations will immediately be suggested. England was by far the more populous and powerful Union partner, and so English ways inevitably triumphed in the construction of British-state identity and ideology. And – in response to the second question – Scots were not disposed to undertake a political mobilisation of their local identity as long as Union (or Union and Empire) was perceived as a gateway to opportunity and prosperity. Clearly, neither of these answers does anything to illuminate actual intellectual and ideological processes.

It is illumination of this kind which Colin Kidd seeks to provide in a recent work entitled *Subverting Scotland's Past*, a detailed account of one aspect of the transformation of Scottish national identity which followed the Union. The focus of Kidd's study is the way in which a particular awareness and interpretation of history figures in identity, and especially the political and ideological force of such a consciousness, or how it functions either to promote or to stifle political options and initiatives.

Kidd addresses two main questions. Why have almost three centuries of Anglo-Scottish union failed to generate 'a comprehensively "British" conception of national identity'?[8] And why, instead of an authentically British or merged Anglo-Scottish identity, did an essentially English or Anglo-British identity triumph? The answers, he suggests, are to be found in the ways of viewing the pre-Union Scottish past which became dominant in (and from) the eighteenth century.

Around the time of the Union, Kidd maintains, it would have been impossible to predict that hegemony would come to lie with a sense of Britishness which is essentially a celebration of English exceptionalism and exemplariness. This identity centres on Crown and Parliament, icons reflecting what are taken to be the English historical peculiarities of unbroken political evolution, trust in custom and tradition, distrust of political rationalism, the immemorial enjoyment of liberty under law, and such popular qualities as love of freedom, tolerance, common sense and decency. For the Scots had their own strong sense of distinct national identity, nourished by an equally rich 'mythistoire' which a vigorous and patriotic historiographical tradition had assiduously cultivated.

This extolled the longevity of the nation and of its existence as an independent kingdom; the martial virtues and love of liberty which had over many centuries repulsed would-be conquerors and preserved national independence; a libertarian political tradition, expressed, for instance, in the notion of a contract between monarch and people; and the purity and exemplarity of the Scottish Reformation, which could be read as evidence of the special role in history assigned to Scots by providence.

This ethnocentric, not to say chauvinistic historiography was potent brew. It constituted, in Kidd's words, 'a formidable ideology of nationhood'.⁹ And such a construct, appealing as it did with such confidence and pride to a positive and forward-looking history, was surely well-equipped to fuse on a basis of equality with English whiggism in the creation of a genuinely British identity, or, later, to engine a liberal-romantic movement for independence in the classic age of European nationalism.

In essence, Kidd's argument – which, as we note later, involves a serious ambiguity – is that this component of Scottish national identity was rapidly hollowed out as a politically viable formation, by the Scots themselves, and principally by the thinkers of the Enlightenment. As a result of this invalidation of the Scottish past as a resource for political ideology and action, by the 1830s Scotland had been deprived of the kind of intellectual and symbolic material required by romanticism and liberal nationalism.

Let us now look briefly at some of the key episodes in this narrative.

The rot had already set in even before the heavy artillery of Enlightenment was trained on the Scottish past. The Kirk would clearly play a crucial role in the cultural-political process. Not only was it a redoubt of Scottish distinctness, but also the home of a radical, libertarian political theory, a theory which had often enough in the past been translated into practice as open rebellion against monarch and state (most recently in the later Covenanting movement). Here surely was a source of inspiration for a Scottish liberal-democratic ideology.

Ironically, this was to prove the Achilles' heel of the Kirk. It was the strength of this very tradition which would occasion the eclipse of the Kirk as an assertive force capable of exercising ideological leadership. For the theory of popular sovereignty, limitation on state authority, and right of resistance – which had been elaborated by George Buchanan and others – was alien and offensive to the patrician and pragmatic ethos of dominant English politics, or what Kidd calls 'conservative Anglican whiggism'. And confronted in the years preceding and following the Union with a vociferous episcopalian campaign which stressed the extremism of Buchananite ideas and identified presbyterianism with fanaticism, antinomianism, threats to due social hierarchy and deference, and even regicide, as the Kirk strove for respectability and a consolidation of its power and position under the new regime, it was obliged to downplay or disown those radical, libertarian, populist and socially critical elements in its tradition which could in any way be construed as a potential menace to social peace and stability. Consequently, 'defensiveness was now the most common characteristic of presbyterian historiography'.[10]

But the really crippling body-blows to Scottish historical confidence and assertiveness – so Kidd's account goes on – were dealt by the eighteenth century *literati*. Few significant aspects of the Scottish past escaped their critical scrutiny, and their damning judgements on that history, Kidd maintains, would effectively finish the Scottish past off as 'a repository of political and institutional value'.[11] At the same time, their endorsement (not always uncritical) of English modes and institutions would serve to cement the hegemony of unionist ideology and Anglo-British identity.

The Enlightenment thinkers spotlighted the faultlines of native institutions which might have been capable of 'contributing some contemporary inspiration and recognisable structure to the revitalisation of a patriotic historiography'.[12] The Scottish Parliament was unfavourably compared to its English counterpart, as weak, inactive and unrepresentative. The failure to divide the parliament into separate chambers for lords and commons had meant an imbalanced constitution, biased towards monarchical and aristocratic interests, and had hindered the extension of popular and personal liberty. The Enlightenment thinkers also drew attention to the deficiencies of the Scottish legal apparatus. They stressed its cruel and oppressive features, and pointed to the survival of the heritable jurisdictions – not finally abolished until 1747 – as evidence of a feudal and archaic order. The old Scottish nobility were depicted as both tyrannical and unenterprising, incompetents who were an insurmountable obstacle to economic improvement.

Scotland's religious past furnished further evidence of the nation's failure to attain modern civility. 'Fanaticism' and 'superstition' were highlighted, while a debunking sociological analysis undermined traditional sources of Scottish pride. William Robertson argued that the origins of presbyterianism were not, as the Scots had fondly imagined, of high, native antiquity, but locatable in the practices of Calvin's Geneva. The Scottish Reformation had been the outcome of particular historical and social circumstances; its principles, therefore, could not be taken to possess special significance let alone absolute and overriding authority. Knox had been a somewhat bloodthirsty type, and the Reform movement's unsavoury side was also clear in the record of iconoclasm. Most damaging of all to a potential whig-presbyterian identity, Anglo-England had proved a site more congenial to the extension of liberty than calvinist Scotland.

Through such exercises in demythology and deflation, as Kidd comments, 'Scotland's literati rendered their native country in a sense a "historyless" nation'.[13] Not only, on their influential view, had pre-Union Scotland been backward and uncivilised, a land of feudalism, fanaticism and failure. Its history could not be worked as a meaningful narrative, that is, a story of progress in commerce and the extension of freedom. The history of England, by contrast, was 'the history of liberty', as one Scottish historian roundly affirmed.[14] The present, therefore, could not be read as the outcome of the Scottish past, but only as the natural consequence of English evolution in refinement, commercialisation, defeudalisation and mixed constitutionalism. It was Scotland's lucky fate to have been plucked from its own native retardation by assimilation to English history and culture.

The Enlightenment thinkers, then, through their historiographic constructions created and succeeded in imposing 'a Scottish version of English Whig identity, based on a commitment to English constitutional history'.[15]

Some attempts were made in the Enlightenment era to make this identity more broadly British by the addition of references to a Scottish heritage of liberty. James ('Ossian') Macpherson, for instance, wished to establish that Scotland could take pride in an ancient past informed by whiggish values. The Celts, he maintained, had been a freedom-loving race. Celtic kings had possessed only restricted powers, and had been accountable to popular assemblies. Macpherson also valiantly defended a more recent Highland past, countering stock contemporary judgements about Highland tyranny and servility by arguing that the clan system displayed democratic features such as a form of common law. Such efforts at 'Scotification' of Anglo-British identity did not bear fruit. Kidd offers this explanation: 'Panegyrics on ancient Celtic government did not compensate for the embarrassing lack of efficient, adaptable and beneficial institutions in Scotland's more recent past'.[16]

Walter Scott is often blamed for (or credited with) reducing Scottish history to a mere museum, an assemblage of customs and characters rich in the colourful and exotic, but wholly devoid of relevance to modernity. But as Kidd's account makes clear, Scott was in no way revolutionary or original in his project of sealing off the Scottish past as a source of contemporary political inspiration. He was heir to an established Scottish tradition of Anglophile deconstruction of Scottish history, and took over its reading of late-seventeenth-century Scotland as a 'half-civilised' society redeemed by assimilation. Indeed, Kidd argues, Scott's predecessors had worked so effectively that by his time no plausible alternative narrative was any longer available. Scots were now, so Kidd states, 'only too well aware that it was the new dawn of Union and Anglicisation which had dispelled the nightmare of Scottish feudal oppression and backwardness'.[17] As a result, on the political plane liberty was now effectively dissociated from self-determination.

This, in rough outline, is Kidd's argument. We now offer a few critical remarks, with a view to placing this contribution within current debates.

Kidd's thesis in fact wavers between two importantly distinct arguments. On the one hand, what is apparently being suggested is that Scotland had indeed – before the process of subversion – enjoyed a politically and ideologically viable history and justified national self-confidence. However, – to spell the case out in a way Kidd does not quite attempt – these were undermined by a sustained campaign of intellectual subversion carried out by an especially critical, detached, and sophisticated intelligentsia, who were promoting their own objectives (and interests), and whose historical vision was naturally shaped and limited by their own ideological commitments. Thus they were inclined to focus on those aspects of the Scottish past which, in terms of their own theory, seemed to provide evidence of backwardness; at the same time, they showed a less than complete appreciation of the darker aspects of the English past (seventeenth-century English treatment of Ireland, for instance).

To repeat, this is not an argument Kidd presents in quite these terms. But some such case can at times be sensed struggling to emerge. Kidd writes, for example, that 'Scotland was an exception to the development of full-blown nationalisms, *in large part* because Scottish patriotic historiography had acquired early a maturity, and a lacerating self-criticism not found elsewhere in Europe' (our emphasis).[18] So Scotland was different, on a reading of Kidd's thesis based on this passage, because here a precociously sophisticated scholarship successfully debunked national chauvinism, whereas other nations, not blessed with, or cursed by thinkers of the calibre of Hume and Robertson could cling to their equally vulnerable legends and construct nationalisms around them. On such an interpretation, Kidd would of course in important ways be distancing himself from the Enlightenment and English-whig (de)construction of the Scottish past.

That this interpretation is correct is suggested by various comments early in the text. He refers, as we have seen, to the Scots enjoying at the time of union 'a *formidable* ideology of nationhood' (our emphasis). Or again: 'Scottish whigs in 1689 possessed *all the ideological ingredients* out of which European intellectuals a century and a half later were to create nationalist movements' (our emphasis).[19]

As the narrative proceeds, however, a quite distinct view is increasingly pronounced, and eventually triumphs. It becomes clear that, for the author, the Enlightenment (de)construction of the Scottish past was more than just effective ideology or propaganda; and Scottish national ideology, it turns out, had not been such a 'formidable' formation after all. The Enlightenment critique was, so to speak, *correct*; it depicts the Scottish past *wie es eigentlich gewesen ist*. Scottish myth-history was not history at all, but pure, undiluted myth. For *in reality* Scottish history had indeed been a meaningless succession of events, a past devoid of institutions, traditions and precedents which could inspire or inform any later rational politics or ideology. The Scottish past, on this second, official argument, was not simply successfully depicted by the Enlightenment theorists as unusable, it *was* unusable – or, at any rate, 'usable only as part of a sentimental or reactionary politics of nostalgia'.[20] At this stage, the reader begins to wonder why the massive machinery of subversion had been necessary (and to fear for the coherence of Kidd's thesis). The Scottish history cupboard had been bare all along, except for a few unappetising scraps. The subvertors had laboured in vain: there was nothing to subvert.

But what is crucial for a placing of Kidd's contribution is its constant underscoring of an Enlightenment and English-whig conception of pre-Union Scotland. Discussing the part played by the Scottish thinkers in the construction of Anglo-British identity, Kidd writes, 'They recognised that political union had allowed Scotland to leap centuries of natural historical development, resulting in the current enjoyment by its people of modern civil liberties'.[21] And they had, we read, 'exposed the Scottish past as an ideologically insignificant saga of events which lacked the backbone of a successful story of legal, institutional or economic development.'[22] Later historians, Kidd also writes, would be unable to 'disguise the ideological bankruptcy of the Scottish past.'[23]

It is necessary to insist on the clear political force of Kidd's study, for he himself is at pains to emphasise its impartiality. He begins his preface with the remark that 'This book is not consciously written on the basis of either a nationalist or a unionist agenda.'[24] We are not privy to the author's conscious designs; but whatever they may be, it is obvious that a text which, as the foregoing quotations show, explicitly and unambiguously endorses the English-whig account of Scottish history can hardly count as politically and ideologically neutral. The text itself – ironically, after this initial plea of impartiality – is a description of how such an account has been so potent in subverting the intellectual resources of Scottish nationalism and, by the same token, so instrumental in sustaining the ideology and politics of unionism.[25]

Kidd's implausible claim of neutrality as to nationalist and unionist allegiances is followed by an appeal to academic 'objectivity'. But objectivity is a matter of rigorous attention to and coherent assessment of relevant data, as these are defined by some determinate conceptual framework and a conception of what constitute significant issues. It is not and cannot be a matter of adopting a vantage point outside all theoretical frameworks – there are no views from nowhere – and hence cannot be a matter of neutrality or impartiality. Marxist historians take to be centrally significant the phenomenon of class conflict, invoke a particular conception of rational conduct, deploy the explanatory category of 'false consciousness', and so on. Whig historians take to be important those events and processes conducive to the emergence of liberal modernity, or a type of society characterised by 'liberty' for 'the individual', on a determinate understanding of these concepts.

Without the deployment of some such set of theoretical presuppositions, there can be no writing or manufacture of history at all. But the adoption of a particular stance means that study is focused on certain aspects of the past, while others are sidelined, ignored, or excluded from view. From the perspective we go on to discuss, the intellectual tradition to which Kidd's study belongs is in fact largely blind to the essential issues at stake in the creation of Anglo-British identity and in the marginalisation of the Scottish past.

4

We have become used to considering intellectual history a relatively discrete field, isolable from social, economic, political and even more broadly cultural processes – a view reflected in established patterns of academic specialisation. It is recognised, certainly, that these fields interact or influence or impinge on one another: economic developments may be seen as, in some sense, 'determining' or 'shaping' the realm of philosophy and ideas, just as the latter can be viewed as standing in a kind of causal relationship to the former (as in the 'protestant ethic' account of the origins of capitalism). What has been excluded from the customary discourses is a conception of thought and social forms as internally related: an understanding of institutional structures as embodying a theory, and doing so in such a way that a society cannot be comprehended except by means of an account of the philosophy of which it is an embodiment. It is this unconventional interpretive principle which is put to work in Alasdair MacIntyre's historical and cultural analysis. Contemporary Western society, he has argued, expresses in many of its procedures and arrangements an emotivist theory of ethics. And MacIntyre brings to his comparison of the two distinct societies which entered a political union in 1707 the same view of the importance of the theoretical presuppositions which are operated in social orders.

That distinctness must, then, according to MacIntyre, be grasped in philosophical terms. It was grounded, to be precise, in rival conceptions of the relationship subsisting between principles, on the one hand, and passions and interests, on the other. 'Conception' is here to be understood in two different senses: as philosophical theory, and as theory-laden social practice. Thus these competing conceptions were articulated explicitly in philosophical texts (the domain, conventionally, of 'intellectual history' or 'history of ideas'), but also – 'and more fundamentally' – in social and political life, 'as alternative modes of shaping social existence, as beliefs systematically embodied in and presupposed by the actions and transactions of institutionalised and political life' (social and political history).[26]

England is the outstanding case in eighteenth-century Europe (argues MacIntyre) of a society in which the passions are accorded priority over principles. The passions are prioritised in several related ways, which involve both normative and epistemological principles.

First, the principles of ethics, justice and politics are understood to serve interests, where interests are the collective expressions of the passions – the desires and aversions – of the individuals who compose the social order. Second, actions are viewed as the products or outcomes of passions. Third, actions are evaluated in terms of their conducing to satisfy or frustrate passions. And finally, since principles are held to be at the service of the passions, standards of just and right conduct are internal to the actually existing social order, in the sense that no appeal to 'a standard expressed in principles whose truth would be independent of the attitudes and judgements of the participants in the order' could be regarded as legitimate, or even intelligible. In other words, 'Nothing is to be accounted a good reason for practical judgement or action . . . unless it can motivate those whose only regard is for the type of satisfaction and benefit which that order provides.'[27]

It was a Scottish thinker who would present the most intricate and persuasive statement of this worldview, which is definitive of modern liberal societies. But we find a clear and simple formulation of the main ideas in Sir William Blackstone's *Commentaries on the Laws of England* (1765), which is regarded as one of the classic expressions of English legal thought.

Blackstone states that it is the motive of self-love, or the pursuit of our own individual happiness, which constitutes the basis of morality and justice. God has shaped human nature in such a way, Blackstone holds, that 'we should want no other prompter to inquire after and pursue the right, but only our own self-love, that universal principle of action . . . he has not perplexed the law of nature with a multitude of abstracted rules and precepts . . . but has graciously reduced the rule of obedience to this one paternal precept, "that man should pursue his own true and substantial happiness". This is the foundation of what we call ethics or natural law . . .'[28] The same point is also expressed by Blackstone in this way: 'the only true and natural foundations of society are the wants and fears of the individual'. That is to say, we do not have and we do not require any criterion of just conduct which is external to our passions. On the foundations of our 'wants and fears', through our need for mutual aid and protection in pursuing our happiness and the satisfaction of our passions, the whole edifice of society, law and ethics can be explained and justified.

(It should be pointed out that MacIntyre is describing what he takes to be the *dominant* conception in the English social order. There were of course as he says dissenting English traditions, from puritan republicanism to Roman Catholic Jacobitism – movements typically tied to theologies less flexible than Anglicanism.)

Scottish society was based on a very different set of presuppositions. Most importantly, it embodied a conception according to which the principles governing the social order possess a validity which is independent of the passions which happen to prevail among its members. Scotland was a type of society, to MacIntyre, 'which is understood by most of those who inhabit it as exemplifying in its social and political order principles independent of and antecedent to the passions and interests of the individuals and groups who compose that society . . .'[29] The nature of these principles will be discussed a little later. What we should note at this stage is that this conception of the relationship between principle and passion implies two further fundamental beliefs, one psychological, and one epistemological. First, commitment to rational principle can motivate to action, even where this action is in conflict with our passions. And second, independent principles of ethics and law can be rationally vindicated, so that, in turn, appeal to such principles is itself rational.

For one formulation of this account, MacIntyre refers us to Lord Stair's *Institutions of the Laws of Scotland*. This was first published in 1681, Stair then being Lord President of the Court of Session, and would long be considered the definitive ascertainment of Scots law. MacIntyre describes it as 'a comprehensive statement of the nature of justice, of law, and of rational and right conduct which articulated the presuppositions of what were to be distinctively Scottish attitudes.'[30] Stair draws on commentary on Roman and Dutch law, but 'No English legal commentator is ever mentioned, nor is any English statute or case.'

MacIntyre underlines that, although Stair's statement might appear to be simply a contribution to legal thought, it in fact articulates a much broader cultural formation: 'No one in the Scottish eighteenth century could engage with these topics [ethics and justice] without in one way or another confronting Stair's theoretical and conceptual scheme, a scheme which expressed in terms of the law of Scotland not only the legal but also the key theological and philosophical doctrines concerning justice, law and rational and right conduct.'[31]

What, then, are the principal features of Stair's system? Firstly, law is 'the dictate of reason', and all human beings apprehend its fundamental principles through the exercise of the reasoning faculty. That is, law is not derived from, based on, justified by or explicable in terms of self-love or any other passion. Stair writes: 'The principles of law are such as are known without arguing, and to which the judgement, upon apprehension thereof, will give it ready and fully assent; such as, God is to be adored and obeyed, parents to be obeyed and honoured, children to be loved and entertained. And such are these common precepts which are set forth in the civil law, to live honestly, to wrong no man, to give every man his due'.[32]

Secondly, there are no legitimate standards of action, such as utility or expediency, which could function in independence of considerations of what is just and right. Third, our primary obligations to God and his law are antecedent to rights. Thus property rights, for instance, are restricted by our obligations to promote the welfare of others. (For Blackstone, by contrast, property rights are absolute.) Finally, the scheme has an ineliminable theological reference. Whereas in Blackstone's account of justice reference to God is an adornment, it is integral to Stair's conception. Reason enjoins us to obey God (rather than the dictates of self-love); moreover, Scripture is as far as Stair is concerned an indispensible aid to our right understanding of and correct reasoning from the principles of the moral law, since our natural or untutored grasp of these principles is defective: 'because through sin and evil custom the natural law in man's heart was much defaced, disordered and erroneously deduced, [God] hath therefore reprinted the law of nature in a viver character in the Scripture, not only having the moral principles, but many conclusions thence flowing, particularly set forth'.[33]

Stair's position is open to a number of obvious and serious objections. There is some tension between the claim that ethical first principles are known to all 'without arguing', and the contention that for a right understanding of them we rely on the study of Scripture. There is also a key difficulty which besets any appeal to self-evident first principles, namely the fact that no non-trivial principles are in reality evident to all human beings. Stair did not go far in attempting to deal with this issue, though he was aware of it.

But the crucial point for our discussion which arises from these and related difficulties is this: a society taken to be guided by principles conceived as possessing an authority which is independent of the passions and interests will require for its survival and successful functioning practices in which these principles can be publicly clarified and given rational vindication. In other words, to quote MacIntyre once more, 'if the sphere of public life is to be understood in the way that it is understood in the *Institutions*, then philosophical debate will have to become central to social and cultural life.'[34]

It is only by reference to the structural requirements of a social order committed to a belief in rationally defensible independent standards of right conduct that we can properly understand a central and well-known feature of the Scotland of the age: the cultural dominance of philosophy. (Conversely, the prioritisation of the passions over rational principle explains why English society had no need of philosophy – and why philosophy would always be a peripheral feature of English culture.)

The dominance of philosophical discussion was established and maintained in two main ways. In the universities, philosophy and in particular moral philosophy enjoyed a privileged status in the curriculum. Here were explored the nature of the rational foundations of Christian, or more precisely Calvinist Christian theology and morals: ' . . . the task of a professor of moral philosophy in eighteenth-century Scotland came to be that of providing a defence of just those fundamental moral principles, conceived of as antecedent to both all positive law and all particular forms of social organisation, which defined peculiarly Scottish institutions and attitudes.'[35]

But philosophical debate was not confined to the universities. It flourished in the wider culture too, most notably through the activities of the many philosophical clubs and societies. Scotland was thus in the enviable position of possessing 'that very rare phenomenon, an educated public, in this case a philosophically educated public . . .'[36]

The fundamental principles which were the focus of inquiry in the universities and beyond, the independent principles which the social order recognised as authoritative, are characterised by MacIntyre as Calvinist-Aristotelian. The dominant Scottish calvinist tradition, he contends, was both in large measure compatible with, and to a large extent informed by Aristotelian ethical theory. This contention may puzzle readers whose understanding of the Scottish past is based on the standard histories and journalistic commentary. These have promoted an image of the orthodox calvinist as a wide-eyed sectarist, and have identified calvinism with distrust of human reason and hostility to philosophical reflection, extreme emphasis on arbitrary saving grace and consequent disregard for the moral law,

and belief in a rigid predetermination of human action. Such representations make for lively copy, and add some colour to drab
recountings of social and economic facts. But as history they are
dubious.

As is already evident from Stair's comments discussed above, adherents of the hegemonic presbyterian tradition neither rejected the use
of reason nor devalorised the moral law. They were concerned, principally through the universities, to provide a rational justification of
their beliefs, and to counter all those philosophical positions which
challenged them. They held to the importance of the moral law, as
indeed they were quite clearly enjoined to do by the catechism: 'The
moral law is the declaration of the will of God to mankind, directing
and binding everyone to personal, perfect and perpetual conformity
thereto . . .' And they also took it to be the case that we are endowed
with a reasoning faculty which enables us to educate and control our
passions, and that we are therefore accountable when we do not in
our conduct observe sound principle.

Like Kidd's, MacIntyre's narrative centres on changes in Scottish
identity effected by intellectual subversion. In MacIntyre's analysis, however, what is subverted is not a myth-history or a set of
legends, but the philosophy embodied in the practices and institutions which defined Scottish identity. The villain of the piece –
MacIntyre is not and makes no claim to be neutral or impartial – is
David Hume. Hume was of course a product of the profoundly philosophical and calvinist culture we have been describing. But MacIntyre
sees his work as involving 'the abandonment of peculiarly Scottish
modes of thought in favour of a distinctively English and Anglicising
way of understanding social life and its moral fabric.'[37]

Frances Hutcheson, the Glasgow professor of philosophy under
whom Adam Smith studied, is a transitional figure in this narrative.
Hutcheson's thought is an expression of the Scottish amalgamation
of calvinism and Aristotelianism. It is clearly theological: Hutcheson
taught that the powers of human reason and moral perception are
means to understanding God's will, and therefore stand to Scripture
as an alternative mode of revelation. Thus, properly applied, these
powers cannot yield conclusions which conflict with theological doctrine. He shared many of Stair's views, agreeing, for instance, that
justice involves principles (as MacIntyre puts it) 'whose truth and
whose claim to our allegiance are independent of the interest or advantage of any person or group of persons.'[38] However, influenced by
writers like Shaftesbury, Hutcheson also broke with a number of central Aristotelian tenets, and thus began an undermining of Calvinist
Aristotelianism.

Here and throughout, readers are urged to turn to MacIntyre's at times demanding account themselves for the complex detail of the argument. But what is crucial at this point is that Hutcheson's system incorporated an appeal to inward feeling as a warrant of rightness, and thereby demoted reasoning and reflection. The 'moral sense', a notion which has no place in any Aristotelian ethics, performs functions which in Aristotle are assigned to rational reflection. Thus we are not required, for example, to reason about our *telos* or chief or ultimate ends: these ends are given by our natural propensities. In MacIntyre's gloss, 'our supreme happiness will in fact result from the pursuit of those ends proposed to us by the moral sense.'[39] Some of the ground had already been prepared for the Humean project.

We can begin to appreciate just how radically Hume departs from Scottish philosophical practice, and even from predecessors such as Hutcheson to whom he was partly indebted, by considering his methodology, and by comparing his conception of the nature of moral inquiry with that inscribed in a framework like Calvinist Aristotelianism. In the latter we can identify a number of central assumptions, all of which are abandoned in Hume's project. Moral inquiry is taken to be the activity of persons belonging to a community which is defined by its adherence to an explicit shared system of belief; the community conducts its inquiry and gauges progress in inquiry with reference to a canonical text or set of texts; inquiry is thus tradition-informed, proceeding in the light of the doctrines of these texts and also of subsequent interpretation in the history of the tradition, interpretation and commentary which the belief-defined community has come to regard as authoritative.

Hume's procedure involves a rejection of all these postulates. His theory is an attempt to account for moral judgements and conduct from the ground up, so to speak – without reference to any tradition or authority, and without the deployment (or so at least Hume supposed) of theoretical presuppositions, let alone of any established and elaborated system of belief. (This is not to say, of course, that Hume does not refer to or incorporate elements of previous theory.) The method employed is nothing more than, as he says, 'cautious observation of human life', that is to say, empirical investigation of human nature in its social environment. This 'scientific' method, Hume believed, would at last place moral inquiry on a rational basis and eventually rid mankind of moral superstition.

In considering now why Hume's mode of inquiry is not only incompatible with but also inadmissible on Aristotelian or Calvinist premises, we can begin to understand further features of his subversive project. By proceeding as he does, through a description of human nature as it is or happens to be, Hume holds and affirms that morality is, so to say,

already established and observable in the customary judgements, sentiments, habits and practices of human beings following the promptings
of their passions. For Aristotelians or Calvinists, on the other hand,
morality is only adequately established and observable among those
persons in whose conduct is reflected an understanding of right doctrine and the acquisition and possession of virtuous character. From
such a perspective, any account based on the observation of human
nature which is untutored in doctrine and virtue will be an account,
not of morality, but of sin or vice. (It is then no accident that, as we
shall see, Hume in fact ratifies a type of social order where a ruling
passion is, on an Aristotelian view, a major vice.) And from these
perspectives ethics is precisely that mode of rational inquiry which
attempts to specify what human nature as it is should become, and
how such a transformation can be achieved.

From a Humean standpoint, any such specification is redundant.
For morality is already in place in conduct flowing from our natural
inclinations as these are shaped by an appropriate social ambience.
Hence in Hume's scheme a conception definitive of preceding Scottish
culture disappears: 'the belief that reason . . . prescribes to the passions
in the light of the knowledge which it affords concerning the true end
of human beings.'[40]

And with this belief falls another. If we do not require rationally-
vindicated principles for the right ordering of self and society, if the
passions, suitably tempered, already conduce to justice, then the activity of philosophy as the elaboration and justification of such principles
can have no sense. Philosophy becomes redundant. And just this of
course is Hume's expressed view.[41] Philosophy is then only meaningful
as a kind of pastime – like, say, chess – which affords those individuals
so inclined a particular form of pleasure and satisfaction (Hume's own
comparisons are with gambling and hunting). It does not even have a
peripheral role in ethics and politics: it is no more significant than
a delightful hobby. The contrast with the Scottish view of philosophy
as culturally necessary and central could hardly be starker.

We can now refine our description of what MacIntyre terms 'Hume's
anglicising subversion' by making a further point about his ethical
theory or 'science of man'. Many later thinkers in the liberal tradition
who, like Hume, reject tradition-informed inquiry, would conceive the
individual, as such, as the locus of moral agency, and so portray moral
value and belief as properly the outcome of personal preference, decision and commitment. But this is not Hume's view. If he naturalises
the source of morality, he also insists that moral sentiment requires
social shaping. Mature moral judgement arises, on his view, neither
from the study of systems nor from the anguished deliberations of an
isolated self, but from participation in social life, where our passions

are reciprocally tempered, adjusted and corrected to achieve the harmonisation of taste and judgement which makes society possible in the first place. However, in Hume it is not social life *per se* which is necessary for morality: what is endorsed is a highly specific social formation.

The presuppositions and values of this formation, so MacIntyre maintains, are what Hume's ethical theory articulates. At the heart of these systems (*i.e.* the theory and the social order which embodies it) is the passion or motive Hume calls pride – or rather, pride and its opposite, humility. Pride is closely connected with love, and humility with hatred, in the sense that those things which cause pride (or humility) in our selves elicit our love (or hatred) towards others in whom they are displayed. Hume in fact famously defined virtue as 'the power of producing love or pride', and vice as 'the power of producing hatred or humility'.[42] MacIntyre comments: 'We confront then a type of social order in which persons are evaluated by reference to those of their qualities which are the objects of pride and humility both in themselves and others'.[43]

What, then, are the things which elicit our pride and love? Hume presents a list of mental and physical qualities, such as wit and learning, beauty and strength. But we also, he says, take pride in our 'gardens, horses, dogs', and in our 'houses, equipage or furniture'. It becomes clear, in fact, that it is *property* which is central to Hume's account. We do not take pride in the qualities of friends or relatives who are poor: we 'are ashamed of any one, that is mean or poor, among our friends and relatives'. Hume can indeed state that 'the relation, which is esteem'd the closest, and which of all others produces most commonly the passion of pride, is that of property.'[44]

As MacIntyre drily comments, Hume took himself – and is still taken by many present-day commentators – to be describing human nature as such, and human civilisation as such. But what he in fact offers is a description of the nature and civilisation of the eighteenth-century English propertied classes – and, we might add, their contemporary spiritual heirs.

Two further points should be made about the social order which Hume endorses and commends. If pride is essentially tied to the possession of property, this is both because property in this order confers status and thus the satisfaction of social esteem, and also because it permits the proprietor to enjoy, as Hume says, 'all the pleasures of life' to which wealth provides access. The type of society which is here being ratified can be variously described. It is an order, in MacIntyre's words, designed to let 'the passions achieve their most extensive and most enduring satisfaction'.[45] In the idiom of a historian who identifies with Hume's views, it is an order where human beings 'devote themselves to the peaceful pursuit of their interests'.[46] Or in a grossly impoverished but related parlance, the now culturally hegemonic discourse of management and marketing, it is a society dedicated to the achievement of consumer satisfaction.

The second point is this: in a social order where the possession of wealth and property occupies the central place which on Hume's account it does, a governing passion will inevitably be what Aristotle designated the vice of *pleonexia*. This can be translated as 'greed' or 'acquisitiveness', and is to be understood as a settled disposition of character to engage in activities aimed at acquisition, for its own sake, and/or for the sake of those pleasures and satisfactions which possession provides. 'The cause of this condition [*i.e. pleonexia*] is zeal for life,' Aristotle comments in the *Politics* – and then adds: 'but not zeal for the good life'.

In order to grasp the broader significance of MacIntyre's interest in the Scottish Calvinist-Aristotelian identity and his highly critical treatment of Hume, we have to set them in the context of the dispute between liberal theorists and neo-Aristotelians (among whom MacIntyre himself is so far the most influential), a confrontation which is at the heart of contemporary philosophy. Briefly, the neo-Aristotelians are attempting to recuperate a conception of ethics as virtue-based and tradition-informed, rather than a matter of individual choice and taste; of the moral self as the bearer of social and historical statuses rather than an individual will; and of politics as a matter of debate over public right and the good rather than a process of bargaining among interest groups.

It might be objected that these are arcane matters far removed from and irrelevant to the 'real' world of social and political life. But in fact it is not only among theorists that we can observe increasing acknowledgment that no worthwhile, dignified or meaningful human life or polity can be built on the commandment, Thou shalt have no other gods save thy wants alone – that ethics and politics require something more than the promptings of contingent individual desire and inclination.

In the context, then, of a growing challenge to the philosophy of liberal modernity, and the rediscovery of Aristotelian moral and political theory, the history of the Scottish social order which Kidd, endorsing the Enlightenment-whig verdict, sees as ideologically bankrupt, is destined to become more rather than less relevant to our predicaments. Of course, to make such remarks is still to invite, from many quarters, predictable forms of ridicule. Our brief response will be to recall what Jacques Maritain once said: only philosophies which are ancient last.

7

The Augustinian Moment

1

Is there a distinctive and significant Scottish contribution to twentieth-century thought? And if so, to what extent do the ideas it presents address our current cultural and political predicaments?

Before any attempt to develop a response to these questions is made, it should be noted that they are surprising and unusual. They are never posed in standard general works concerned with recent Scottish history, which have little to say either about intellectual culture in general or, more specifically, about developments in philosophy and theory. Where these topics are dealt with at all in such texts, the accounts offered are extremely meagre. Why should this be so?

In order to explain this relative neglect, we have to draw out two assumptions which are at work in typical accounts by historians.

One is that Scottish intellectual and philosophical production in the modern period has itself been meagre, and consequently does not merit any extended discussion. Let us look, by way of illustrating how this assumption operates, at the treatment of culture in a book we have already referred to in previous sections, *A Century of the Scottish People, 1830–1950*, by T. C. Smout. The justification for taking this particular text as an example is that it is in a sense now *the* history of modern Scotland – without much doubt the most widely-read and most influential, among students, teachers and a wider reading public, both in Scotland and elsewhere. It is a product, therefore, which we have to take with great seriousness, and read with great care.

As in other works on Scotland of this type, the treatment accorded to cultural developments is cursory, as the author admits. His main concern, as he states, and as the text more than amply bears out, is with the 'world of deprivation' in which, on his account, the majority of the Scottish people in the period concerned lived. However, Professor Smout does acknowledge that there is much more to be said about artistic, scientific and intellectual endeavour than he himself attempts. He concedes, as we have already seen, that

> . . . a book could be written about the achievements of the Scots from the Edinburgh Reviewers and Thomas Carlyle to the poets of the Scottish Renaissance, from the scientists like Clerk Maxwell and D'Arcy Thompson to the doctors like Simpson and Lister and the divines like Robertson Smith and David Cairns.[1]

The choice of names here is rather idiosyncratic, and it is tedious to have to point out that the list omits many figures – artists, scholars, scientists, philosophers, theologians, writers and so on – whose work is of outstanding interest and importance. The passage is also curiously lacking in perspective: in terms of intellectual stature, James Clerk Maxwell is hardly someone to be mentioned in the same breath as the other figures indicated here. Maxwell's peers in the history of culture are generally taken to be Newton and Einstein: Einstein himself stated that Maxwell's work was 'the most profound and the most fruitful that physics has experienced since the time of Newton'. Professor Smout's comment seriously distorts Maxwell's stature.

More importantly, the seemingly innocuous, even generous remark that 'a book could be written' about Scottish intellectual life in his period contains a deeper layer of significance. It betrays the assumption, and by implication conveys the message, that the Scottish cultural production of the period was of comparatively limited value and interest. In order to see that this is the case, we only have to consider how unlikely it would be that Smout, or any other historian, in a book entitled, say, *A Century of the English People, 1830–1950*, should make the observation that

> a book could be written about the achievements of the English from Dickens and Arnold to George Orwell, from divines like Newman to scientists like Darwin and philosophers like Bertrand Russell, and from poets like Browning and A. E. Housman to composers such as Elgar.

The second assumption concerns philosophy or theory in particular. It is that philosophy is a highly specialised type of cultural activity, properly of concern only to professionals in the field, a kind of inquiry which has an at most marginal influence on other events and developments. And from this follows a further notion: that the history of these other domains – political, social, economic, and cultural – can be written independently of the history of theory. We can return to Professor Smout's text to demonstrate the point. His objective, he states, is to describe 'what life was like for most Scottish people' in the historical period under consideration. Matters of theory or high culture, he takes it, are largely irrelevant to such a project.

However, Smout's account of the Scottish 'world of deprivation' contains occasional references to other aspects of Scottish life,
including the intellectual world. One of these repays a little detailed
consideration. In the section Smout devotes to the churches, we find
this short passage on the work of the churchman and theologian John
Baillie:

> In the twentieth century it [the Church of Scotland] bravely
> strove to reconcile philosophy, science and biblical scholar-
> ship with religion, and its most noted theologians, especially
> John Baillie, who held chairs in the USA and Canada as well
> as in Scotland, had a worldwide reputation among those
> who still cared for such things.[2]

This is a splendid exercise in damnation by faint praise. It successfully conjures an image of worthy but slightly dotty individuals, bent
over musty tomes and obsessed with questions which – to enlightened
minds like Professor Smout and his readers – are patently archaic and
futile, if not absurd. Of particular interest is the notion implied by the
final dismissive clause: the issues which concern a theologian, being
of interest only to a small minority, are of little significance – as if
importance were something to be measured by market research and
opinion polls, or gleaned from a study of government statistics.

But let us now say something about John Baillie himself, both to
provide an alternative perspective to Smout's liberal condescension,
and to raise some questions about the assumptions of 'social history'.
William Storrar has recently drawn attention to the part played by
Baillie in a Church of Scotland commission which reported annually
to the General Assembly from 1941 to 1945. As Storrar indicates, it
has been argued that these reports, which articulated a strong social
conscience in the Kirk, had some influence in the creation of demands
for a more egalitarian social structure, the climate of public opinion
which led to the Labour victory of 1945 and the subsequent extension
of state welfare provision. However this may be, what is of greater
relevance to the present discussion is the commission's diagnosis of
Scottish society as by now a largely secular one. What is meant by
'secular'? The commission offered the following definition:

> ... secular means 'pertaining to an age', and the age here
> meant is this present world – that is, the day-to-day round
> of our present transitory existence. The secularist outlook
> thus differs from all previous outlooks whether pagan or
> Christian, in being without any kind of far horizon, any
> ultimate background of belief, any final sanction for the
> routine of present behaviour.

People, it stated, go on 'living decently', but 'they are living in a
sort of void, without any general frame of reference to give their lives a

meaning'.[3] It is at once clear from these quotations that some at least of the questions which concerned Baillie, far from being matters of peripheral or antiquarian interest, are of quite central importance, and not least to the writing of history. For if our objective is to understand and describe 'what life was like for most people', the consideration that in recent times many have lived 'without any general frame of reference' is surely significant. And it might also be the case that Baillie had, in fact, brought out in its proper light – as a profound and critical cultural phenemenon – the process of breakdown in overall patterns of belief which Smout deals with, in breezy fashion, by talk of 'the death of hell'.

In his other writings, Baillie, like some other recent Scottish thinkers, connects this crisis to movements in theory: to the intellectual dominance of naturalistic modes of thought, the worldview which found expression, for instance, in the kind of ethical theory propounded in Baillie's day in analytic philosophy, according to which moral beliefs are not based on reason but on personal taste and pre-rational inclination. To posit such a link between philosophical developments and their wider social environment is not to claim that, among the general populace, there is a vast and avid readership for the *Proceedings of the Aristotelian Society*. But it is to recognise both that theory expresses concepts already incorporated in forms of social practice, and that all human actions and forms of life are theory-laden, informed by schemes of belief, and not intelligible without reference to such beliefs. And it is therefore to recognise also that the history of a period cannot be written adequately if it takes no account of the history of ideas. 'Social history', by contrast, tends to proceed on the reductivist assumption that preconceptual needs and interests function in social practice independently of agents' theory-informed beliefs about the role of such interests.

But it is possible, of course, to acknowledge that ideas play a crucial role in history, and at the same time to believe that the kind of worldview expressed by Baillie no longer represents any significant community and has ceased to have much influence on events, at least in those societies which take themselves to be and are generally perceived to be advanced and sophisticated. Such ideas, surely, belong in the past; and to this extent at least, it seems, Professor Smout's verdict on Baillie is safe.

The most momentous events of recent years – the revolutions in eastern Europe – at first sight confirm the thesis that human actions are now governed, not by the ideas of a man like John Baillie, but by the pragmatic ethic which is most at home in modern liberal capitalist societies. And just this, of course, is the standard interpretation placed on 1989 by men and women of affairs, media experts and other self-defined realists. But if it is true that people are generally concerned to improve the material conditions of their lives, such an interpretation leaves out of account a different and striking feature of the eastern revolutions which challenges this liberal complacency.

For what these movements also demonstrated, precisely, is the power and 'relevance' of traditions of thought and action which are completely alien to the pragmatism and ethical premisslessness of liberal modernity – that absence, to employ Baillie's words, of 'any final sanction for the routine of present behaviour'. In Romania, it was the moral intransigence (or, in liberal code, 'fanaticism') of a Calvinist pastor in Timosoara which set the popular revolt against Ceaucescu in motion. In the Czechoslovakia of the 1980s, the dissent of such groups as the clandestine universities fed on the study of classical and Christian thought, on Plato and Augustine. And in Czechoslovakia and elsewhere, dissidence and opposition depended on the responsibility felt by Havel and others to the ethical imperative of 'living in the truth'.

Such people were, of course, in their time dismissed by sociologists and others who pride themselves on their no-nonsense understanding of human affairs as dreamers and utopians, members of that laudable but insignificant minority who 'still care for such things'. And what this may suggest is that those whose values, beliefs and attitudes are rooted solely in the present, and who take to be real and significant only what the majority of the inhabitants of contemporary liberal society consider to be so, can understand the present no more than they can understand the past, and are blind to the fundamental issues which confront us.

This blindness will form the subject of their most fitting obituary.

2

There are few knowledgeable interpreters of Scottish thought in the post-Enlightenment period, and to date there has been only one sizeable treatment of philosophy in the twentieth century, George Davie's *Crisis of the Democratic Intellect*. This study presents a challenge to the widely-held assumption that Scottish contributions to theory over the past century have been of negligible value and importance. As contrasted with the meagre, dismissive and often seemingly ill-informed accounts *á la* Smout, this text, like Davie's earlier writing on nineteenth-century thought, involves a detailed and complex reading of Scottish intellectual culture. It opens up tracts of cultural history which have been left unexplored by mainstream histories, and so at the same time serves to stimulate much further inquiry and discussion.

Part of Davie's project is to unearth a position which is common to major Scottish intellectual production through the century. His view is that there is a distinctive orientation in this work, and, moreover, that this has been of outstanding relevance to contemporary theoretical argument. Since Davie's work is not as well-known and as widely studied as it deserves to be, we will begin by offering a summary of part at least of his account. Our main aim here, however, is not to provide a commentary on Davie, but to the develop his thesis; for his argument, as we will later try to show, can now be extended in a very substantial way.

Davie's view is at first sight, no doubt, a startling, even absurd one. It is that what is most distinctive and valuable about twentieth-century Scottish contributions to theory involves a re-working, in more or less secular form, of the nation's theological inheritance. This will strike many readers as a bizarre conception, because we have all long been led to believe, by historians, textbook-writers, journalists and other opinion formers, that Scottish religious traditions embody little more than philistinism, bigotry and a set of discourses pathetically irrelevant to modern debate. Davie takes issue with these liberal *idées reçues*.

The re-elaboration of Scottish religious discourse takes the form, on Davie's account, of an anti-modernist, anti-Enlightenment position which stresses, against the assumptions of modern progressivist optimism, the extent of the limitations of human potentialities. In more strictly theological terms, what is involved here is a re-assertion of Calvinist ideas, and in particular the doctrine of original sin, as against the Pelagian view that man is in possession of resources which enable him to attain a state of moral perfection.

Given the particular ideological configuration which prevails in Scotland, we should perhaps pause here to mention an objection which will immediately be raised by some readers (including those who labour in that minor academic industry devoted to the detection and analysis of religious intolerance in Scottish society). Any such appeal to Calvinism as in some way definitive of Scottish intellectual culture, so it will be argued, is suspect for at least two kinds of reason: first, it does not take into account the other major religious force in modern Scottish history, Catholicism; and second, because of this exclusion, such an interpretation is tainted by, and can only serve to bolster, a religious sectarianism. From this kind of perspective, Davie's thesis runs the risk of stoking 'tribal emotion' and stirring up 'sectarian rivalry' – to use typical dreary clichés of sociologism.[4]

Something will be said in the course of the discussion to suggest that the philosophical assumptions which base the cosy self-congratulation inherent in such charges are unsustainable. But at this point we need note only that the objections, at least as far as Davie's thesis is concerned, do not have any force. For in his account nothing turns on whether we refer to a Calvinist or an Augustinian inheritance; on whether, in other words, we refer to reformed or unreformed Augustinianism. And in fact Davie tends to use the words 'Calvinist' and 'Augustinian' interchangeably. The justification for this practice is supplied by a commonplace of theological scholarship: that Calvin was at one with Augustine in the essential features of his teaching. As one scholar writes, the reformer 'considered himself in accord with St Augustine on all fundamental issues, and willingly underlined this harmony when responding to his critics'.[5]

In Davie's history, one of the twentieth-century re-statements of anti-Pelagianism is to be found in the work of Norman Kemp Smith. Kemp Smith was appointed professor of philosophy at Edinburgh in 1919, after teaching for many years in the USA. He would establish himself as a major interpreter of both Hume and Kant; and it is on his contributions to Humean and Kantian scholarship that his fame now rests. Davie, however, draws attention to some neglected and surprising aspects of Kemp Smith's work in order to develop his thesis.

In the early 1920s, Kemp Smith dedicated part of his time to taking discussion of his ideas beyond the university, and in particular, in an exemplary exercise in democratic intellectualism, to a working-class audience. In public lectures and in courses organised by the Workers' Educational Association, he sought to bring some philosophical depth to the debates then engrossing more intellectual sectors of the working class. Prominent in these discussions were the marxist ideas of the day. While by no means hostile to working-class demands for social change, or to greater degrees of state intervention and planning, Kemp Smith thought it necessary to try to raise popular political debate above the level of marxist orthodoxies, and to undermine over-sanguine conceptions about the possibility of social and human transformation.

The inspiration behind Kemp Smith's remarkable interventions in a wider public forum was his sense of the continuing significance of the ancient quarrel between Augustinians and Pelagians. In a letter to the Catholic thinker von Hügel, written at the beginning of this period, Kemp Smith had written:

> For some years I have been ambitious to write upon what I should describe as 'traditional views of human nature' – meaning the Christian doctrine of original sin and the Enlightenment (or Pelagian) doctrine of human perfectibility – on the lines of a plea for a better understanding of the former view.[6]

At the same time as his participation in debate with the workers, in his lectures on epistemology in the university Kemp Smith was arguing for a conception of knowledge incompatible with the assumptions of

progressivist optimism. Knowledge, he taught, is not a matter of incre-
mental evolution, and the human mind does not begin as a *tabula rasa*.
Rather, we start from illusion, and illusions permanently threaten to
invade and distort whatever knowledge we attain. So there can be no
question of straightforward progress in knowledge; there is, instead,
only a constant struggle against error and falsehood. The underlying
message here, once more, was a warning against rosy views concerning human potentialities, the kind of easy optimism about the human
condition then being advanced in Scottish educational circles (and later
projected to an international audience of educationalists) by A. S. Neill.

Let us at this point listen to how Davie himself summarises these
aspects of Kemp Smith's thought:

> The original feature of Kemp Smith which marked him off as
> quite different from other representatives of his generation
> was his deeply felt conviction that the new ideas deriving
> from men like Freud and Nietzsche, when they were properly
> understood, assimilated and developed, pointed forward
> not to the kind of brave new world of liberated happiness
> expected by men like A.S.Neill, but rather to the necessity
> of critical revaluation of the kind of ideas associated with
> Calvin, so as to bring out what they had of value, separating
> it from what was out of date. In short, the new idea behind
> Kemp Smith's philosophy which made it surprising and
> interesting was a sort of secularised version of the doctrine
> of original sin.[7]

This 'secular calvinist' position, as Davie terms it, was subsequently
developed and sharpened – so the narrative continues – by John
Anderson: a native of Lanarkshire, Glasgow graduate in physics and
philosophy, and one-time colleague of Kemp Smith in the Edinburgh
department of philosophy. For Davie, Anderson is the star of modern
Scottish theory, although most of his work was done during his long
tenure of a chair at the University of Sydney. (In recent times, Davie
has remarked elsewhere, the Scottish philosophical tradition has been
much more alive outside rather than within the Scottish universities.)

To many of his Australian colleagues and students, Anderson
seemed 'a critic of almost inhuman acuteness and pertinacity, a corrosive mind . . .'[8] He became a belligerent arch-foe of *bien pensant*
progressivism in all its different hues and forms: of statism and wel-
farism in politics, for instance, and of modernism in education. He
made what is a still unsurpassed contribution to the articulation of a
classical, critical-humanist philosophy of education.

Anderson's verdict on marxism – which is still, incidentally, perhaps
the most judicious available – permits us to grasp something of his
anti-Pelagian social theory:

The doctrine of history as struggle is at once the liberal and scientific part of marxism: the doctrine of socialism as something to be realised ('classless society') is its servile part. The point is not merely the drabness that might result from attempts to eliminate social struggles, but the impossibility of eliminating them – and therewith, the loss of independence and vigour which can result from the spreading of the belief that they can be eliminated.[9]

Society, that is, is a site of conflict and struggle among different and irreconcilable interests, values, beliefs, philosophies and ways of life; and, *pace* what Anderson named the 'solidarist' conceptions and aspirations of socialists, planners and the techno-bureaucracies of modern states, we have no grounds for belief in the possibility of any ultimate stable state of collective harmonious contentment where such divisions will have been abolished. What is more, such a conflict-free condition would represent, from a cultural point of view, a catastrophe; for in a monist world there would be no possibility of comparison, no way of 'seeing ourselves as others see us', and hence no way for any group to develop a critical attitude towards its own practices. That commonplace of bars and boardrooms the world over – socialism is all very well in theory, but doesn't work in practice – is thus shown to be false: we have strong theoretical reasons for rejecting socialism.

Anderson has been enormously influential in Australian intellectual life; and what Davie terms 'Anderson's reassertion of the limitations of human nature as opposed to the doctrine held by the apostles of progress and perfectibility' would in turn be taken up by some of his students there. Of special interest in this connection is John Passmore's essay on the history of ideas, *The Perfectibility of Man*, which, as its author attests, is shaped by the Andersonian perspective.

This brief summary may serve, we hope, to convey something of the richness and interest of Davie's thesis that there is a distinctive Scottish contribution to recent theory which takes the form of a secularised Augustinian anti-modernism. The argument, of course, raises a host of questions, and points to the need for much further investigation and analysis.

It would be illuminating, for instance, to compare this Scottish Calvinist contribution with the ideas of Dutch neo-Calvinism, as represented in the work of figures like Abraham Kuyper. We also require some study of the similarities between Davie's secular Calvinists and theologians like Thomas Torrance. There are more critical issues to be explored too. It could, for example, be argued that Anderson's anti-modernism is classical rather than Christian, inspired more by Heraclitus, and a Heraclitean sense of conflict as 'the father of all things', than by Augustine or Calvin. Davie's thesis also provokes a more general challenge. For a strong case could be made that what is most representative of modern Scottish thought is a position which combines a critique of naturalism with the development of personalist ideas – a movement represented by, among others, Macmurray, MacQuarrie and R. D. Laing.

But such matters must be left, for now, to one side. What we would like to do here is show how Davie's particular thesis can be extended. The argument, it will be suggested, may be amplified and modified in the light of the remarkable recent contributions to theory made by the most gifted Scottish-born philosopher since Anderson himself. We are referring, of course, to the work of Alasdair MacIntyre.

It has by now become common to bracket MacIntyre's name with those of Habermas and Foucault, as one of the handful of recent and present-day thinkers whose work is of exceptional interest and importance. MacIntyre's reputation as a theorist of this order was established by *After Virtue: a Study in Moral Theory*, which was first published in 1981. There he argued that in modern liberal society moral discourse has become a quite mysterious phenomenon. Moral rules, injunctions and concepts have been split off from other beliefs and practices in such a way that their sense and force are now largely inexplicable. Intelligibility can only be restored to ethics, he claimed, if we recover something similar to the Aristotelian conception of a *telos*, or goal of human life, and revive an Aristotelian-type moral discourse in which the moral and intellectual virtues play a central role. In other words, questions about what we ought to do can only be given proper sense within a wider framework of belief which concerns the nature of the good life, or questions about what we ought to be or become.

The position elaborated in *After Virtue*, then, was both strongly anti-modernist and strongly Aristotelian. MacIntyre described its 'central thesis', in the postscript added to the 1985 addition, as the view that

> the Aristotelian moral tradition is the best example we possess of a tradition whose adherents are rationally entitled to a high measure of confidence in its epistemological and moral resources.[10]

In his more recent work, however, while developing his anti-modernist and anti-Enlightenment stance, MacIntyre now speaks from a position he himself describes as 'Augustinian Christian'.[11]

The relevance of MacIntyre's ideas to Davie's thesis is immediately obvious, as is the way in which the thesis requires some qualification in the light of these ideas. MacIntyre's work can be viewed as a further instance of the Augustinian anti-modernism Davie analyses in Kemp Smith and Anderson; but this work, at the same time, obliges us to revise the thesis insofar as it stresses the secular nature of this neo-

Augustinian tradition. We are concerned with a theoretical moment which has both a secular and a theological dimension.

The fundamental question we must now pursue is this: if the anti-modernism of Kemp Smith and Anderson was an important contribution to theory, as a response to the deficiencies and limitations of the progressive orthodoxies of their day – in the shape, for instance, of marxism, or of modernist philosophies of education, in what way or ways does MacIntyre's Augustinianism represent a vital response to our own, in some respects very altered intellectual and ideological predicament? It is with some remarks on the theoretical contours of the contemporary situation that we can most usefully continue.

3

The decline of the marxist/socialist tradition as a political and ideological force is by now a familiar theme: over the past few years we have been treated to a flood of analyses and commentaries on the demise of the socialist regimes and the crisis afflicting the socialist movement, or the left, as a whole. It is important, for our purposes, to underline some of the implications of these developments at the level of theory and ideas.

The most obvious question which confronts us here is whether anything at all of this intellectual tradition can now be salvaged. But if socialism can survive the material and moral bankruptcy of the ex-socialist states, what shape will socialist-marxist thought now take? Let us look briefly at recent contributions by two leading representatives of socialist theory in order to indicate some current trends in this tradition.

In *The Ideology of the Aesthetic* the English marxist Terry Eagleton appears to offer a re-affirmation of marxism's perfectibilist moment (precisely that feature which Anderson diagnosed as its central weakness). Eagleton here gives perfectibilism an aesthetic twist. What marxism holds out is a vision of a future world of collective 'enjoyable self-realisation'[12] where for the first time human beings will be able to experience a full sensual life. He quotes Marx: 'the society that is fully developed produces man in all the richness of his being, the rich man who is profoundly and abundantly endowed with all the senses . . .'[13] Only with the establishment of a society whose members can all enjoy this complete aesthetic fulfilment will real human history begin. This vision prompts a gloss on the marxist perspective whose evaluation of past and present human life is astonishingly dismissive:

The only truly historic event would be to get history started,
by clearing away the obstacles in its path. So far, nothing

particularly special has occurred: history to date has simply been the same old story, a set of variations on persisting structures of oppression and exploitation.[14]

But how will the rupture from our present pre-history to real human history be made? No answer is supplied, but Eagleton seems to take the view that the transformation will be carried out by those social groups which are most oppressed:

> How can history be turned against itself? Marx's own response was the boldest imaginable. History would be transformed by its most contaminated products, by those bearing the most livid marks of its brutality. In a condition where the powerful run insanely rampant, only the power-less can provide an image of that humanity which must in its turn come to power, and in doing so transfigure the very meaning of that term.[15]

It is difficult to see in this passage anything except confirmation that Eagleton's work, as represented here, is a flight from social and historical analysis and philosophy to mysticism and blind faith. It is true that, as Hannah Arendt once wrote, warmth and humanity are 'well-known characteristics of all oppressed people. They grow out of suffering and they are the proudest possessions of all pariahs. Unfortunately' (she adds) 'they have never survived the hour of liberation by even five minutes.'[16]

It is a relief to turn from Eagleton's Pelagian fantasies to the measured considerations of Jürgen Habermas, even if, once more, what we find here is a demonstration of the relative resourcelessness of socialist theory. In an essay on the future of socialism, Habermas makes a central positive proposal which is in some ways surprising. The main socialist task now, he holds, is to extend the ethical dimension of political discussion. He expresses regret over 'the de-moralisation of public conflicts', and talks of the need to 're-think topics morally' and to 'introduce morality' into political debate.[17] It is by no means clear, though, how this project represents a distinctively socialist approach, or how it forms a continuation of the socialist-marxist tradition. But however this may be, the main problem is that Habermas talks as if moral discourse were consensual and monolithic. Hence he does not confront the central issue raised by his proposal: whose ethics and which morality are we to rely on? As Charles Taylor has recalled recently, Habermas's own theory, which asks us to consider what norms of social and political organisation would be agreed upon by people who could reflect together in conditions of unrestrained communication, is capable of generating, like utilitarian and Rawlsian procedures, only an account of social obligation. It is silent about the deep concerns of ethics, questions about the good life and about the things which should be objects of our love and allegiance.[18]

If we take a broad view of developments on the left, what is observable is a process of theoretical dissolution. One of the comically sad symptoms of this process, at more mundane levels, has been the British Labour Party's frantic, if so far vain, effort to make itself 'electable' by tossing overboard as much as possible of its traditional ideological ballast. But the phenomenon is a very general one. A self-proclaimed 'socialist' posture now survives mainly in the form of the defence of the rights of disadvantaged or oppressed groups, and of protests against social inequality in the name of vague concepts of solidarity and justice. 'Socialism' is becoming, in other words, an essentially defensive and reactive stance which possesses no clear or defined theoretical underpinnings: it no longer represents anything resembling a coherent, worked-out intellectual position, a political philosophy. Hence the admissions about the need for 'enormous theoretical revisions' by E. J. Hobsbawm *et al.*

But so what? Why should any of this matter? Surely we are describing here only a crisis internal to the socialist tradition? If this were the case, the matter could safely be left in the hands of those committed to rescuing and reviving the socialist case – to *New Left Review* contributors and other faithful remnants.

In reality, the crisis in the socialist tradition has much wider implications. For most of the twentieth-century, in the developed West at least, socialist thought has been the main counterforce to the values and practices of the established social and intellectual orders. In the work of the Frankfurt School, for instance, it has provided some of the most penetrating critical analyses of the culture of capitalism; and readers will be able to supply their own examples of other contributions from within the tradition to our social understanding and critical awareness. If, therefore, as seems to be the case, the movement is in terminal decline, what is at stake is something which concerns not only socialists. For the question then arises of where we are to find resources for coherent theoretical dissent and critique to confront what has become an overwhelming political and cultural hegemony.

Socialism's critical force was fuelled by a conception of the good life, a vision of what human life properly consists in. True, that conception never received any detailed elaboration; notoriously, socialism has always been weak on ethics, concerned as it has been principally with collective, class action and salvation rather than close issues about the personal. Nevertheless, however hazy, superficial or banal the formulations have been, socialist thought has served to keep alive the conviction that there is a way of life to which we ought to aspire in virtue of our humanity: there is a form of life, it asserts, in Marx's own words, which is 'worthy of human nature'.[19] Integral to the intellectual ethos of modern liberal societies, by contrast, is a deep scepticism about such notions. Anticipated in the thinking of the sophists, and developed by modern philosophers in positivist and pragmatist traditions, the view that there is no standard of right action which is independent of the empirical wants and preferences of individuals is now an axiom of liberal thought.

The decline of the socialist tradition and the triumph of such liberal ideas form part of a wider intellectual history, whose origins can be traced to the eighteenth-century Enlightenment.

Two features of the Enlightenment project here deserve emphasis. The Enlightenment thinkers aimed to establish a set of principles for the regulation of personal and social conduct which would make no appeal to tradition or authority, save the authority of reason alone; and the principles to be established were such that they would receive universal assent – or, at least, the assent of all persons able and willing to think rationally. The *Aufklärer* assumed not only that there is available to us an ethical standpoint which is independent of all inherited and traditional patterns of belief, but also that it is from this standpoint alone that a rational morality can be developed. Here they were partly motivated by the conviction (which was, no doubt, in many ways well-founded) that local loyalties and commitments to tradition were sources of obscurantism and prejudice – the 'superstition' and 'fanaticism' which attached to religious practices, for instance – and so inimical to intellectual and social progress. In any case, the Enlightenment aspiration – to create a universal ethics independent of historically contingent tradition – would define the subsequent history of moral philosophy, and it still haunts thinking and discussion about moral issues today, both within and beyond the universities.

Developed in out-of-the-way places such as Scotland, Enlightenment notions would be taken up by the self-nominated centres of culture and civilisation and become a powerful instrument in their ideological hegemony over other regions. 'Enlightenment' or rationality came to be seen as the characteristic of metropolitan life, and 'darkness' that of the peripheries, a darkness defined in terms of the brute irrationality or *Urdummheit* taken to inhere in the natives' commitments to their ancient traditions and prejudices. Even today, of course, and especially in inwardly imperial states like Britain, this ideology is by no means dead: we are all familiar with the denunciations, made by newspaper editors, members of parliament and other exemplars of rational man, of the tribalism and obscurantism which still survive in the dark corners of the realm (among Irish nationalists, Highland Free Presbyterians, and other backwoodspeople).

But our concern here is less with the articulation of pure reason in the history of power than with the ultimate fate of the great project of Enlightenment. It was, in intellectual terms, a failure. For all the ingenious philosophical systems it was to produce, and for all the outstanding and generous minds which sought to bring it to fruition, the project has in the end been unable to fulfil its own declared objectives.

The universal ethical standpoint has not been found – or rather, to make the metaphor slightly more accurate, all the maps indicating its location have been declared defective by other cartographers. The various systems of universal principles of action proposed have all failed to attain universal assent. The evidence for this is not hard to find. On any serious personal or social issue – for example, abortion, capital punishment, the distribution of wealth, the justifiability of war, etc., etc. – , societies whose culture has been profoundly influenced by Enlightenment modes of thought are marked by glaring lack of consensus. And were the principles underlying different and conflicting views on these and other issues to be made explicit, we would encounter a further and deeper level of dissensus. Some might be tempted to object that this situation is simply due to a failure to diffuse adequate doses of enlightenment and rationality among the populace. But this response is not convincing, for, to put the matter mildly, no more consensus is to be found, either at the level of particular issues or of theoretical position, in those arenas where, if anywhere, Enlightenment rationality is at home – in, for instance, the debates of professional academic philosophers.

In historical perspective, socialist thought is properly seen as one major stage in the development of the Enlightenment programme. Its debt to the worldview of the eighteenth-century *philosophes* is evident in the requirement that people free themselves from the irrationality and 'false consciousness' of religious and other traditional schemes of thought, and from tribal and national identification and related forms of petty particularism. Minds unencumbered by such outmoded and parochial loyalties, socialists believed, would perceive the truth of their account of man and society, and unite to construct a rational social order.

The failure of the project is inscribed in the spirit and the agenda of that more mature product of the Enlightenment which constitutes the now dominant theoretical-ideological structure, contemporary liberalism. David Hume died regretting that he had been unable to complete the great task of liberating Scotland from 'the Christian superstition'. Contemporary liberals, by contrast, are quite happy to tolerate Christianity, and indeed any and every other philosophy, belief and form of life (as long, of course, as their adherents are not sufficiently serious as to challenge the legitimacy of the liberal ordering of society). Today's liberal theorists profess strict agnosticism concerning the nature of the good life, and insist that disputes over such conceptions are futile, since rationally unresolvable, and that they must therefore be excluded from debates in political and legal theory. Liberal thinking then goes to work on the reality of the empirical wants, choices, tastes and inclinations of the individual: all such desires and preferences, insofar as they do not conflict with the interests of other individuals, are to be granted equal legitimacy. In liberalism, then, ethical rationality is conceived as procedural rather than substantive: that is to say, the scope of practical rational debate is restricted to the task of establishing principles of social organisation acceptable to all individuals irrespective of their conceptions of the good life.

The very brief sketch of the contemporary theoretical scene we have offered here is of course inadequate in many ways. We have not discussed, to mention one outstanding omission, those currents of contemporary thought, represented for example by the work of Foucault and Derrida, which derive from Nietzsche. Nietzschean perspectives are centrally relevant to the themes of this essay. They have been summarised forcefully and succinctly in these terms by Christopher Norris: 'Behind all the big guns of reason and morality is a fundamental will to persuade which craftily disguises its workings by imputing them always to the adversary camp. Truth is simply the honorific title assumed by an argument which has got the upper hand – and kept it – in this war of competing persuasions.'[20]

However, in the present context this merely perfunctory reference can be excused if we accept the view that liberalism is a variant – 'a genteel and half-hearted expression', to use Onara O'Neill's phrase[21] – of the Nietzschean position that no rational vindication of a substantive ethics is possible. So perhaps enough has been said to permit a proper focus on MacIntyrean theory, to which we now turn.

4

If the Enlightenment project has not succeeded in establishing the foundations of a substantive rational ethic, we are obliged to accept that many of our deepest and most cherished beliefs – about justice, about the way we should live, about the nature of the good society, and so on – do indeed lack a rational basis, and reflect not, as we would like to believe, the operations of intellectual inquiry and mature reflection, but acts of faith, pre-rational preferences, individual inclination, or (the Nietzschean view) the devious and self-deluding mechanisms of a will to power. So, at least, it appears; and so it has long and widely been assumed.

It is MacIntyre's central concern to challenge this assumption. He does so by proposing an alternative to the concept of practical reasoning which has informed modern moral philosophy since its origins in the Enlightenment. The crucial differences between this and the MacIntyrean model concern, first, the relationship between ethics and tradition, and secondly, the role of foundationalism in moral inquiry. Let us approach these separately.

Put very simply, MacIntyre contends that rationality about practical issues is achieved, not against, but within traditions; rationality, to use an alternative formulation, is always contextualised in the sense that it is embodied in a historical tradition. This is how he announces his project in *Whose Justice? Which Rationality?*

> What the Enlightenment made us for the most part blind to and what we now need to recover is . . . a conception of rational inquiry as embodied in a tradition, a conception according to which the standards of rational justification themselves emerge from and are part of a history in which they are vindicated by the way in which they transcend the limitations of and provide remedies for the defects of their predecessors within the history of that same tradition.[22]

Whereas from the perspective of Enlightenment-modernist thought practical rationality is a function of minds liberated from all particularism, from all concrete personal, social, historical and cultural circumstances, MacIntyre's view is that only through participation in historically contingent traditions of debate can we fruitfully conduct our ethical inquiries and achieve development in ethical understanding.

In a culture so long and deeply shaped by Enlightenment patterns of thought, this must inevitably seem a very strange notion indeed; and so one of MacIntyre's tasks is to explain the depth of resistance to any thesis about the rationality of traditions. Part of the explanation, of course, is to be found in the vigorous and successful propaganda of the Enlightenment crusade itself, where tradition was portrayed as nothing more than superstition, and the opponents of the cause depicted as – in Diderot's phrase – the 'enemies of philosophy'.[23] A second reason is that there have been very few attempts among modern thinkers to develop a theory of the rationality of traditions. Newman explored such a theory, but he did so in the kind of theological context which mainstream modern philosophy has tended to sideline or ignore. A third important factor is that many champions of tradition – Edmund Burke being an outstanding example in the British context – have themselves embraced the notion that tradition and reason are contradictory principles. The idea influentially propagated by the likes of Burke (or, in a more profound way, by de Maistre) is that conduct in accordance with tradition is unquestioning and unreflective.

MacIntyre is of course aware that there are traditions which do not embody practices of reflective inquiry. And there are no doubt those who take themselves to be adherents of (inquiry-constituted) traditions who appropriate these traditions in an unquestioning and unreflective way. But such appropriation, for MacIntyre, is radically defective. As he writes, glossing Aquinas' view: 'the practical life . . . is a life of inquiry by each of us into what our good is, and it is part of our present good so to enquire'.[24] On MacIntyre's interpretation, to participate in a tradition is to be involved in the continuation of a debate, to be a member of an interpretive community: 'A living tradition . . . is an historically extended, socially embodied argument.' If the kind of tradition extolled by Burke is 'always dying or dead', a living tradition involves as well as some measure of continuity (defined in terms of certain shared basic texts, assumptions and beliefs) also an ongoing internal debate or conflict or set of debates and conflicts, which will typically centre on rival accounts of the fundamental goals the tradition sets itself, competing interpretations of those goods 'pursuit of which gives to that tradition its particular point and purpose'.[25]

A tradition of reflective inquiry will be able to look back, then, on a history of theorising and debate, of discussion prompted, for instance, by the discovery of contradictions or omissions in the canonical texts and judgments which are shared by its adherents and which are partially definitive of the tradition; by the emergence of conflicting interpretations of key texts and concepts; by the discovery of inadequacies in the tradition's theoretical resources; by challenges posed by rival traditions; and so on. This will be a history, that is, of revision, reformulation, innovation and developing theoretical sophistication, in the course of which the tradition will have elaborated its own dialectical procedures and a set of standards for the evaluation of positions advanced within it.

MacIntyre's second major disagreement, which is implicit in this account of the nature of the rationality of traditions, is with the assumption that practical reasoning is foundationalist. Enlightenment thought involves the attempt to establish foundations or unassailable first principles for conduct, universally valid truths which are independent of social, historical and cultural circumstance and inherited traditions of moral inquiry. We have good reason to believe, as we have seen, that no such principles can in fact be established. The conclusion to be drawn from this, however, is not that ethical beliefs lack rationality, but rather that we need to acquire a better understanding of the nature of practical reasoning.

The model proposed by MacIntyre can perhaps be glossed in the following way: practical rationality is a matter of developing better, more adequate accounts of what we actually believe within the ethical world, the tradition or traditions, we already inhabit. We begin from who we are, where we are: in other words, MacIntyre's position involves a principle of particularism (or, in his own terms, a principle of 'contingent positivity').

Charles Taylor has recently advanced a very similar anti-foundationalist model of practical reasoning, and his concepts of 'reasoning in transitions', 'epistemic gain', and 'error reduction' are extremely useful in making such an account clearer.[26]

Practical reasoning is reasoning in transitions. Here we do not attempt to establish absolute truths, but proceed comparatively, by showing that some belief, description or position X is better than some other, Y, in the sense that, for example, X avoids a confusion or contradiction detectable in Y, or takes into account some significant relevant factor neglected in Y. Argument can bring us to abandon our commitment to Y and to accept X instead, because we perceive this move as error-reducing. The transition involves epistemic gain. We do not arrive at absolute and certain truths through this process, but we do arrive at 'the best account so far', both of ourselves and others. This reasoning process therefore provides the means, in the life of a person as in the history of a tradition, for a person or a tradition to develop in ethical understanding.

Rationality, in other terms, is always historically and socially contextualised. As MacIntyre summarises the position near the end of *Whose Justice? Which Rationality?*

> The conclusion to which the argument has so far led is not only that it is out of the debates, conflicts, and enquiry of socially embodied, historically contingent traditions that contentions regarding practical rationality and justice are advanced, modified, abandoned, or replaced, but that there is no other way to engage in the formulation, elaboration, rational justification, and criticism of accounts of practical rationality and justice except from within some one particular tradition in conversation, cooperation, and conflict with those who inhabit the same tradition. There is no standing ground, no place for enquiry, no way to engage in the practices of advancing, evaluating, accepting, and rejecting reasoned argument apart from that which is provided by some particular tradition or other.[27]

But we now have to consider what appear to be two quite devastating objections to MacIntyre's position. Firstly, if there is no neutral ground, no Archimedean point, outside of all tradition, from which to appraise the degree of rationality or irrationality of any particular ethical tradition; if, instead, standards of rationality are internal to traditions, must this not mean that each tradition is locked into a history of vacuous self-confirmation? Do not traditions become, on this account, immune to criticism, failure and defeat? And is it not precisely such vulnerability, and the possibility of such failure, that we ordinarily take to be a minimal but fundamental mark of rational belief-systems, as distinct from mere dogma and superstition? The suspicion arises, in other words, that MacIntyre's attempt to demonstrate the rationality of substantive ethics rests on an unconvincing redefinition of the nature of rationality. Secondly, the position seems to be inescapably relativistic. For if moral argument can only take place within traditions, there can be no way of showing how one tradition provides a better or truer ethical understanding than any other. And if this is the case, we do not after all have any response to the sceptical relativism inscribed in liberal theory and Nietzscheanism.

Moral philosophy, it is relevant to note at this point, is generally regarded and conducted as an isolable cultural activity, an academic specialism or sub-specialism. MacIntyre rejects this conventional demarcation: 'moral inquiry,' he writes, 'extends to historical, literary, anthropological, and sociological questions.' As we will now see, his work shows not only the strength which philosophical thinking derives from social and historical awareness and understanding, but also how these can be indispensable to the achievement of progress in theoretical understanding. This work is therefore also, incidentally, a powerful argument for more generalist modes of education in the humanities.

The reply to the first objection described above is essentially cultural-historical. If we look at the history of inquiry-constituted traditions, MacIntyre argues, we find that they do not function in a constantly self-confirming and self-perpetuating way. Periodically they undergo crises, crises which they may or may not be able to overcome. They may cease, in their own terms, to make progress, or be confronted by problems to which they are unable to generate solutions.

One example provided by MacIntyre of just such an epistemological crisis concerns the fate of the Scottish Common Sense tradition in philosophy in the American setting into which it had been imported, and where, in the nineteenth century, it was widely influential in the colleges and beyond. It was a central tenet of the school that the basic principles of morality are both universal and evident to all plain persons of sound mind. Variations in particular moral judgements are due to the different material, social and cultural conditions which prevail in different communities. Thus radical moral disagreement within a single culture, from this perspective, was impossible to explain. When, therefore, in the pre-bellum period American society was deeply divided over the issue of slavery, this ethical tradition foundered. It could neither plausibly account for the type of profound disagreement which then surfaced, nor offer persuasive reasons based on its own principles and procedures as to why one side was in the right or was mistaken. The present difficulties affecting the marxist-socialist tradition provide a further example of epistemological crisis. In this case, many different problems are involved: a central one, especially damaging to a political theory like marxism, which has always stressed the primacy of its practical orientation over its interpretive ambitions, is the apparent impossibility of constructing institutions which accomplish the objectives set by the tradition itself. This failure in turn triggers further questions, for example about the adequacy of socialism's philosophical anthropology; and so on.

Such difficulties may not prove insuperable. But if they do, many marxists, or former marxists, may acknowledge that these difficulties, inexplicable in terms of marxism's own shared premises and assumptions, can very well be explained in terms of the concepts and beliefs of some other, rival tradition, or traditions. And what such a situation demonstrates is not only that traditions of reflective inquiry are vulnerable, but also that one tradition can be vindicated as rationally superior to another. The reply to the charge of relativism, then, once more, appeals to historical and social evidence; and the evidence shows that the objection fails.

So far, then, the argument has been concerned with affirming the rationality of traditions and demonstrating the nature of that rationality, and with refuting the objections that the theory entails both relativism and the invulnerablity of traditions. We can now turn to more concretely personal issues, and to what could be described as the existential dimensions of MacIntyre's case for commitment to tradition-informed reflection.

MacIntyre resists two views about philosophy which have been endemic in recent Anglo-American culture. One, already mentioned above, is that theory is in some way isolated from and without influence on its social setting. The other, which complements the first, is that academic philosophers have no responsibility to attempt to supply answers to questions concerning the lives of the members of that wider society. As we might expect, then, he offers both a diagnosis of some of the broader cultural consequences of developments in Enlightenment-liberal thought, and a prescription, from his own anti-modernist Augustinian position, concerning how the predicament which correlates with these developments can be overcome.

The failure of the Enlightenment project, and the consequent agnosticism in liberal theory about conceptions of the good, are reflected in a wider social phenomenon: the dominance of sceptical pragmatism. Doubt concerning the possibility of giving rational validation to any general philosophy or theory of the self and society is prevalent. Allan Bloom has remarked that in contemporary American universities,

> There is one thing a professor can be absolutely certain of; almost every student entering the university believes, or says he believes, that truth is relative . . .That anyone should regard the proposition as not self-evident astonishes them, as though he were calling into question 2+2=4.[28]

This sceptical relativism is conjoined with a reluctance to look beyond the realm of everyday affairs and practicalities, and a tendency to regard those committed to wider schemes of belief as victims of self-delusion. We commonly encounter, in MacIntyre's own words,

> the kind of post-Enlightenment person who responds to the failure of the Enlightenment to provide neutral, impersonal tradition-independent standards of judgment by concluding that no set of beliefs proposed for acceptance is therefore justifiable. The everyday world is to be treated as one of pragmatic necessities. Every scheme of overall belief which extends beyond the realm of pragmatic necessity is equally unjustified . . . Such an individual therefore views the social and cultural order, the order of traditions, as a series of falsifying masquerades.[29]

Such persons may pride themselves on having avoided the self-deception they take to be the basis of allegiance to some wider philosophy or pattern of belief. But they are characteristically unaware of the personal impoverishment their own stance involves. They inhabit a world which lacks coherent stable belief. Here there is little conviction about anything: these are selves with many half-convictions and very few fixed beliefs. This absence of conviction can of course be paraded as tolerance – but liberal tolerance is very often indistinguishable from indifference.

It is hard to detect in such selves any web of belief: their opinions are typically compartmentalised. They draw on different scraps and fragments of various traditions, theories and moralities – Aristotelian, Christian, Kantian, utilitarian, Freudian – applying one principle here, another there, regardless of the incoherence involved, 'a fundamental incoherence which is too disturbing to be admitted to self-consciousness except on the rarest of occasions.'[30] Where a philosophy should be, there is instead a clutter of unrelated and unrelatable postures, a rag-bag of assorted superficialities.

Is there any escape from this condition of moral-intellectual impoverishment? MacIntyre distinguishes the predicament of two distinct types of liberal self. On the one hand there are those who, because of their background, are to some minimal extent already responsive to the idiom and ethos of a particular tradition, a tradition in whose debates they can recognise means for understanding themselves and their history. The rational approach for such persons is to test whether this tradition does indeed furnish the best available account of their lives by engaging in the tradition's own ongoing internal arguments and in the arguments it conducts with rival traditions of inquiry.

But there is a second kind of modern self, whose plight is more extreme. This is the person who is estranged from all types of tradition-constituted inquiry, and whose attitude to all of them is thoroughgoing scepticism. What is required here, MacIntyre says, is a profound transformation and re-ordering of the self, based on the self's realisation of its own impoverished state, a transformation of the kind described in Augustinian tradition as conversion.

> Such a transformation, understood from the standpoint of any rational tradition of inquiry, would require that those who adopt this stance [post-Enlightenment scepticism] become able to recognize themselves as imprisoned by a set of beliefs which lack justification in precisely the same way and to the same extent as do the positions which they reject but also to understand themselves as hitherto deprived of what tradition affords, as persons in part constituted as what they are up to this point by an absence, by what is from the standpoint of traditions an impoverishment. From a Humean point of view they have warped their sentiments in such a way as to render themselves incapable of reciprocity; from an Aristotelian they have refused to learn or have been unable to learn that one cannot think for oneself if one thinks entirely by oneself, that it is only by participation in rational practice-based community that one becomes rational; from an Augustinian point of view they have ignored even that standard internal to mind in whose light we are able to know our own deficiencies and consequently our inability to remedy them.[31]

For such a person, awareness of his or her own impoverishment and incoherence will be a pre-condition of entering into dialogue with traditions, with a view to discovering which tradition best provides the self-understanding he or she has so far lacked.

> The catalogues of virtues and vices, the norms of conformity and deviance, the accounts of educational success and failure, the narratives of possible types of human life which each tradition has elaborated in its own terms, all these invite the individual educated into self-knowledge of his or her own incoherence to acknowledge in which of these rival modes of moral understanding he or she finds him or herself most adequately explained and accounted for.[32]

5

In a recent article in the American journal *Applied Philosophy*, MacIntyre has been described as 'the greatest iconoclast of modern life – its philosophy, education, culture, society, economics'. Here we have touched on some aspects of MacIntyre's critique of modernity: his diagnosis of the impoverishment and incoherence of the liberal self, and his analysis of the resourcelessness of contemporary philosophy – its inability to provide a grounding for ethics other than what people happen to want.

His particular judgments – or restatement of judgments belonging to the tradition – are often destined to shock. The following are some examples, which demonstrate how his commitment to Augustinian and Thomistic conceptions of the good involves radical dissent to many of the values and practices of the liberal capitalist order. Exorbitant fees charged by lawyers and the like are a form of theft. Banking, insofar as it involves usury, is an ethically unacceptable practice. Business activity is only legitimate if undertaken for the sake of the public good. The right to property is limited by the necessities of other members of society.

But to see MacIntyre primarily as a critic is to distort. The iconoclasm is rooted in an enterprise which, as we have tried to sketch, is immensely constructive, and reconstructive. The principle of 'contingent positivity' and the idea of 'the best account so far' base an alternative to the conventional model of practical reasoning, as the search for universally valid foundations conducted by individuals abstracted from the particularities of their history, and allow us to understand and articulate, as against the different forms of scepticism and nihilism inscribed in modernist and postmodernist positions, the way in which substantive ethical beliefs can be a function of intellectual inquiry.

Furthermore, the project involves the recovery and reconstruction of certain specific, pre-Enlightenment traditions of ethical inquiry which in modern liberal societies have been marginalised or lost. The argument of *After Virtue* was that classical, and in particular Aristotelian ethical theory displays a richness and coherence which our current views lack, while the more recent writing draws attention to the resources of Augustinian and Thomist theory.

It is through a re-engagement with these and other pre-modern traditions of ethical, social and political thought, MacIntyre's work proposes, that we can now best confront the emptiness of liberalism and the exhaustion of modern sources of critique.

8

Radical Traditionalism
in Educational Theory

1

Education, it has been said, is the real battleground:[1] the site where the struggles between different conceptions of culture – or, as it would perhaps be more accurate to say about the contemporary scene, in Scotland and elsewhere, the arena where conflicts between cultural and anti-cultural forces, are most evident and most influential. Certainly such a view of the significance of educational issues can be read from Scottish cultural history. Due in part to the influence of the Reformers, and the keen sense of the value of learning they imparted, education has at least until fairly recently been regarded across Scottish society as a matter of great importance. And in any appropriate history of twentieth-century Scottish culture, a large space would have to be devoted to the work of educationalists. The contribution of A. S. Neill, one of the pioneers of 'progressive', 'child-centred' educational methods, is perhaps the most famous instance, and perhaps also, in the history of recent educational practice, the most influential.

It is a distinctive and remarkable feature of twentieth-century Scottish culture that many of the country's outstanding thinkers and scholars, not educationalists by profession, have taken a deep interest in educational issues. It is, indeed, for reasons a cultural history would have to explain, in the work of philosophers and classicists – John Burnet, John Anderson, A. D. Lindsay and George Davie, for instance – that we find some of the most complex and interesting statements in educational theory. Among these philosophers of education, Anderson is an outstanding figure. Reacting against utilitarian, vocationalist or what he named 'practicalist' approaches, on the one hand, and 'progressive' trends which emphasise personality development and the nurturing of psychological well-being, on the other,

Anderson formulated a humanist conception which stresses the intellectual nature of education and defines as its prime task the formation of critical intelligence. Such a type of education, he argued, could best be maintained and fostered through classicism, understood as both the study of Greek and Roman culture, and immersion in literary and philosophical tradition.[2] George Davie would be largely responsible, in the 1980s, for bringing Anderson's thought to wider public attention in Scotland. Earlier, in a work which has greatly shaped recent intellectual and cultural nationalism, *The Democratic Intellect* (1961), he had charted the gradual extinction in the Scottish universities of a type of higher education which encouraged breadth of study and, through compulsory philosophy, a concern with theory and ideas. The specialising and overly empiricist modes now dominant in the universities, he suggested, were out of tune with the local traditions in education which had based Scottish intellectual achievement in the past, and which had been defended in the nineteenth century by figures such as J. S. Blackie and James Lorimer, and in the early twentieth century by Anderson's mentor, the St Andrews classicist John Burnet.[3]

We cannot here offer the kind of comprehensive account of educational ideas in twentieth-century Scotland we hope one day will be written. Our present, much more modest objective is to outline a thesis which might inform such an account: namely, that the most valuable and distinctive Scottish contributions to the philosophy of education in the recent period are based on a position we will call, for reasons which should become clear, radical or critical traditionalism. To illustrate this argument, we would like to set alongside the work of Anderson and Davie the more recent reflections on education offered by Alasdair MacIntyre. These were first made public, appropriately, in a Scottish university, in the form of the 1988 Gifford lectures.

What, then, are the characteristics shared by different positions within radical traditionalism? We should distinguish at least four. First of all, such positions appeal to some pre-modern conception of education. Anderson looks to and reformulates the ideals of the tradition of classical humanism; Davie invokes the same tradition, but in its more specifically Scottish mode, what he terms 'the presbyterian inheritance'; and MacIntyre – in a way even more alien to current intellectual fashions – finds in thirteenth-century Thomist education a model for the reconstruction of the contemporary university. At the same time, in each case a tradition-informed conception of education involves a critical attitude towards modernist and contemporary educational theories.

Secondly, each of these three thinkers takes philosophy to be central to education. For Davie, the distinguishing characteristic of the old Scottish universities, and the key to their intellectual dynamism, was the 'commanding position' which philosophy occupied in the curriculum – what D. D. Raphael calls 'the Scottish university tradition of philosophy for all'.[4] For Anderson, the educated life is the philosophical life, the life of questioning and criticism which is made possible by acquaintance with the categories, distinctions and insights of philosophical tradition. In MacIntyre's work we are presented with the belief that education essentially involves systematic inquiry into the nature of the good and the means of its attainment.

Third, education is humanistic, in the sense that what is involved is a process of development in moral and intellectual understanding which radically determines the kind of person the student will become. A contrast here is with a conception of education as training, the mere learning of different skills, or with education as the appropriation of different sorts of factual knowledge or information. Thus, in Anderson, criticism and questioning are also self-criticism and self-questioning, and what is at stake in education is nothing less than the 'way of life' the person will adopt. And in MacIntyre, as we will see in more detail later, education involves a fundamental interrogation and transformation of practice, judgment and character. There is therefore also a contrast here with conceptions according to which the humanities are nothing more than sites for scholarly investigation into history, art, literature and other specialisms.

Finally – disclosing a conviction about the significance of the educated life – these thinkers oppose the splitting off of education and educational centres and of philosophy from their broader social setting and from public discussion. The critical role of education can only properly be fulfilled through engagement with the wider community. Part of the meaning of Davie's famous ideal of 'democratic intellectualism' is the need for dialogue between learned and unlearned: one example he gives of this ideal being put into practice is the contribution made by the philosopher Norman Kemp Smith to political discussion in the Scotland of the 1920s.[5] Anderson, too, believed in and practised active intervention in public debate. For MacIntyre, the frequent failure of academic philosophy to connect with general concerns, and the exclusion from philosophical discussion of a wider audience, represent a major cultural deformation. The philosopher, he writes, can be 'an active participant in the forums of public debate . . . appealing to standards shared by or at least accessible to a generally educated public'. But in contemporary liberal societies, 'professionalized academic philosophy makes the rational discussion of questions of fundamental import the prerogative of an academic elite with certified technical skills, using a vocabulary and writing in genres which are unavailable to those outside that elite . . .' As a result, in the forums of popular life rhetorical effectiveness in persuasion and manipulation prevails against rational argument.[6]

MacIntyre's views, which form part of a more general onslaught on the presuppositions, beliefs and practices of contemporary liberalism, are highly controversial and provocative, and to many, no doubt, shocking; but at the same time there can be little doubt that they represent an outstanding intervention in current controversies, and offer a coherent response to what is rightly perceived as a deep crisis in education.

2

If, in current debates about education, there is little dispute regarding the importance of the sciences, there is very little agreement on questions which concern the value and role of the humanities. And over the last decade or so, in particular within higher education, the humanities have been subjected to criticism and attack in a way which is perhaps unprecedented in the present century. In many places the traditionally central subjects of the liberal university are being gradually marginalised, and a new type of institution is emerging, where resources and student and staff numbers are concentrated in the practically-oriented disciplines – an institution which is more of a training school than a university in any traditional sense.

In the UK, the era which commenced with the Conservative assumption of power in 1979 has been characterised by a particularly virulent and overt practicalist approach to education, involving the reduction in size, or even the closure of departments of subjects whose benefits are not readily measurable in terms recognised by or recognisable to accountants. For instance, entire departments of philosophy have been closed, to save a shilling. (It is difficult, of course, in the Scottish context, not to indulge a certain *Schadenfreude* over the fate of the universities when we bear in mind how hostile many academics were in the 1970s both to the idea of Scottish autonomy and to any proposal that control of the universities be removed from London were a Scottish Assembly established – a singular case of sheep bolting for the abattoir.)

However, if the naked nature of this philistinism was something of a novelty, these attacks are not in themselves a matter which ought to surprise us. Philistinism is always with us, and the modern liberal state has no interest in the furtherance of education (as distinct from, say, training, or social control) except to the extent that education is indispensable to the achievement of its own different and distinctive objectives, which require the fostering of at least some forms of intellectual ingenuity and dynamism. What ought to have been surprising, though it has received all too little attention, was the fact that the half-literate statements and policies penned by civil servants and politicians were never effectively answered by those whose duty it is to defend the culture of the university: chancellors, vice-chancellors, principals, professors and other academic dignitaries. Confronted with an ideology based on such sophisticated notions as value for money and the needs of *homo economicus*, the seats of learning were unable to articulate any clear and coherent statement in defence of culture around which resistance within the universities and among wider sections of the population could have been organised. What is truly remarkable is that the thugs were battering down an unlocked door.

All the universities could offer by way of reply was – in MacIntyre's harshly-worded judgment – a series of 'stuttering ineptitudes'.[7] Worse, some dignitaries would soon themselves be echoing the discourse, and discharging the functions of the money-savers and fund-raisers. Academics of humbler station, thus bereft of leadership, and abandoned to their fate, were reduced to the unseemly strategies of *sauve qui peut*. There was left only the small consolation of revenge exacted by the refusal to grant the traditional honorary titles to those who wield political power – a pitiful, schoolboyish gesture which betrayed that the academics had no conception of the extent to which the universities' own incoherence had drained such titles of any value they might once have possessed.

Charity would dictate that a veil be drawn over these and related grotesque proceedings, were not matters of fundamental import involved, and did they not help us to understand the nature of the deeper crisis which afflicts the humanities. As the sheer scale of the defeat suggests, the failure of the universities' spokesmen and spokeswomen to respond effectively to the neo-practicalist attacks cannot be attributed to any merely personal deficiencies. It is highly unlikely that, given the current condition of the humanities in the universities, any account of what they represent and of why they should matter would be able to secure more than local and minoritarian agreement. Why?

In natural science there is a large and fundamental area of agreement about what constitutes both acceptable investigative method and progress in knowledge. The situation in the humanities is very different. Here there is agreement on relatively narrow and detailed matters within each discipline (for example, on what constitutes valid historical evidence and on what kind of technical scholarly skills candidates for particular academic posts should possess). But this consensus co-exists with a wide area of doctrinal disagreement and conflict both within and across subjects. Academic posts are occupied by deconstructionists, socialists, Christians, feminists, anti-theoretical empiricists, Freudians, behaviourists, nationalists, liberals, marxists, Moslems and no doubt adherents of many other intellectual and ideological movements. (The same divergences in ideological persuasion are also to be found, of course, among the student body.) Moreover, when conflicts over these wider commitments are brought into the open, they seem not to be susceptible of rational resolution. They tend, instead, to give rise only to inconclusive and interminable forms of disagreement and polemic, debate which is not genuine in that it does not yield evidence of the superiority of any of the competing views. Such apparently ineradicable forms of profound doctrinal divergence would make it very difficult to construct a defence of the humanities capable of securing wide assent even within the academies.

This brings us to another fundamental issue: the serious contradiction at the heart of the conduct of the humanities in the university. Despite the deep and apparently unresolvable doctrinal and theoretical conflicts, both within and across disciplines, we continue to speak and act as if the university, or the humanities, or the 'academic community' were homogeneous entities; and indeed such central university institutions as the lecture would only make proper sense if it were indeed counter-factually the case that lecturers and their audiences shared to a great extent the same universe of discourse and belief. 'We still behave for the most part as if the university did still constitute a single, tolerably unified intellectual community', MacIntyre writes.[8] And this situation, he continues, testifies to the power of 'encyclopedism', a type of discourse whose history, MacIntyre suggests, has an especially close connection with nineteenth-century Scottish culture. For the great modern expression of encyclopedism is of course a Scottish, or more precisely an Edinburgh product, the *Encyclopedia Britannica*. The Ninth Edition, publication of which began in 1875 and ended in 1889, was the encyclopedia's apogee, the canonical formulation of notions about the nature of knowledge and of rationality which have centrally shaped cultural history.

3

The view of Scottish intellectual history which historians tend to convey to general readers is both highly implausible and highly influential. The account runs something like this: before the eighteenth century, there was little intellectual production of any note; in the eighteenth century there was a sudden, brilliant flowering of thought – the Scottish Enlightenment; thereafter, the country reverted to a condition resembling its pre-Enlightenment intellectual drabness ('theological squabbles', etc), so that post-eighteenth-century Scottish thought merits little investigation or discussion. One historian – William Ferguson – goes so far as to assert that the nineteenth century witnessed 'a virtual collapse of Scottish culture'.[9] Echoing such analyses, the Marxist scholar Tom Nairn talks of 'the relatively sudden disintegration of a great national culture'.[10]

As far as the pre-Enlightenment period is concerned, this oft-told tale has been thoroughly discredited by such work as Alexander Broadie's on sixteenth-century Scottish philosophers like John Mair, a thinker of European renown in his day who taught Calvin and Loyola at the University of Paris.[11] Now, it is to be hoped, MacIntyre's focus on nineteenth-century thought will stimulate reconsideration of the post-Enlightenment period and the kind of more extensive studies we still lack. For MacIntyre, the Ninth Edition reflects the remarkable intellectual energy and creativity of later-nineteenth-century Scotland – reflects, indeed, what MacIntyre terms a second Scottish Enlightenment.

The contributors to the Ninth Edition included, among other notable figures, James Clerk Maxwell, J. G. Frazer, and William Robertson Smith, who was also for a time editor of the encyclopedia. Maxwell was undoubtedly the main star of the second Scottish Enlightenment. In the current, fifteenth edition of the *Britannica*, he is said to be 'regarded by most modern physicists as the scientist of the nineteenth-century who had the greatest influence on twentieth-century physics; he is ranked with Sir Isaac Newton and Albert Einstein for the fundamental nature of his contributions'.[12] Maxwell's work, concerned principally with electromagnetism, and carried out in the course of a comparatively short life, prepared the way for the special theory of relativity and quantum physics; Maxwell also laid the groundwork of such disciplines as cybernetics and information theory.

James George Frazer was one of a group of Scottish thinkers – among them Robertson Smith, Andrew Lang and John Ferguson McLennan – who played a prominent role in the development of anthropology, and its establishment as a form of intellectual inquiry[13] – Frazer was the first scholar in anthropology to become a fellow of the Royal Society (in 1920). Frazer's intellectual training was in classics, and from the point of view of contemporary scholarship his finest work, perhaps, is his early, massive commentary on Pausanius, and the edition of Ovid's *Fasti* he produced towards the end of his life. Accustomed, throughout most of his adult life, to devoting some thirteen hours a day, fifty weeks a year, to scholarly labour, he was one of the very few classical students in the Britain of his day who could take on such titans of German classical scholarship as Doerpfeld and Wilamowitz.

His anthropological writing is no longer held in high esteem by professionals, for a number of reasons. It is informed by little sociological sense, it deals with examples of customs wrenched from their cultural settings, and its concern to place behaviour in some grand evolutionary scheme is no longer in intellectual fashion. However, in terms of the impact of his work on the modes of thought of his own age, Frazer the anthropologist must be considered a thinker of the first importance.

The work for which he was and is most famous, *The Golden Bough*, the third edition of which spanned twelve volumes, is a monument not only of Scottish but European scholarship. It made Frazer the world's most famous anthropologist and it is one of the key texts in the formation of recent European consciousness, diffusing among a wide readership the notion of human intellectual history as a process of development from magic through religion to science and rationality. Frazer's readership included not only fellow-anthropologists, poets and novelists, and thinkers in other fields (Freud's *Totem and Taboo* was inspired by *Totemism and Exogamy*), but also a non-specialist reading public whom Frazer was always at pains to accommodate without compromising the 'scientific' nature of his writings. These included articles in the Ninth Edition, contributed at the instigation of his friend and the then editor, Robertson Smith, the *Britannica* too being a project (in the tradition of democratic intellectualism) which strove to make scholarly and scientific findings available and comprehensible to the layperson.

On the astonishing reception and impact of *The Golden Bough* itself, we would like to quote Frazer's most recent biographer.

> As the volumes appeared, and its immense scope began generally to be appreciated, it was universally acclaimed despite its inadequacies as one of the intellectual monuments of the age. It was often said that *The Golden Bough* as a whole had fundamentally changed the way that educated people understood both human history and contemporary behaviour and institutions. Because the volumes of the third edition received such extensive critical attention, Frazer's ideas – or at least their general drift, along with a few central images and metaphors – quickly passed into intellectual currency in the English-speaking world in the 1920s. In addition, many people who could not afford the ten-shillings-per-volume price sought the work out in the public libraries. He had something for everyone: educated persons enjoyed his prose style and were impressed and moved by the immense intellectual sweep of the work, which seemed to comprehend and clarify so much . . . ; the new and not-

so-well-educated middle class were told by the newspapers that *The Golden Bough* ... was one of those books that any thoughtful person had to know about; the self-educated among the working class and aspiring intellectuals and radicals read *The Golden Bough* for its explanation of how society and religion had begun in primitive confusion and misunderstanding.[14]

T. S. Eliot referred to Frazer as 'unquestionably the greatest master', and Frazer's formative influence on modernist literary culture deserves special mention. Robert Crawford has recently shown how Frazer's work, both in form and content, prepares the way for Eliot, Pound, Borges and Alasdair Gray. Frazer's 'cultural assemblages, his juxtapositions of civilised and savage, and his curious combination of conscious literary style and factual encyclopedic scope' anticipate the modern movement; in turn – Crawford also convincingly argues – these features of his work partly derive from the youthful Frazer's immersion in the novels of Walter Scott.[15]

Frazer, like his friend and fellow-member of the Cambridge 'Scottish contingent', Robertson Smith, came from a Free Church family. Unlike Frazer, however, Robertson Smith remained a Calvinist throughout his life, despite the notoriety he came to enjoy among more conservative factions of Scottish presbyterianism. Frazer's attitude to religion was ambivalent. His work was widely read as supporting the rationalist cause, and as evincing hostility to religion in general and Christianity in particular as forms of superstition and irrationality. This is shown by the fact that the Rationalist Press was keen to bring out *The Golden Bough* under its aegis. Frazer, however, had no sympathy for the devotees of easy certainties, and gave the proposal short shrift: he could not identify with what he called 'arid rationalism'. His real position, as a recent commentator observes, was scepticism, but a scepticism which was sceptical also of itself. If he enjoyed indulging his ironic sense of humour at the expense of clerics, in the end his perspective was alien to rationalism, and involved recognition, it has been suggested, that 'religion is part of the mind; the world cannot be understood without it'.[16]

It is fair to say that William Robertson Smith is now a largely forgotten figure. He is likely to be known in today's Scottish universities only to students of nineteenth-century Scottish history, as the defendant in the last major heresy trial to be conducted in Britain. This was occasioned by some of his articles in the Ninth Edition of the *Britannica*. These drew upon the new Continental criticism, which approached the Bible as a socially-, historically- and culturally-bound text, and thus challenged orthodox conceptions that it constituted a pure revelation of divine truth which could and should be read in a straightforwardly literal fashion. The storm raised by these ideas was such that Smith was removed from his Aberdeen Free Church college chair of Hebrew; though ultimately vindicated in the trial itself, Smith moved to Cambridge, and became Professor of Arabic there. (It is interesting to note that one of Smith's allies in the story, Professor T. M. Lindsay, was the father of the classicist and educationalist A. D. Lindsay). The trial was an epic affair which dragged on over five years. From the standpoint of liberal and 'progressive' historians, the prosecution of Smith is a clear symptom of the comparative darkness and backwardness of the Scottish society and culture of the time. It is possible, however, to see the matter in a rather different light. An English church historian has written of the Smith trial:

> The proceedings at each stage were reported at length in the daily newspapers, and excited immense interest all over Scotland. The debates were followed and reproduced in railway carriages, workshops, and country smithies. Not even Mr Gladstone's Midlothian campaign, which greatly moved the Scottish people at this time, was able to overshadow their absorption in the theological controversy that was raging.[17]

Such public and press interest indicate a level of intellectual seriousness across Scottish society which is surely admirable and remarkable; today's cultural scene – to judge, for instance, by the press and other media – seems by comparison trivial and unsophisticated. But, to return to Smith himself, if we restrict our attention solely to his role in the trial of 1876–81, we cannot begin to understand his real significance in cultural history. Something of Smith's intellectual stature is suggested by a comment of Frazer's. Early in their friendship (which was largely responsible for Frazer's becoming an anthropologist), Frazer attempted on one occasion to argue against what Smith was saying, but 'was immediately beaten down, in the kindest and gentlest way, by his learning . . .' Frazer continues: 'I never afterwards, so far as I can remember, attempted to dispute the mastership which he thenceforward exercised over me by his extraordinary union of genius and learning.'[18]

Smith's astonishing erudition and intellectual gifts were applied in different fields; in biblical scholarship and theology where, partly through the many articles he wrote for the Ninth Edition, he exerted enormous influence; and in sociology and anthropology, in particular the sociology of religion. Here Durkheim was an admirer, and credited Smith with establishing the principle of religion as a social phenomenon, functioning for the preservation and welfare of the social group.[19] And as a student of Semitic culture, so it has recently been argued, from a highly critical perspective, Smith's role in the construction of recent Western culture is of great importance. For the Palestinian critic Edward Said, Robertson Smith is the main architect of that complex of Western attitudes to the Middle East which Said terms 'Orientalism'. '. . . Smith, I think, was a crucial link in the intellectual chain connecting the White-Man-as-expert to the modern Orient. None of the encapsulated wisdom delivered as Oriental expertise by Lawrence, Hogarth, Bell, and the others would have been possible without Smith.'[20]

But it is now time, after this brief excursion through some of the cultural background, to return to our main theme, and ask: what does MacIntyre mean by encyclopedism?

4

In the confidence shared by Robertson Smith and his fellow contributors to the Ninth Edition that they represented a more advanced stage of human evolution than contemporary Moslems, Polynesian Islanders and other backward or 'savage' (pre-literate) groups – an attitude now generally castigated as racist, Eurocentric and complicitous with imperialist designs – we have the most obvious feature of their thought which differentiates their cultural world from ours. It is instructive, however, to follow MacIntyre in probing a little deeper, beyond these cliched charges, and examine the epistemological presuppositions which based the outlook of the encyclopedia.

Its contributors and readers shared a view, first of all, that moral inquiry or the study of how we ought to conduct our personal and social affairs is coordinate with the study of the natural world. In making the bequest which provides for the lectures still given in his name, Adam Gifford, a prominent figure in the Edinburgh cultural scene of the time, wrote that 'I wish the lecturers to treat their subject as a strictly natural science . . . wish it to be considered just as astronomy or chemistry is'. The subject was natural theology, 'in the widest sense of that term, in other words the knowledge of God' and 'of the foundation of ethics'.[21] Related to this conception of the scientificity of moral inquiry was a second presupposition of encyclopedism: that the history of ethics, like the history of any other branch of inquiry, is a history of continual progress in knowledge. Today, such notions appear very strange: far from regarding ethics as a science, we tend to question to what extent, if any, substantive moral beliefs can be rational at all; and no-one looks to university philosophy departments to supply new discoveries in practical philosophy in the way we look, say, to physicists and biologists to contribute ever more sophisticated accounts of the natural world. This situation marks, not only an area of difference between our cultural world and that of Gifford and the Ninth Edition, but also the extent to which the encyclopedist project has failed.

This failure, MacIntyre argues, is related to the falsity of a further central principle of encyclopedism: the idea that rationality is universal, in the sense that all rational persons will understand the world in the same way. As MacIntyre points out, the universalism of the Scottish encyclopedists did not derive from an empiricism *à l'anglais*: they had learned too much from Kant, and also Reid, Stewart and Hamilton for that. But although they did not believe in the possibility of pure observation, they held that the categories through which the mind perceives the world are the same for all rational minds – that is to say, minds not clouded by commitment to some outmoded or irrational scheme of belief. Thus the philosopher Andrew Seth could say of the Scholastics, in Volume 17 of the Ninth Edition, that 'They appear to contemplate the universe of nature and men not at first sight with their own eyes but in the glass of Aristotelian formulae'.

The principle of the unity of rationality was crucial in legitimating the move from the pre-liberal to the liberal university, that is to say in the abolition of moral and theological tests. The defining (and, so it has turned out, false) thesis of the liberal university is that 'human rationality is such and the methods and procedures which it has devised and in which it is embodied are such that, if freed from external constraints and most notably from the constraints imposed by religious and moral tests, it will produce not only progress in inquiry but also agreement among all rational persons as to what the rationally justified conclusions of such inquiry are'.[22]

Basic to MacIntyre's position is the view that today – in the light of arguments offered by such diverse thinkers as Bachelard, Wittgenstein, Kuhn and Quine, and given the manifest absence of ideological consensus in liberal societies, both within the university and beyond – the thesis of the unity and universality of rationality is no longer theoretically sustainable. Aspects of reality can indeed be described in simple ways which may be universal. But conceptualisation which serves the interests of theoretical inquiry always involves prior commitment to some categorial system which is incompatible or incommensurable with some other rival scheme or schemes. To illustrate this idea, let us consider the study of human conduct. Within the academic subject of psychology we find such rival, and incommensurable approaches as behaviourism and Freudianism. On a broader front, a Freudian interpretation of conduct is in conflict with an Augustinian reading: where a Freudian may see in some feeling or action the operations of the superego, for instance, an Augustinian may see evidence of *synderesis*, the fundamental grasp of natural law possessed by all human beings which can never be wholly lost. There is no way of adjudicating between such schemes by appeal to the observation of some basic 'facts', for the descriptions relevant to the inquiry will already presuppose one or another of the theories in dispute. It will also be the case, clearly, that behaviourists, Freudians and Augustinians have no way of reaching agreement on what constitutes the achievement of progress in the study of human conduct. Such examples of incompatible paradigms or discourses could be multiplied by considering the humanities in general.

Nevertheless, it is very rarely that the existence of such profound kinds of disagreement within the university is openly acknowledged by academics. Indeed, the rhetoric of academic 'neutrality' and 'impartiality' is still widely in use, and testifies to the enduring strength of the encyclopedist worldview. This rhetoric has a clear ideological value, especially where what is involved is inquiry which engages with political conflict beyond the university – the writing of Scottish history is an example. But 'the notion of a single neutral nonpartisan history is one more illusion engendered by the academic standpoint of the encyclopedist.'[23] When historians or other academics claim to speak from a position of neutrality, we have to see such claims – here at least MacIntyre goes along with Nietzschean genealogism – not only as illusions, but as masks for a will-to-power, the disguised furtherance of some particular interest or set of interests.

One of MacIntyre's central and most radical educational proposals is based on the conviction that the inevitably partisan nature of inquiry must be taken seriously – that we fully recognise the fact that 'the neutrality of the academic is . . . a fiction of the encyclopedist'. The proposal is then that institutions of inquiry in the humanities be re-ordered and differentiated according to the theoretical and doctrinal allegiances of those who research, teach and study within them. The idea is a bold, and no doubt to some a preposterous one. But MacIntyre, in its defence, asks us to consider how inquiry in the natural sciences proceeds. Departments of natural science exclude astrologers, palm-readers, believers in a flat earth, and indeed also laypersons uninitiated in the mathematical techniques and theoretical knowledge required for the undertaking of scientific research: everyone, that is to say, not committed to a certain body of doctrine and versed in certain procedures of inquiry. So also, argues MacIntyre, a Catholic university should exclude non-Catholics, a marxist university should exclude liberals, and so on. Hume, on MacIntyre's view, was rightly passed over for the university chair at the presbyterian University of Edinburgh in favour of James Cleghorn.

The point of the contrast with the natural sciences is, of course, that these normally display constant progress in inquiry. In the humanities, the variety of doctrinal allegiances within the universities is a massive obstacle to the achievement of theoretical progress. Consider, by way of example, the condition of contemporary academic philosophy. Here the characteristic activity is the application of logical skills to 'problems' treated in piecemeal fashion, and detached from their place in overall systems of belief. (It is no doubt significant that the philosophical primer long in use in British universities should be entitled 'The Problems of Philosophy'.[24]) Such 'problems' ('the mind-body problem', 'the free-will – determinism problem', etc) typically prove resistant to resolution, in the sense that all solutions proposed prove highly contestable. Thus, ever more logically-sophisticated solutions are countered by ever more sophisticated objections and ever more sophisticated statements of rival solutions.

That this should be so is related to the diversity of ideological commitments. Since philosophers have wider commitments (as Catholics, liberals, positivists, marxists, etc), disagreement over the acceptability of solutions is bound to be ineradicable. For instance, a philosopher with a materialist kind of worldview will naturally be disposed to accept and argue for certain types of solutions to philosophical 'problems' which will be unacceptable to, say, a philosopher influenced by Christian notions about human life. Discussion in such circumstances, inevitably, is interminable and inconclusive. As against current academic philosophy – where inquiry is concerned with problems abstracted both from systematic belief and the realm of human practice, where disagreement is interminable, and no general directedness can be identified – MacIntyre wishes to re-establish the Thomistic conception and practice of philosophical inquiry as 'long-term cooperative activity in the construction of a systematic overall understanding of theory and practice'.[25] An institution dedicated to such a conception of philosophy would have as its task the continuation of a debate or tradition which attempts to provide ever more adequate answers to those questions recognition of the primacy of which in part constitutes both membership of the tradition and fitness to take part in the debate, questions such as:

> What is the *telos* of human beings? What is right action
> directed towards the *telos*? What are the virtues which issue
> in right action? What are the laws which order human
> relationships so that men and women may possess those
> virtues?[26]

But for that task to be carried forward, for the reach of the tradition to be extended, MacIntyre insists, there can be no place in such an institution for liberals, sceptics, Moslems, calvinists or others whose fundamental commitment is not to the Thomist tradition. They require their own institutions. This does not mean, however, that MacIntyre is proposing a series of universities which work in strict isolation from each other. The postliberal university would have two functions, one internal and one public. One task, as we have seen, would be the advancement of inquiry from one particular point of view (liberal, Thomistic, calvinist, marxist, feminist or whatever). But at the same time, each university would be required to take part in periodic public debate or disputation with other universities.

> The second task would be to enter into controversy with other rival standpoints, doing so both in order to exhibit what is mistaken in that rival standpoint in the light of the understanding afforded by one's own point of view and in order to test and retest the central theses advanced from one's own point of view against the strongest possible objections to them to be derived from one's opponents.[27]

5

The ghost of encyclopedism which haunts the contemporary university appears in different guises; and in the development of his conception of an alternative kind of university, MacIntyre takes issue with a number of encyclopedist theses which are not only still inscribed in current practices, but form part of taken-for-granted academic truth. These concern, chiefly, the relationship between inquiry and the kind of person who engages in inquiry, and our relationship to the past, or to tradition.

One is the belief that the kind of person the student or teacher is is irrelevant to that person's capacity to achieve right reasoning and to engage in the pursuit of knowledge. As against this notion, MacIntyre holds – following a conception first elaborated by Plato and Aristotle – that the moral and intellectual virtues are inseparable, and therefore that the possession of certain moral virtues is a necessary condition for entry into the philosophical community. On such a view – again alien to the assumptions of liberal modernity – intellectual error is founded in moral defect. It follows, therefore, that 'the enquirer has to learn how to make him or herself into a particular kind of person if he or she is to move towards a knowledge of the truth about his or her good and about the human good'.[28] What this position implies is a conception of philosophy as a virtue-guided *techne,* or *ars,* or craft, a conception of philosophy which informed inquiry from Plato's time to that of Aquinas. It corresponds to a conception of the beginner as an apprentice; and here we come to the strong sense of 'humanistic' which has to be applied to MacIntyre's theory of education. What the apprentice must first do, according to the Augustinian conception of moral inquiry, is achieve a kind of re-ordering of the self through the acquisition of the virtue of humility.

> The intellect and the desires do not naturally move towards that good which is at once the foundation for knowledge and that from which lesser goods flow. The will which directs them is initially perverse ... hence the acquisition of that virtue which the will requires to be ... guided, humility, is the necessary first step in education or in self-education.[29]

Without this transformation of the will, the intelligence cannot be rightly directed. 'Will is more fundamental than intelligence, and thinking undirected by a will informed by humility will always be apt to go astray.'[30] Implied by such a view is another notion which is unacceptable in the culture of encyclopedism and the liberal university. Here it is assumed that all rational persons are able and fit to read any book whatsoever. But on the Augustinian view, this is not the case. We must – in moral and theological terms – become a certain kind of person before we are able to read aright.

The humility we must initially as apprentices acquire involves the acceptance of authority: the authority of the teacher, the master of the craft of philosophical inquiry: ' ... we shall have to learn from that teacher and initially accept on the basis of his or her authority within the community of a craft precisely what intellectual and moral habits it is which we must cultivate and acquire if we are to become effective self-moved participants in such inquiry.'[31]

To many readers, this kind of remark will be offensive – an expression of an authoritarian conception of education and learning, which conflicts head-on with such central assumptions of the modernist worldview as that education should foster independence or autonomy and that rationality is a matter of being able to think for oneself. In response, MacIntyre could appeal, once more, to the situation in that most prestigious and indubitably successful contemporary form of inquiry, natural science. For, contrary to romantic popular conceptions of scientists as lonely geniuses and bold sceptics, science, as Thomas Kuhn has emphasised, proceeds through a training which (to quote one commentator) 'is unusually authoritarian and dogmatic, precisely in order to produce the highest possible degree of commitment to paradigms and the least possible inclination to think and act outside them'.[32] Scientific pedagogy does not cultivate scepticism, open-mindedness, critical thinking, or individual autonomy, as these are generally understood; it inculcates, instead, commitment to the values, beliefs and traditions of inquiry of a community.

For the encyclopedists, as for their predecessors of the eighteenth-century Enlightenment and for their present-day heirs, the order of traditional belief represents an intellectual moment which modern man has overcome. The history of human inquiry on this conception, as we noted in a previous section, is a story of progress from superstition to ever higher and purer forms of rational belief. Unencumbered by the conceptions, or misconceptions fostered by tradition, the inhabitants of modernity have for the first time in human history achieved rational knowledge. The past, therefore, is something on which we pass judgment: 'tradition presents itself to us to be sifted and evaluated by our standards.' As against such a view, MacIntyre asserts the Augustinian position 'that we have to learn from authoritative tradition how to sift and evaluate ourselves'.[33] The task, in other words, is not to put to the question traditions of intellectual inquiry, but first of all to allow such traditions to put us to the question.

It is important at this point to distinguish MacIntyre's position here from the – in some ways rather similar – kind of educational theory and proposals recently advanced by Alan Bloom and others.[34] The latter involve the view that studies in the humanities ought to be restructured in such a way that what is central is immersion in literary and philosophical traditions, becoming acquainted with what they have to say about fundamental personal and political issues (the kind of view, in fact, it is possible to read from the work of Anderson and Davie also). If MacIntyre is willing to describe such a position as 'the most plausible remedy [for the crisis in the humanities] so far advanced by anyone speaking from a position of authority',[35] it is still, for him, too much in thrall to encyclopedistic assumptions. For it posits that there is some non-partisan standing-ground from which texts can be selected, interpreted, debated and evaluated. In reality, no such neutral ground exists. 'There is not and never was available any single neutral mode of such appropriation and it was indeed one of the illusions of the encyclopedist's standpoint to believe that there was . . .'[36] How the past is appropriated inevitably depends on the particular, contestable and contested theoretical site the reader him- or herself occupies.

6

'What good is a university?' 'What are universities for?' When faced with these and related questions, the universities, as we have recently learned, find it very difficult to respond. For MacIntyre, this inability reflects the fundamental disorder at the heart of the liberal university: the exclusion of substantive moral philosophical inquiry – inquiry concerned, precisely, to establish rational responses to questions of the form 'What good is an x?' or 'What are ys for?'

Such exclusion is inevitable in an institution where limitless ideological divergence prevails. Historically, toleration of such disagreement was legitimated by the belief that conflict and dissensus would gradually be overcome as rational inquiry proceeded. But, contrary to the expectations of the encyclopedists, this has not occurred, and the history of the liberal university, again contrary to their expectations, has thus not been one of progress in ethical inquiry. The history of the humanities has involved, instead, the gradual abandonment of what MacIntyre sees as the university's true vocation – 'the development of systematic moral and theological or antitheological inquiry'.[37] To the exclusion of substantive moral inquiry there then correspond the triviality and vacuity of much contemporary academic endeavour.

But – even readers in sympathy with MacIntyre's general position will want to say – the proposal to make systematic philosophical inquiry once again central in university education, like the proposal that universities be restructured in such a way as to regulate and make coherent doctrinal and ideological conflict, is surely hopelessly impractical, or utopian. And if such views have received some support, and not only among those who would share the conception of moral inquiry as a virtue-guided craft, or wish to be members of a MacIntyrean, tradition-informed university,[38] we can hardly expect them to be regarded with great seriousness among today's politicians and educational administrators, or among educational experts in universities and colleges. But, quite possibly, this is less an argument against MacIntyre and the kind of educational tradition he has restated than an indication of the moribund condition of conventional educational thinking, and of how far such thinking is from allowing us even to be able to locate where the crucial educational issues lie.

9

Therapism, Sociology and Tradition-Informed Inquiry

In Colin Kirkwood's *Vulgar Eloquence* and David McCrone's *Understanding Scotland* we have two wide-ranging recent books about Scotland which discuss a variety of political, historical and cultural questions. They also, in representing two different types of intellectual position, which give rise to very different general diagnoses, raise the further issue of how Scotland's cultural predicament is best to be approached. A dominant discourse in Kirkwood's collection of essays is therapism, and the analysis offered is a rather sombre one which underlines the need for processes of liberation. McCrone's text, though also admirably generalist, expresses a sociological perspective, which, in this particular case, involves a relatively sanguine view of Scotland's cultural condition. In this essay, from a position distinct from those exemplified in *Vulgar Eloquence* and *Understanding Scotland*, we would like to focus on certain aspects of these analyses, and to describe some of the central problems and limitations in the discourses they embody.

1

The radicals of 1968 sought a totalising revolution which would transform both the public and the private realms of human existence. Liberation, they believed, required the overthrow of the existing political, social and economic orders, and at the same time profound changes in the structures of personal life. Forms of direct democracy should replace the regime of managers, bureaucrats and career-politicians, and, in more personal spheres, the pleasure principle was to displace those moral and religious codes which had hitherto repressed human desire, thwarted self-expression and impeded the achievement of happiness and fulfilment. This process would at the same time end dependence on the *ersatz* delights mongered by the culture industries. The bourgeoisie, the superego and television would perish together, and real human history finally begin.

These aspirations now seem to belong to a very distant past, such have been the rate and depth of political and intellectual change in the last two decades. Marxism, in all of its traditional garb at any rate, has entered a period of accelerated and irreversible decline, both as a political and intellectual force; socialism is now presentable only as a more generous form of social democracy; politicised Freudianism has died; critical concepts such as 'liberation', central to the projects of 1968, have lost purchase on political discourse, at least in prosperous parts of the world; English radicals now quote Tom Paine instead of Poulantzas, and instead of demanding the instauration of the millennium are now content with demanding the abolition of the monarchy. Only specialists and nostalgics now study Sartre and Guevara, Fanon and Marcuse, and many of us who came to what we naively took to be intellectual maturity while reading them now wonder at how innocent, ignorant and uncritical we then were.

The idealistic spirit which informed the radicalism of 1968, moreover, has no place in what Gilles Lipovetsky has aptly termed our present *ère du vide*.[1] Such an ethos is alien to the various forms of nihilism which now prevail in intellectual discussion – the neo-conservatism which draws on garbled cribs of Adam Smith, for instance, or the different fashions in 'postmodernist' thought which titillate those who pride themselves on being in the intellectual avantgarde.

Is the radicalism of 1968, then, now of no more than historical interest? Or does it still have something to teach us? These are some of the questions prompted by Colin Kirkwood in *Vulgar Eloquence: from Labour to Liberation*.[2] This is, in the present political-intellectual climate, an unfashionable contribution to Scottish debate; for it is not unfair, we think, to see the book as a record of engagement, in the realm of practice, with some of the central ideals of 1968, and an attempt to establish the ways in which these ideals remain viable. The first essay, written in 1969, recounts the author's experience as a teacher being challenged by students who demanded 'democratic' and 'non-authoritarian' forms of learning. The book goes on to chart a number of practical explorations in the two decades following, in such fields as adult and community education and counselling. The guiding theme of these inquiries and reflections is the meaning and possibility of human liberation, in both a political and personal sense, and in particular within the specific circumstances of Scottish society.

The political argument, baldly, is for a kind of populist politics beyond labourism. For the Labour Party, the author holds, the political function of the people is no more than that of an electorate, those shepherded, at the occasional appointed times, into the polling stations in order to ensure that the Honourable Member is 'returned' to those high realms whence blessings for the poor and needy are bestowed. Labour's excessively, or exclusively welfarist and statist conception of politics has fostered a spirit of dependency and a sense of personal powerlessness among its constituents. Some sections of the People's Party have, of course, recently come to acknowledge the force of such criticisms, at least in the rhetoric designed for public consumption. But Kirkwood has long argued that the left must reclaim such ideals and values as personal responsibility, initiative, enterprise, self-reliance and independence, a language traditionally surrendered by Labour to the right. With the recovery of such principles, he argues, forms of popular political organisation and action could develop, leading to greater local and popular control of resources, services and amenities.

Perhaps the outstanding achievement of the People's Party in Scotland has been the creation of large housing estates which serve to segregate the riff-raff from respectable sections of society. The author inquires: 'How many Labour MPs, councillors and apparatchiks choose to live in the houses they provide for their voter-natives?' This touches on a wider picture and history: the divide between the people and their representatives in the People's Party. The upper echelons of the party have never been conspicuously occupied by people drawn from the toiling masses: they have been and are dominated by posh types with scant personal experience of either toil or hardship.

Another task for a radical, populist leftism, therefore, is to challenge the monopolisation of political debate by such 'representatives', other *Berufspolitiker* and media professionals. Structures must be created for 'vulgar eloquence' to be heard, the voices of the poor, the unemployed, and other oppressed and neglected people, those who are seldom listened to, or even permitted, in public forums, to speak.

But given all the obvious practical obstacles, what are the chances for this kind of *basismo*? In the Scottish context, we believe, there is one glimmer of hope, hope at least of conditions more favourable to the development of the demotic type of politics the author advocates. The achievement of Scottish self-government would represent a shift towards more popular power for at least two reasons. First, popular political participation and the exercise of popular pressure on and control over government are much more feasible in a small state, if only because those with political power are closer and more visible.

Secondly, and crucially, the new Scottish polity will be based on conceptions of the state alien to UK regalism – Calvinist and Catholic conceptions, to be precise, rather than Anglican ones. The constitution will assert – in line with the traditions of Scottish constitutional law – the principle of the sovereignty of the people, an idea which the People's Party, strange to relate, has never embraced, preferring to grant its allegiance, instead, throughout its history, to the distinctly anti-popular and anti-democratic doctrine (and reality) of the absolute sovereignty of 'the Crown in Parliament' – an allegiance sealed by enthusiasm for the whole sorry panoply of royalism: Palace tea parties, ennoblement, the Garter, and what-not. There should also be in an autonomous Scotland an important change in political symbolism, government and state being conceived and projected as agencies of the people, and not, as now, as 'Her Majesty's' this or that.

The climate created by such changes, it hardly needs to be stressed, would favour 'vulgar eloquence' in a way which is inconceivable within the regal-patrician state and culture of the UK. Kirkwood refers to Tom Nairn's work in his bibliography, but his nationalist argument could have been greatly strengthened by an integration of Nairn's analysis of Ukanian regalism.[3]

But like the radicals of 1968, Kirkwood stresses that there are internal, personal obstacles to human freedom as well as the more public, political structures of oppression. What, then, of the personal, psychological dimensions of liberation?

We are presented with a number of practical principles which define the process by which we can move towards a more liberated way of life. But here there is none of the easy optimism of the 1968 revolutionaries: like Bonhoeffer's grace, liberation is not cheap, but costly. It must also be said – since we are insisting that *Vulgar Eloquence* is in some central ways a product of 1968 radicalism – that the perspective which informs the book is hostile to the mandarinism which characterises, for example, the work of such 1968 liberationists as Marcuse. Our author would agree that there can be no liberation 'from above'; liberation is always self-liberation.[4]

The most important of the practical principles of self-liberation presented in *Vulgar Eloquence* can be summarised under the following terms: growth, feelings, autonomy, reflection. These concepts are not explained in any systematic way in the text, nor elaborated in any great detail. But they are clearly central to the discourse which defines the author's position; and we can most usefully extend the discussion *Vulgar Eloquence* sets in motion by unpacking these notions a little, and by asking a few critical questions about them.

The concept of personal growth or personal development, entrenched in the discourses of therapy, counselling, modernist philosophies of education and the language of popular handbooks which proffer guidance on better living, is open to a variety of interpretations. It is sometimes over-optimistically taken to involve 'the full development of the personality', an ideal which founders on the fact that different types of development may not be compossible. Growth as an artist may not be consistent with growth as a partner or parent, for instance (the Gauguin case). We might then think of growth as the development of all or many of the self's mutually consistent capacities. The immediate problem here is that not all types of development seem desirable or legitimate. For example, what about the capacity for enjoying pornography, or for indulging in forms of cruelty? In other terms, we need a set of criteria to distinguish capacities which should be cultivated from those which should be allowed to wither.

The author probably has in mind a more integrated, goal-oriented kind of development: growth towards maturity, or fulfilment, or happiness, or whatever. But then, obviously, we need some wider theory of the self which provides an account of these ideas. The questions raised here are not intended to suggest that personal growth is not a meaningful ideal. The point, rather, is that the ideal can only be made properly operable in a philosophy, or, to be more precise, an ethical theory, an account of the human good and how it can be attained.

According to David Hume's science of man, feelings, those 'original facts and realities', as he took them to be, are the only source of human action. As Hume puts it in a famous passage, 'reason is . . . the slave of the passions, and can never pretend to any other office than to serve and obey them'.[5] It follows that, as he insists, our moral actions too must be motivated by some feeling or feelings. Curiously, most recent moral philosophers, in Anglophonia at least, have restricted ethics to the study of moral language and moral reasoning, in an intellectualist approach which excludes that wider personal reality, including motivation and feeling, within which moral debate and reflection are set. It should be obvious that an adequate ethics cannot divorce the attempt to articulate a consistent theory of the good from the study of what we are and how we can come to attain the good for ourselves and others. Unfortunately, just as philosophers tend to disregard psychology (in the sense of Hume's science of man), psychoanalysts, therapists and counsellors are rarely conversant with the traditions of ethical inquiry we need for a full theory of the self.

The author of *Vulgar Eloquence* enjoins us to be 'in touch with our feelings'; but little guidance is offered as to how we are to meet this obligation. Let us consider one possible interpretation. Part of 'being in touch with our feelings' is coming to understand what it is we really want, as a basis for action aimed at fulfilling our real desires. However, experience teaches us that, very often, once we get what we want, we discover that it is not really what we wanted after all, or is no longer what we want. This platitude points to a less obvious consideration, which has far-reaching consequences: that our untutored wants, or, more generally, feelings, may not be the most reliable guide to conduct. But nothing in *Vulgar Eloquence* suggests any recognition that there could be standards of the good and standards of right action – for instance those elaborated in philosophical and religious traditions – which conflict with what people in general happen to want. From the perspective of tradition-informed inquiry, this is the fatal weakness of therapism as a whole.

What is the role of feeling and motivation in ethics? To many readers, certainly, the very idea that morality can be harmonised with our feelings (pleasures, pains, wants, felt needs, etc) will appear paradoxical. We inherit a very powerful conception, which derives in great measure from Kant, that pleasure and morality are conflicting principles. To use Kantian terminology, we think that duty and inclination are generally or at least very frequently in opposition: typically what we (morally) ought to do is not what we 'feel like' doing or what will bring us pleasure and contentment. Doing what is required of us from the moral point of view, on this conception, normally involves a degree of self-abnegation. This view has been reinforced by the most pervasive and influential twentieth-century belief system concerning the self, Freudianism, with its desperately crude picture of the person as little more than a site where blind libidinous urges war with a repressive internalised authority.

Such simple antitheses are alien to Aristotelian ethical theory, still, it has recently been argued by a number of philosophers, the best starting-point for any discussion of the role of feeling in ethics (and, indeed, for ethical thinking in general). For Aristotle – we sketch the view here in caricature – the good person takes pleasure in doing good, and would be pained by performing actions which are base or ignoble. In him or her, generosity, courage, honesty, self-control and the other virtues are accompanied by positive, strong, motivating feeling; and he or she abstains from dishonest, mean, cowardly and other types of vicious action because they are associated with negative feeling. Such things are incomprehensible to the person who has not acquired the virtues. He or she simply does not know the feelings involved in their practice, just as, to use a very rough analogy, the person who has only ever read comics does not know the pleasures afforded by the reading of literature.

From such a perspective, the crucial question then is: why do some people take pleasure in doing good, while others do not? The Aristotelian answer places great weight on early training. Before the age when we can reason maturely and understand why virtuous conduct is the best for us, we have to have acquired certain habits of feeling, such that we take pleasure in right action. To quote one recent gloss on Aristotle's position, 'a good upbringing makes the noble a part, perhaps the chief part, of the pleasant for us.'[6] Without this correct early habituation, Aristotle believed, nothing much could be done: he did not believe in preaching or moral exhortation, in trying to persuade crooks and scoundrels to mend their ways.

If this particular step in Aristotle's argument is pessimistic, what is striking about the position overall is its optimism. It is impossible for us today to believe that all problems can be solved through good upbringing. For there is such a thing, which the Augustinian-Calvinist tradition above all has emphasised and allowed us to articulate, as knowing the good, but choosing to do evil: 'For the good that I would I do not: but the evil which I would not, that I do.'

Autonomy, the third ideal presented in *Vulgar Eloquence*, seems uncontroversial. Surely the adult, mature person is one who has achieved independence from the beliefs, roles and statuses inculcated by the family, tradition, education, the media and other 'socialising agencies'? To use a phrase from the text, liberation involves 'choosing our own values'. The idea has been fleshed out, in its most extreme forms, in some versions of existentialism (a philosophical movement which has exerted considerable influence on the development of therapist discourse). Since neither God nor a fixed human nature exist, we are compelled to create our own values and identity. Assuming this responsibility is the mark of genuine selfhood, whereas the heteronomy involved in acquiescence in received beliefs and statuses denotes inauthentic existence.

However, this conception leads straight to a painful dilemma. If, in choosing our values, our choice is not purely arbitrary, we must select according to certain pre-existing values or criteria. If these in turn have been chosen, there must have been a yet prior set of criteria; and so on. So either there is here an infinite regress, or else the only conceivable basis of autonomy is some criterionless choice or arbitrary act of commitment.

Whatever the force of this objection, it is certainly the case that the discourse of moral 'autonomy' and 'choice' is now firmly established in the life of liberal societies. This reflects the belief, or assumption, that questions about how we ought to live, about 'the chief end of man', to quote the Kirk's catechism, are not resolvable by rational means. And since we have no way of showing – so the argument runs – how one answer or set of answers to such questions is rationally superior to any other, we can only accept the free play of individual taste and inclination. Although it is now largely obscured by such taken-for-granted ideas, there exists, of course, a quite different conception of ethics. This is at home, for instance, in Aristotelian thought, in Thomism, and in certain personalist schools. From the perspective of such positions, our nature as human beings is such that, if we are to make progress towards our good, we have to act and develop in certain ways. And this implies that we are required to learn, from the texts and teachers of an ethical tradition, how it is that we have to live and act in order to attain the good. So, as contrasted with the god-like self of existentialism, who brings his morality into being by free decision, the self must here set out by submitting to the authority of tradition, and by acquiring first of all the virtue of humility. (The author acknowledges that he is no longer happy with the naive anti-authoritarianism of the 1960s and 1970s. But it is not clear what role he sees for authority and tradition in ethics. If these are granted importance, the strong emphasis in *Vulgar Eloquence* on personal autonomy and choice requires substantial qualification.)

Such ideas may have greater relevance to the routine concerns of psychotherapy than at first sight appears. For many people who seek help of this kind are in fact preoccupied by questions which are essentially moral or ethical, questions about the kind of life which is worth living, or about what constitutes a meaningful life. For various reasons, however, therapists tend to be averse to any suggestion that they are concerned with ethics or should provide ethical guidance. This would conflict with therapism's scientific and professional pretensions, that is, its claim to provide a special and distinctive skilled service which is based on objective and value-free knowledge of human beings. At the same time, many therapists no doubt share the view that ethics is a matter of personal choice and preference; they may also see in the exercise of this choice a condition of maturity and authenticity. Finally, 'morality' has very often been conceived by psychoanalysts and therapists as a repressive force and an obstacle to well-being; and similar connotations attach in such discourses to 'tradition' and 'authority'.

In a recent essay, Charles Guignon has suggested that psychotherapy must revise many of these assumptions if it is to be of genuine use to those who seek counselling. The ideal of unbounded freedom or autonomy, he suggests, is self-defeating: 'For where all things are equally possible, nothing is really binding, and so no choice is superior to any others.'[7] Freedom is then, in Philip Rieff's words, the 'absurdity of being freed to choose and then having no choice worth making'. Drawing on Heidegger, Guignon goes on to argue that the notions of moral authority and tradition are in fact indispensable to counselling which addresses the needs of its recipients. Essential to this argument is the idea that in making sense of ourselves and others we are forced to understand a life as a narrative. In Charles Taylor's words, 'In order to have a sense of who we are, we have to have a notion of who we have become, and of where we are going'.[8] Psychotherapists frequently deal with people who suffer from feelings of an absence or loss of meaning and direction in their lives. What this amounts to, on the view being described, is that they cannot see their actions and activities as part of a unified narrative structure. And this predicament, Guignon's argument implies, corresponds to that very detachment from moral and cultural tradition which many psychotherapists have portrayed as emancipation, autonomy and authenticity. For it is in the particular stories, commentaries, and ethical debate of a historical community – in the 'well-springs' of a 'heritage', as Heidegger says – that we encounter the narrative structures, the accounts of possible ways of living a life, without which our own lives cannot be given a sense.

Reflection is another seemingly uncontentious ideal: the mature person is one who strives for self-knowledge by reflecting on his or her experience. But once more complex and controversial issues lie just below the surface. For the self can only reflect on its experience by using certain concepts and categories, beginning with some determinate concept of the self. So the question arises: which concepts and categories?

The answer suggested in *Vulgar Eloquence* is: the concepts of object relations psychoanalysis, the movement associated with Fairbairn, Guntrip, and Sutherland. But – whatever the merits of this particular discourse – no arguments are presented as to why it is superior to, say, Aristotelian, Thomistic or Kierkegaardian theories of the self. It is interesting to note here that the most famous recent Scottish psychologist, R. D. Laing, who himself had some connections with the object relations school, came to emphasise the need for categories drawn from religious and ethical tradition.[9] An example Laing gives is 'sin', the concept in Christian thought which names 'that rooted tendency to disobedience in the will and distraction by passion', the recognition of which, for Aquinas, is 'a necessary condition for one's reception of the virtues of faith, hope and charity'.[10] But this kind of idea is hardly insertable into any scheme of thought based on Freud or Fairbairn.

We are faced, then, with rival, conflicting and in some cases incommensurable theoretical frameworks for understanding the self. How are we to choose between them? What makes one such theory superior to another? Here we would like to quote Charles Taylor's recent illuminating discussion in *Sources of the Self* for one response to this question. The best theory, in Taylor's formulation, is the one which provides us with

> those terms which on critical reflection and after correction of the errors we can detect make the best sense of our lives. 'Making the best sense' here includes not only offering the best, most realistic orientation about the good but also allowing us best to understand and make sense of the actions of others.[11]

The view that, in this regard, modernist psychodiscourse has superior resources to those found in religious and philosophical tradition seems to us to be erroneous – which is not to deny, of course, the contemporary dominance of this idiom, among reputedly educated members of society, in discussions concerning the human personality and human relations. But the main point here is the falsity of the assumption present in *Vulgar Eloquence*: that there is some neutral intellectual framework for understanding the self, on which all well-intentioned, rational and reasonable persons can be brought to agree. Positions here are inevitably partisan.

Back, in closing, to our initial questions about 1968. If the ideas and ideals of that year are no longer in fashion, and if most of them need, in any case, to be rejected, it has to be stressed that at least one important lesson which the student movement had to teach has not been learned.

> The student radicals of the late 1960s and early 1970s failed to understand many things, and their own intellectual poverty reflected the poverty of much, if not all, of that against which they rebelled. But they had understood this and those who defeated them by the use of political as well as academic power still fail for the most part to understand it. The rejection of the liberal university signaled by that revolt of the 1960s was a response to the barrenness of a university which had deprived itself of substantive moral inquiry . . . '[12]

Substantive moral inquiry, or the posing of questions about the good, the good person and the good community, and the attempt to explore and provide systematic answers to such questions, is a practice as rare in the universities today as it was before 1968. It is rare even in the small and diminishing space occupied by moral philosophy, where questions about the nature of the good life have long and effectively been sidelined by academic philosophers' concentration on narrow issues about social obligation. And outside the universities there are few forums where ethical inquiry can or does take place. The liberation we now most urgently require is from this cultural vacuity.

2

David McCrone's *Understanding Scotland* is clearly a very important book. It is set to become, among academics, students and others, one of the most widely-read and widely-discussed serious works on Scotland to appear in recent years. Its usefulness as a summary of different positions in sociological, historical and cultural debate will ensure that it is an indispensable textbook for beginners. It has been highly praised by reviewers (and comes with a blurb blessing from Tom Nairn, no less). For such reasons alone, quite apart from its intrinsic qualities as a stimulating and thoughtful discussion of Scottish affairs, it is a text which calls for close study and attention.

Our comments here are intended to deepen (one area of) debate, and not to question the value and interest of McCrone's contribution. In any case, we do not want to attempt any full review or analysis of the book; what we have to say will be directed at only a small part of McCrone's argument – albeit, as it seems to us, a crucial part. One more initial disclaimer is in order: whereas McCrone is a professional academic sociologist, and *Understanding Scotland* appears in the *International Library of Sociology* series, we are not sociologists of any kind, and our comments should not be read as an intervention in 'sociological' debate.

Our main argument, moreover, will be that a central weakness of McCrone's position is due to its circumscription within the universe of discourse of 'sociology'; and so it is with some comments on this particular form of inquiry that we begin.

In his introduction, McCrone draws attention to the role of eighteenth century Scottish thinkers such as Adam Ferguson and Adam Smith in the founding and development of what would later come to be called the social sciences. McCrone writes: ' . . . there is a strong case for claiming that sociology was invented in Scotland, for the Scottish Enlightenment founded its knowledge upon "sociological" assumptions about mankind.'[13] However, he correctly notes that the thinkers of the Scotttish Enlightenment had a broader conception of the nature of their inquiry than that which informs modern sociology: their 'science of man', he comments, 'took in more than the social sciences currently defined'.[14] This would appear to carry the implication (not actually spelled out in the text) that modern sociologists, in shedding the wider interests and concerns of thinkers like Smith, have made of their discipline a more satisfactory type of investigation. This seems to us, as should become clear, a highly contestable view.

In any case, McCrone's qualification that Scottish eighteenth-century social inquiry and contemporary social science are not coterminous is important. But it needs much heavier underlining: McCrone does not go nearly far enough in bringing out the 'epistemic break' or 'paradigm shift' which separates the two.

In the former project, we can identify four significant general features which are relevant to our discussion. First, obviously, the inquiry was concerned with observing social phenomena, and the processes of social change; second, it drew upon and attempted to elaborate more adequate accounts in philosophical anthropology, or a theory of the person; third, it made use of this philosophical dimension to evaluate the social changes it recorded; and finally, this ethical-critical base generated prescriptions of a political nature. It is doubtful whether the practitioners of this type of intellectual inquiry would have made any sense of the suggestion that one or other of these aspects could usefully be excised or treated in isolation.

To illustrate, let us turn to certain famous passages in *The Wealth of Nations*, those where Smith is concerned with some of the human consequences of the division of labour. As specialisation in the production process extends, Smith remarks, 'the employment of the far greater part of those who live by labour, that is, of the great body of the people, comes to be confined to a few very simple operations, frequently to one or two.'[15] Then, after noting the formative role exercised by our occupation, or 'ordinary employments', on the quality of our intellectual life, Smith immediately moves to an evaluation of the consequences of the division of labour: 'The man whose whole life is spent in performing a few simple operations . . . has no occasion to exert his understanding . . . He naturally loses, therefore, the habit of such exertion and generally becomes as stupid and ignorant as it is possible for a human creature to become.' Governments are consequently obliged, Smith claims, to 'take pains' to ensure that the labouring population does not fall into such a condition.

Smith's warnings are based on a philosophical and ethical foundation; they clearly invoke a conception of the kind of life which human beings, on account of their nature, as described in the best available analysis, ought to pursue. Shortly after the sentences just quoted, he writes: 'A man without the proper use of the intellectual faculties of a man is, if possible, even more contemptible than a coward, and seems to be mutilated and deformed in a still more essential part of the character of human nature.' Smith then repeats his moral-political message: 'Though the state was to derive no advantage from the instruction of the inferior ranks of people, it would still deserve its attention that they should not be altogether uninstructed.'

The kind of discourse exemplified by these quotations – in which social analysis, philosophy, moral evaluation and political prescription intermesh and proceed together – did not of course die out with the thinkers of eighteenth-century Scotland. It defines much nineteenth-century social inquiry, too, the most striking and significant instance being the work of Marx (this is not to overlook such profound differences as those between the realism of an Adam Smith and the Pelagian, messianic spirit of Marx). Significant social theory and commentary in the twentieth century has also operated within similar parameters, most obviously in the writings of thinkers in the marxist and socialist traditions.

Mainstream modern academic sociology is a very different animal. Here the predominant tendency has been to delimit the investigator's role to the observation and description of social phenomena, in isolation from ethics and philosophy, and to attempt to bracket as far as possible the observer's personal moral and political commitments in the interests of scientific 'neutrality'. Sociologists have of course been concerned with ethics and morality, but here their role has typically been that of observing, recording, analysing, classifying and tabulating the moral attitudes and pronouncements of those who come under their scrutiny.

This is not the place to undertake an account of the process, and its different motivations, which led to the establishment of twentieth-century sociological discourse. But the general outline of the trajectory and its determinants seems clear enough: the successes and prestige of natural science, which encouraged attempts within the *Geisteswissenschaften* too to emulate an impersonal and supposedly 'value-free' form of inquiry; the professionalisation and bureaucratisation of intellectual labour, which promoted the demarcation of a zone with its own distinct lexis, techniques and procedures, where the competence of laity could plausibly be denied; the ubiquitous influence of emotivist views of ethics, propounded for instance in positivism and analytic philosophy, which denied the rational nature of ethical commitments and theories, and so made the assumption of ethical neutrality a condition of scholarly respectability; and the development within social science itself of forms of theory according to which ethics is explicable as a product of other social and economic processes and 'forces'.

These remarks are not meant to suggest, something which is not true, that McCrone's text is an exercise in sociological positivism, or that it reflects a dully academic, specialising mentality. But the book operates within the paradigm of normal sociology at least in the sense that social and cultural analyses are here largely divorced from any wider theoretical framework; and what we do want to suggest is that such analysis is both limited and deficient in critical power.

In saying this, we should not be (mis)taken as aligning ourselves with calls for 'interdisciplinary' forms of inquiry. Such calls betray subscription to the essential priority of the academic discipline, the *Fach*, whereas what ought to be questioned, and what indeed is now being questioned by many thinkers, is the logic of conventional academic compartmentalisation and its ability to generate discourses adequate to address the issues which confront us. With reference to the contemporary intellectual scene in the USA, Richard Bernstein has recently written that 'there has been an explosion of study and discussion groups that cluster about new constellations of texts and themes that cut across disciplines .. .There is no longer the presumption of a distinctive disciplinary approach to a given problem – as if there were a unique philosophic, literary or anthropological point of view . . . It is almost as if there is a "counter-disciplinary" movement developing which no longer finds the disciplinary matrices that have shaped our academic departments helpful in dealing with intellectual problems.'[16] And in support of the validity of this 'counter-disciplinary' movement, a case could be made for the thesis that a distinguishing feature of the work of the most significant recent and contemporary thinkers is that it is not categorisable in terms of established academic 'subjects'. (Start the list with Habermas, Apel, Foucault, Derrida, Gellner, Taylor.)

In the light of the intellectual developments to which the quotation from Bernstein draws our attention, McCrone's book seems in central respects a rather old-fashioned work; and it is ironic that he should wish to stress that his position – as contrasted, for example, with ours – properly takes account of current cultural realities, when his discourse discloses no awareness of the need for a type of inquiry whose focus is broader than that available from within 'sociology' (or any of the other conventional disciplines). Some ten years ago, Alasdair MacIntyre expressed the view that there is a 'tension between the professionalisation of philosophy and its flourishing'; and in the same article he declared that 'there is no separate discipline of philosophy'.[17] For reasons sketched out below, it is perhaps time for our sociologists to ask themselves whether serious reflection on society is best achieved within the confines of 'sociological' discourse – whether, in other terms, there can now be any meaningful separate discipline of sociology.

In his chapter concerned with arguments about Scottish culture, and in some later sections of the book, McCrone takes issue with a number of ideas he imputes, or appears to impute, to us (among others). These include the notion that there was once some Golden Age of Scottish culture against which the present is to be judged (and found wanting); a belief in the possibility of a 'Scottish national culture' as a monolithic, homogeneous and conflict-free entity; an essentialist view of nationhood, as some mysterious inner essence or *Geist* which is not explicable in terms of historical and cultural contingency; and the judgement that Scottish culture can and should be sealed off from all foreign or non-Scottish influence.

It is impossible to take any of these ideas seriously, and in reality McCrone is here engaged in combat with a batallion of straw men. Certainly they are not views we happen to hold, or have ever tried to articulate or defend. However, an examination of some of McCrone's comments on cultural matters, and their implications, does uncover an area of real and profound disagreement between himself and us, as we now want to indicate. The differences centre on questions concerning tradition and identity.

As some readers may recall, in *The Eclipse of Scottish Culture* we put forward the view that among the Scottish intelligentsia a number of highly negative perceptions of Scottish history, culture and traditions had become entrenched. At the same time, we expressed our disagreement with forms of purely pragmatic nationalism, which ignore or sideline issues of tradition and identity. We then attempted to argue for a reconsideration of certain cultural traditions, and for the recovery and re-assertion of such practices as bases for the construction of contemporary identity. While we can see no good reason to revise our position in any fundamental way, as then presented it was in some respects seriously flawed. We offered no worked-out account of what we meant by tradition, nor did we explore in any detail what would be involved in the 'recovery' or 're-assertion' of tradition(s). But these are not the types of criticism McCrone wants to make: his opposition to our view is of a much more wholesale character.

McCrone, it seems clear, sees little sense in undertaking any such project, in the sense we intend, as the recovery, retrieval, re-assessment or re-assertion of tradition(s). But it is important to notice here that the conception of tradition deployed by McCrone, if a common one in the discourse of sociologists and social historians, is severely limited. 'Tradition', on this view, is closely associated with 'myth', 'legend', 'symbol', 'image'. Thus, for instance, McCrone can write that 'in Scotland and Wales, different ethno-histories are on offer from the dominant Anglo-British one, and these mobilise their own myths, legends and traditions'.[18] Raymond Williams is quoted here to the effect that tradition is a 'selective version' of the past. That is to say, it is a part or form of ideology, which idealises the past in order to create group identity, to guide action, and (here McCrone quotes Patrick Wright) 'to re-enchant a disenchanted everyday life'.

McCrone's understanding of 'tradition' is made clear in the following passage:

> Traditions and myths provide meaningful though partial interpretations of social reality and social change. They involve selective inclusion and exclusion, and thereby become a contemporary and active force providing a reservoir of legitimation for belief and action . . . Traditions, then, legitimise institutions, symbolise group cohesion, and socialise others into the appropriate beliefs and values.[19]

The rational approach to traditions, therefore, is to observe and understand their social functions: 'The task is . . . to show how and why they are put to such telling use.'[20]

No-one would wish to deny the fairly obvious truth of the thesis that selective accounts of a national past can shape contemporary consciousness and political action. The interesting point about McCrone's discussion here is that, as an account of 'tradition', it is itself highly selective, and excludes a quite different conception: an understanding of a tradition as a history of reflective inquiry, as 'an historically extended, socially embodied argument'.[21] What traditions in this sense supply are not more-or-less distorted images of the national past, but rather the means by which the self is introduced to and can become educated into a form of concern and reflection which addresses his or her status as a moral agent. A tradition in this sense is an ethical discourse, which will provide, for instance, a particular account of the virtues, a conception of the good, for the self and the community, and a vocabulary for self-understanding. And such traditions will provide for the self to achieve a particular form of identity or selfhood, as a participant in the interpretive community through which the tradition continues and is extended. Traditions, in this sense, do not present themselves as objects to be observed and explained from some superior plane of rational inquiry: they are, rather, conditions of the self being able to attain practical rationality.

It goes without saying that the notion that the self should find its identity through an encounter with some locally available tradition of rational practical inquiry, that tradition is identity-constitutive, has no place in McCrone's understanding of selfhood and identity. Not only, on McCrone's view, is there no need for the self to construct its identity by reference to a tradition, there is no general requirement that the self should aspire to any single or stable identity. The self of postmodernist, pluricultural societies becomes, rather, a consumer of different identities, as this key comment makes clear: 'What is on offer in the late twentieth-century is what we might call "pick'n'mix" identity, in which we wear our identities lightly, and change them according to circumstances.'[22] In allusion to the passage where Hume talks of the person as 'a bundle . . . of different perceptions', Ernest Gellner once dubbed the concept of the self articulated in empiricist discourses the 'Bundleman'.[23] Now, thanks to McCrone, we can coin the expression 'Pick'n'mix man' to capture the notion of the self inscribed in postmodernist sociology.

Actually, the example McCrone offers of such a self, whose life ideally consists in a gay, ludic donning and discarding of various identities, is a woman: 'black, Glaswegian and female' (an example given, no doubt, as testimony to the author's political rectitude). What the example is intended to suggest is a person who lives, so to say, betweeen and across different cultural traditions and identities, equally at home (or homeless) in all of them, with allegiances to several systems of meaning and belief, and no stable or constant allegiance to any. Now it may well be that such a condition, and effective alienation from tradition (in the sense of the term we are emphasising) and communities of tradition-informed practical inquiry in which the self can be educated into a determinate understanding of the virtues and the good, is in fact the situation (or, from an alternative perspective, the predicament) of many people who inhabit contemporary liberal societies. For McCrone, this self's condition is not only unproblematic: it is entirely proper, and indeed worthy of emulation. He does not consider the possibility that Pick'n'mix man might represent, instead, a self in a state of profound disorder.

This possibility cannot be raised within McCrone's discourse, and not only because raising it might risk breaching the orthodoxies of labourist and progressive thought. This is so, first, because although it now seems permissible for the sociologist to profess benign sentiments towards current social trends, a critical appraisal of Pick'n'mix man could not be undertaken without seriously and flagrantly compromising the ideal of ethical neutrality, or ethical non-judgmentalism; and second, because such an appraisal would necessarily involve invoking criteria of a philosophical kind which normal sociology regards as beyond its domain of competence.

Since *we* see no compelling reason to confine discussion within the boundaries of sociological discourse, we now want to ask what seems to us the crucial question raised by McCrone's position: why should we accept and share his endorsement of Pick'n'mix man? In what way or ways is this model of selfhood better than or preferable to other conceptions of the self? It is interesting and important, if hardly surprising, that McCrone himself offers no actual arguments in support of his endorsement – it is not surprising, obviously, for the reason that any such argument would have to go beyond the mere description and tabulation of social fact, and draw on a theoretical frame of reference external to 'sociology'. What we are offered, in place of argument and theory, is an appeal to fashion: 'Those who would argue for the paramountcy or even the exclusivity of a single identity have a hard time of it in the late twentieth century.'[24]

Paradoxically, one of the most famous critical accounts of the kind of self McCrone holds out as paradigmatic for our time is to be found in classical sociology itself. For one of the forebears of Pick'n'mix man is the individual whose condition was analysed by Durkheim in terms of anomie, or normlessness. But what for Durkheim was a pathological state is now, for postmodernist sociologists, an exemplary form of life. 'Anomie', as Durkheim characterised it, was a form of deprivation, of a loss of membership in those social institutions and modes in which norms, including the norms of tradition-constituted rationality, are embodied. What Durkheim did not foresee was a time when the same condition of anomie would be assigned the status of an achievement by and a reward for the self, which had, by separating itself from the social relationships of traditions, succeeded, so it believed, in emancipating itself.[25]

A striking feature of this 'emancipated' liberal or postmodernist self is what could be termed intellectual anomie: the condition of the self who applies, for instance, marxist categories to the understanding of history, Freudian notions to the understanding of the mind and of human relations, utilitarian patterns of thought to political issues, and Kantian principles in the raising of his or her children. Such intellectual incoherence undermines the possibility of settled conviction and commitment: with so many semi-commitments and half-allegiances, this self has effective allegiance to no system of belief.

There is a final feature of *Understanding Scotland* with which we must take issue. McCrone affects to speak with academic impartiality, to view the historical and cultural questions with which he is concerned from a site of rational inquiry which is neutral as to conflicting theoretical approaches. In reality, no such neutral or impartial site is available; and there is no way of 'understanding Scotland' which uniquely embodies standards of objectivity and rationality. McCrone's text represents one more discourse, one more position, with a particular set of questions and problems taken to be significant, a particular view of the self, and so on. And, we have been suggesting, what that text most effectively demonstrates, at least to those committed to traditions of substantive ethical inquiry, is the relative poverty and resourcelessness of the discourse it articulates.

Notes

Chapter 1

1. David McCrone, *Understanding Scotland: the Sociology of a Stateless Nation*, London, 1992, p. 30.
2. Peter Burke (ed.), *A New Kind of History: From the Writings of Febvre*, London, 1973, p. 41.
3. R. D. Laing, Wisdom, Madness and Folly, London, 1985, p. 35.
4. Without embarking on an extended discussion of methodological questions, we ought perhaps to say a word about the concept of 'discourse', which has become central in cultural analysis and plays a central role in our discussion too.

   The meaning given to the term (and related expressions such as 'paradigm' and 'problematic') varies from author to author. We mean by it, briefly, a way of seeing, of interpreting, of knowing, which deploys a particular, developed system of concepts, identifies what count as significant facts and processes, and specifies what types of questions and problems are worthy of investigation, and what kinds of solutions to such problems are acceptable. (So, for example, 'scientific discourse', or 'marxist discourse'.) The concept has also been put to different uses, a common one being that of relativising claims to the truth or importance of any position or belief, as having validity, not absolutely, but only in terms of criteria internal to some determinate discourse. While we reject the kind of absolute or ultimate relativism such arguments are often taken to support, we certainly agree with the basic notion that no discourse, no way of describing and attempting to understand the world, can plausibly be seen as 'neutral' or 'impartial', or free of theoretical assumptions, or uniquely endowed with standards of rationality and objectivity.

   The issues involved here are rather complex, but they are fundamental to contemporary theoretical argument (and are taken up at various points in the essays which follow). Moreover, if they can only be adequately discussed at a somewhat abstract level of analysis, the issues impinge directly on day-to-day cultural life. For those who overlook the inevitably partisan nature of any intellectual position succumb to a common set of illusions – that certain beliefs and attitudes have a unique claimto rationality, that all rational and well-intentioned persons will agree on fundamental questions, that those who dissent from the judgments of this imaginary consensus are victims of irrational prejudices or feeblemindedness, and so on. Such notions are now theoretically archaic, but they continue to inform a certain type of historiography, and they can be encountered on a daily basis in the leader columns of liberal metropolitan newspapers.

Chapter 2

1. T. C. Smout, *A Century of the Scottish People 1830–1950*, London, 1986, pp. 32–57.
2. *Ibid.*, p. 33.
3. *Ibid.*, p. 35.
4. *Ibid.*, p. 53.
5. *Ibid.*, p. 36.
6. *Ibid.*, p. 39.
7. *Ibid.*, p. 54.
8. Quoted, *ibid.*, p. 40.
9. *Ibid.*, p. 57.
10. *Ibid.*, p. 52.
11. *Ibid.*, p. 53.
12. William Ferguson, *Scotland 1689 to the Present*, Edinburgh and London, 1968.
13. See, for example, *ibid.*, p. 379.
14. *Ibid.*, p. 349.
15. *Ibid.*, p. 330.
16. *Ibid.*, p. 301.
17. *Ibid.*, pp. 332–3.
18. *Ibid.*, p. 402.
19. *Ibid.*, p. 318.
20. *Ibid.*, p. 217.
21. *Ibid.*, p. 319.
22. Sydney and Olive Checkland, *Industry and Ethos*, London, 1984.
23. *Ibid.*, p. 5.
24. *Ibid.*
25. *Ibid.*, p. 51.
26. *Ibid.*, p. 30.
27. *Ibid.*, p. 27.
28. *Ibid.*, p. 143.
29. *Ibid.*, see pp. 135, 136, 140.
30. *Ibid.*, p. 55.
31. *ibid.*, pp. 53–4.
32. Rosalind Mitchison, *A History of Scotland*, London, 1971.
33. *Ibid.*, p. 403, our italics.
34. *Ibid.*, pp. 403–4.
35. *Ibid.*, p. 408.
36. *Ibid.*, see pp. 380–1.
37. *Ibid.*, p. 393.
38. *Ibid.*, p. 394.

39. *Ibid.*, p. 394.
40. Christopher Harvie, *No Gods and Precious Few Heroes. Scotland Since 1914*, London, 1987.
41. *Ibid.*, pp. vi-vii.
42. *Ibid.*, p. vii.
43. *Ibid.*, p. viii.
44. S. G. Checkland, *The Upas Tree*, Glasgow, 1976.
45. *Ibid.*, Preface.
46. *Ibid.*, p. 18.
47. *Ibid.*, pp. 18–19.
48. *Ibid.*, p. 24.
49. *Ibid.*, p. 22; see also p. 43.
50. *Ibid.*, p. 27.
51. *Ibid.*, p. 99.
52. *Ibid.*, p. 3.
53. *Ibid.*
54. *Ibid.*, p. 6.
55. *Ibid.*, p. 86.
56. T. C. Smout, *op. cit*, p. 275.
57. *Ibid.*, p. 275.
58. Christopher Harvie, *op. cit*, pp. 135–6.
59. Sydney Checkland, *op. cit*, p.
60. G. S. Pryde, *Scotland, 1603 to the Present Day*, 1962.
61. *Ibid.*, p. 236.
62. *Ibid.*, p. 252.
63. *Ibid.*, p. 260
64. *Ibid.*
65. *Ibid.*, p. 277.
66. *Ibid.*, p. 303.
67. *Ibid.*, *see* pp. 233–4.
68. Michael Lynch, *Scotland. A New History*, London, 1991, pp. 406–7.
69. *Ibid.* See, for example, his description of a reform procession in 1884, p. 418.

Chapter 3

1. T. C. Smout, *A Century of the Scottish People 1830–1950*, London, 1986, p. 5.
2. *Ibid.*
3. Colin McWilliam, *Scottish Townscape*, London, 1975, p. 141.
4. *Ibid.*, p. 145.
5. *Ibid.*, p. 148.
6. *Ibid.*, p. 163.
7. *Ibid.*, p. 163.
8. *Ibid.*, p. 164.
9. Robert Macleod, *Charles Rennie Mackintosh: Architect and Artist*, London and Glasgow, 1983, p. 23.
10. *Ibid.*, p. 25.

11. *Ibid.*, p. 79.
12. *Ibid.*, p. 51.
13. *Ibid.*, pp. 66–7.
14. *Ibid.*, see pp. 27, 92.
15. *Ibid.*, quoted p. 112.
16. *Ibid.*, pp. 114–15.
17. J. G. Dunbar, *The Architecture of Scotland*, London, 1966, p. 164.
18. see F. Sinclair, *Scots Style: 150 years of Scottish Architecture*, Edinburgh, 1984.
19. J. G. Dunbar, *op. cit.*, p. 166.
20. Peter Savage, *Robert Lorimer and the Edinburgh Craft Designers*, Edinburgh, 1980, p. 13.
21. *Ibid.*, quoted p. 33.
22. *Ibid.*, p. 39.
23. *Ibid.*, p. 35.
24. William Hardie, *Scottish Painting 1837–1939*, London, 1976, p. 18.
25. *Ibid.*, p. 37.
26. *Ibid.*, p. 51.
27. *Ibid.*, p. 63.
28. *Ibid.*, p. 82.
29. Agnes Ethel Mackay, *Arthur Melville, Scottish Impressionist*, 1951, p. 78.
30. William Hardie, *op. cit.*, p. 82
31. Agnes Ethel Mackay, *op. cit.*, p. 78.
32. *Ibid.*, pp. 95–6.
33. *Ibid.*, p. 102.
34. William Hardie, *op. cit.*, p. 67.
35. Roger Billcliffe, *The Scottish Colourists*, London, 1989, Introduction.
36. William Hardie, *op. cit.*, p. 93.
37. *Ibid.*, p. 96.
38. *Ibid.*
39. *Ibid.*, p. 104.
40. *Ibid.*
41. *Ibid.*
42. Colin McWilliam, *op. cit.*, See pp. 160–170.
43. *Ibid.*, p. 167.
44. J. S. Marshall, *The Life and Times of Leith*, Edinburgh, 1986, pp. 180–1.
45. J. G. Dunbar, *op. cit.*, p. 158.
46. Charles McKean *et al.*, *Central Glasgow: An Illustrated Architectural Guide*, 1989, p. 4.
47. Allen Wright, 'Transatlantic City of Culture', *The Scotsman*, 4 December, 1989.
48. J. G. Dunbar, *op. cit.*, p. 155; see also F. Sinclair, *op. cit.* pp. 74–5.
49. F. A. Walker, 'Glasgow Squanders Wealth of its Banks', *The Scotsman*, 13 December 1989.
50. Charles McKean, *op. cit.* p. 6.
51. Tom Weir, *Tom Weir's Scotland*, Harmondsworth, 1982, Introduction
52. *Ibid.*, Introduction.

53. *Ibid.*, Introduction.
54. R. Aitken, *The West Highland Way*, pp. 41–2.
55. Anna Blair, *Tea at Miss Cranston's. A Century of Glasgow Memories*, London, 1985, p. 8.
56. *Ibid.*, p. 6.
57. T. C. Smout, *op. cit.*, p. 149
58. Anna Blair, *op. cit.*, p. 4.
59. Sidney Checkland, *The Upas Tree: Glasgow 1875–1975*, Glasgow, 1976, p. 68.
60. *Ibid.*, p. 74.
61. T. C. Smout, *op. cit.*, p. 150–1.
62. *Ibid.*, p. 151.
63. Tom Weir, *op. cit.*, p. 12.
64. T. C. Smout, *op. cit.*, p. 158.

Chapter 4

1. Alexander Broadie, *The Tradition of Scottish Philosophy: A New Perspective on the Enlightenment*, Edinburgh, 1990; David Allan, *Virtue, Learning and the Scottish Enlightenment*, Edinburgh, 1993, p. 4.
2. W. Donaldson, *Popular Literature in Victorian Scotland: Language, Fiction and the Press*, Aberdeen, 1986.
3. Tom Nairn, *The Break-Up of Britain*, 2nd edition; London, 1981, chs 2 and 3; Lindsay Paterson, 'Scotch Myths', *Bulletin of Scottish Politics*, Vol. 1, No. 2, spring 1981; Colin McArthur, 'Breaking the Signs: "Scotch Myths" as Cultural Struggle', *Cencrastus*, No. 7, Winter 1981–2.
4. P. H. Scott, 'Scotch Myths', *Bulletin of Scottish Politics*, Vol. 1, No. 2, spring 1981.
5. Colin Kirkwood, *Vulgar Eloquence: from Labour to Liberation*, Polygon, 1990, p. 342.
6. E. P. Thompson, *Whigs and Hunters: the Origin of the Black Act*, London, 1970, p. 258.
7. Nairn, *The Break-Up of Britain*, p. 148.
8. Tom Nairn, *The Enchanted Glass: Britain and its Monarchy*, London, 1988, p. 239.
9. Bruce Lenman, *Integration, Enlightenment and Industrialisation: Scotland 1746–1832*, London, 1981, p. 1.
10. William Ferguson, *Scotland, 1689 to the Present*, Edinburgh, 1968, p. 147.
11. G. S. Pryde, *Scotland from 1603 to the Present Day*, Edinburtgh, 1962, p. 66.
12. Lenman, *Integration, Enlightenment and Industrialisation: Scotland 1746–1832*, p. 144.
13. David McCrone, *Understanding Scotland: the Sociology of a Stateless Nation*, London, 1992, p. 175.
14. Nairn, *The Break-Up of Britain*, p. 168.

15. McCrone, *Understanding Scotland*, p. 184.

16. Eric Hobsbawm, 'Introduction: Inventing Traditions', in Eric Hobsbawm and Terence Ranger, eds, *The Invention of Tradition*, Cambridge, 1992, pp. 1 and 2.

17. Hugh Trevor-Roper, 'The Invention of Tradition: the Highland Tradition of Scotland', in Hobsbawm and Ranger, eds, *The Invention of Tradition*, p. 15.

18. *Ibid.*, p. 19.

19. Michael Lynch, *Scotland, a New History*, London, 1992, p. 331.

20. Quoted in Bruce Lenman and John S. Gibson, *The Jacobite Threat – England, Scotland, Ireland, France: A Source Book*, Edinburgh, 1990, pp. 197–8.

21. Quoted in Winifred Duke, *The Rash Adventurer*, London, 1952, p. 106.

22. Trevor-Roper, 'The Invention of Tradition: the Highland Tradition of Scotland', *The Invention of Tradition*, p. 16.

23. But it is only fair to point out that one of the veteran Scotch Mythers, Colin McArthur, in 'Scottish Culture: a Reply to David McCrone', *Scottish Affairs*, No. 4 summer 1993, seems now to acknowledge the force of such criticisms.

24. That Jacobitism was 'historically meaningless' (whatever this might mean) is David Daiches' judgement in *The Paradox of Scottish Culture*, London, 1964, p. 16.

25. J. C. D. Clark, *English Society 1688–1832*, Cambridge, 1985, p. 143.

26. Quoted *ibid.*, p. 144.

27. Quoted *ibid.*, p. 142.

28. Quoted *ibid.*, p. 5.

29. H. T. Dickinson, *Liberty and Property: Political Ideology in Eighteenth-Century Britain*, London, 1977, p. 71.

30. Nairn, *The Enchanted Glass*, p. 152.

31. Murray Pittock, *The Invention of Scotland*, London and New York, 1991), p. 76.

32. Lenman, *Integration*, p. 126. A less jaundiced judgment on MacPherson is to be found in Malcolm Chapman, *The Gaelic Vision in Scottish Culture*, London, 1978 p. 48: '. . the Ossianic poems were written largely by MacPherson . . . they did, nevertheless, have a genuine Gaelic basis in both documentary and oral evidence, with which MacPherson was familiar.'

33. Pittock, *The Invention of Scotland*, p. 63.

34. Andy Stewart/Jimmy Blae, 'Song of Freedom', Lochside Music, 1975.

35. Quoted in J. C. D. Clark, *Revolution and Rebellion*, Cambridge 1986, p. 197.

36. F. McLynn, *The Jacobite Army in England, 1745*, Edinburgh, 1983, p. 197.

37. Ferguson, *Scotland, 1689 to the Present*.

38. Lynch, *Scotland, a New History*, p. 336.

39. *Ibid.*, p. 337.

40. Eric Linklater, *The Prince in the Heather*, London, 1965, p. 13.

41. Pittock, *The Invention of Scotland*, pp. 52–3.

42. Bruce Lenman, *The Jacobite Cause*, Glasgow, 1986, p. 117.
43. Lenman, *ibid*.
44. F. McLynn, *Charles Edward Stuart: A Tragedy in Many Acts*, London, 1988, p. 149.
45. John Prebble, *Culloden*, Harmondsworth, 1967, p. 288 and p. 290
46. McLynn, *Charles Edward*, pp. 159–60.
47. Clark, *Revolution and Rebellion*, pp. 62–3.
48. Lynch, *Scotland, a New History*, p. 338.
49. *Ibid.*, ch. 19.
50. Pittock, *The Invention of Scotland*, p. 95.
51. *Ibid.*, p. 117.
52. Lenman, *Integration, Enlightenment and Industrialisation*, p. 117.
53. *Ibid.*, p. iv.

Chapter 5

1. John Lough, quoted in David Allan, *Virtue, Learning and the Scottish Enlightenment*, Edinburgh, 1993, p. 4.
2. Neil McCallum, *A Small Country: Scotland 1700–1830*, Edinburgh, 1983, p. 57.
3. Nicholas Phillipson, quoted in Allan, *op. cit.*, p. 5.
4. Charles Camic, *Experience and Enlightenment*, 1983.
5. See for example Bourdieu's *Distinction* (1979) for his use of the concept.
6. Allan, *op. cit.*, p. 128.
7. Quoted *ibid.*, p. 56.
8. *Ibid.*, pp 170–1.
9. *Ibid.*, p. 54 .
10. Quoted *ibid.*, p. 80.
11. Quoted *ibid.*, p. 61.
12. Quoted *ibid.*, p. 62.
13. *Ibid.*, p. 80.
14. *Ibid.*, p. 85.
15. *Ibid.*, pp 85–6.
16. *Ibid.*, p. 96.
17. Quoted *ibid.*, p. 96.
18. *Ibid.*, p. 97.
19. Quoted *ibid.*, p. 96.
20. Quoted *ibid.*, p. 63.
21. Quoted *ibid.*, p. 63.
22. *Ibid.*, p. 127.
23. Quoted *ibid.*, p. 150.
24. *Ibid.*, p. 158
25. *Ibid.*, p. 174.
26. *Ibid.*, p. 176.
27. Quoted *ibid.*, p. 158.
28. Quoted *ibid.*, p. 175.
29. *Ibid.*, p. 175.
30. Quoted *ibid.*, p. 171.

31. *Ibid.*, p. 203.
32. *Ibid.*, p. 172.
33. Quoted *ibid.*, p. 172.
34. Quoted *ibid.*, pp 188–9.
35. *Ibid.*, pp 192–3.
36. Quoted *ibid.*, p. 216.
37. *Ibid.*, p. 213.
38. *Ibid.*, pp. 232–3.
39. *Ibid.*, p. 232.
40. *Ibid.*, p. 234.
41. *Ibid.*, pp. 234–5.
42. Angus Calder, 'Throwing light on a dark age of Scottish scholarship', *Scotland on Sunday*, July 25, 1993.

Chapter 6

1. Dean Ramsay, *Reminiscences of Scottish Life and Character*, London, n.d., quotations from conclusion.
2. Edwin Muir, *Scott and Scotland*, 1936; Polygon edition, Edinburgh, 1982, p. 113.
3. Andrew O'Hagan, 'Scotland's Fine Mess', *The Guardian*, July 23, 1994.
4. Angus Calder, 'A Song of Our Own', *The Scotsman*, June 25, 1994.
5. David McCrone, *Understanding Scotland: the Sociology of a Stateless Nation*, London, 1992.
6. John Osmond, *The Divided Kingdom*, London, 1988, p. 193.
7. Linda Colley, *Britons: Forging the Nation, 1707–1837*, New Haven and London, 1992.
8. Colin Kidd, *Subverting Scotland's Past: Scottish Whig Historians and the Creation of an Anglo-British Identity, 1689–c.1830*, Cambridge, 1993.
9. *Ibid.*, p. 29.
10. *Ibid.*, p. 69.
11. *Ibid.*, p. 215.
12. *Ibid.*, p. 129.
13. *Ibid.*, p. 209.
14. Sir John Dalrymple, quoted *ibid.*, p. 210.
15. *Ibid.*, p. 214.
16. *Ibid.*, p. 245.
17. *Ibid.*, p. 267.
18. *Ibid.*, p. 280.
19. *Ibid.*, p. 28.
20. *Ibid.*, p. 79.
21. *Ibid.*, p. 208.
22. *Ibid.*, p. 207.
23. *Ibid.*, p. 256.
24. *Ibid.*, p. ix.

25. We have presented our criticisms of what we here call the English-whig conception of pre-Union Scotland in *The Eclipse of Scottish Culture*, Edinburgh, 1989, especially chs 1–3. For other critical comments on this conception, see, for example, K. E. Wrightson, 'Kindred Adjoining Kingdoms', in R. A. Houston and I. D. White, eds, *Scottish Society 1500–1800*, Cambridge, 1989, and David Allan, *Virtue, Learning and the Scottish Enlightenment*, London, 1993.

26. Alasdair MacIntyre, *Whose Justice? Which Rationality?*, London, 1988, p. 214.

27. *Ibid.*, p. 217.

28. Quoted *ibid.*, pp. 228–9.

29. *Ibid.*, pp. 222–3.

30. *Ibid.*, pp. 226–7.

31. *Ibid.*, p. 227.

32. Quoted *ibid.*, p. 227.

33. Quoted *ibid.*, pp. 232–3.

34. *Ibid.*, p. 235.

35. *Ibid.*, p. 239.

36. *Ibid.*, p. 248.

37. *Ibid.*, p. 280.

38. *Ibid.*, p. 277.

39. *Ibid.*, p. 272.

40. *Ibid.*, p. 269.

41. See *A Treatise of Human Nature*, 1, iv, 7.

42. Quoted in MacIntyre, *op. cit.* p. 294.

43. *Ibid.*

44. Quoted *ibid.*, p. 294.

45. *Ibid.*, p. 309.

46. Nicholas Phillipson, *Hume*, London, 1989, p. 141.

Chapter 7

1. T. C. Smout, *A Century of the Scottish People, 1830–1950*, London, 1986, p. 5.

2. *Ibid.*, p. 207.

3. Quoted in William Storrar, *Scottish Identity: a Christian Vision*, Edinburgh, 1990, pp. 74-5.

4. These particular phrases are taken from a recent example of the genre: Graham Walker, 'The Orange Order in Scotland between the Wars', *International Review of Social History*, XXXVII, 1992, No. 2.

5. Luchesius Smits, *Saint Augustin dans l'oeuvre de Jean Calvin*, 2 vols; Assen, 1957–8, p. 259.

6. Quoted in George Davie, *The Crisis of the Democratic Intellect*, Edinburgh, 1985, p. 52.

7. *Ibid.*, p. 50.

8. P. H. Partridge, 'Anderson as Educator', in John Anderson, *Education and Inquiry*, ed. D. Z. Phillips; Oxford, 1980, p. 6.

9. Quoted in Davie, *op. cit.*, p. 86.
10. Alasdair MacIntyre, *After Virtue: a Study in Moral Theory*, 2nd edition, London, 1985, p. 277.
11. Alasdair MacIntyre, *Whose Justice? Which Rationality?*, London, 1988, p. 10.
12. Terry Eagleton, *The Ideology of the Aesthetic*, Oxford, 1990, p. 228.
13. *Ibid.*, p. 202. Italics in original.
14. *Ibid.*, p. 215.
15. *Ibid.*, p. 230.
16. Hannah Arendt, personal letter to James Baldwin, quoted in James Campbell, *Talking at the Gates: a Life of James Baldwin*, London, 1991, p. 162.
17. Jurgen Habermas, 'What does Socialism Mean Today?', English version in *New Left Review*, No. 183, September–October, 1990.
18. Charles Taylor, *Sources of the Self: the Making of Modern Identity*, Cambridge, 1989, p. 79.
19. Karl Marx, *Capital*, Vol. III, ch. 48.
20. Christopher Norris, *Deconstruction: Theory and Practice*, London, 1982, p. 61.
21. Onara O'Neill, *Constructions of Reason: Explorations in Kant's Practical Philosophy*, Cambridge, 1989, p. 145.
22. Alasdair MacIntyre, *Whose Justice? Which Rationality?*, p. 7.
23. Quoted in Peter Gay, *The Enlightenment: an Interpretation*, Vol. 1, *The Rise of Modern Paganism*, London, 1970, p. 23.
24. MacIntyre, *Whose Justice? Which Rationality?*, p. 193.
25. MacIntyre, *After Virtue*, p. 222. The concept of a tradition is notoriously problematic. For further details on MacIntyre's definition, see the MacIntyre symposium in *Philosophy and Phenomenological Research*, Vol. LI, No. 1, March, 1991, and in particular there Schneewind's criticisms and MacIntyre's response.
26. Taylor, *op. cit.*, p. 72.
27. MacIntyre, *Whose Justice? Which Rationality?*, p. 350.
28. Allan Bloom, *The Closing of the American Mind*, Harmondsworth, 1987, p. 25.
29. MacIntyre, *Whose Justice? Which Rationality?*, p. 395.
30. *Ibid.*, p. 397.
31. *Ibid.*, p. 396.
32. *Ibid.*, p. 398.

Chapter 8

1. The phrase is used by G. W. R. Ardley in describing the philosophy of education of William Anderson, the Scot (and brother of John Anderson) who was Professor of Philosophy at Auckland (1921–58). See Ardley's 'William Anderson as Educator', *Chapman*, No. 58, 1989.
2. John Anderson, *Education and Inquiry*, ed. D. Z. Phillips; Oxford, 1980.
3. George Davie, *The Democratic Intellect*, Edinburgh, 1961.

4. D. D. Raphael, *Adam Smith*, Oxford, 1985, p. 102.
5. George Davie, *The Crisis of the Democratic Intellect: the Problem of Generalism and Specialisation in Twentieth-Century Scotland*, Edinburgh, 1986, pp. 51–3.
6. Alasdair MacIntyre, *Three Rival Versions of Moral Inquiry: Encyclopaedia, Genealogy, and Tradition*, London, 1990, p. 168.
7. *Ibid.*, p. 221.
8. *Ibid.*, p. 8.
9. William Ferguson, *Scotland 1689 to the Present*, Edinburgh and London, p. 217.
10. Tom Nairn, *The Break-Up of Britain: Crisis and Neo-nationalism*, London, 1981, p. 116.
11. Alexander Broadie, *The Tradition of Scottish Philosophy: a New Perspective on the Enlightenment*, Edinburgh, 1990.
12. *Encyclopedia Britannica*, 15th edition; Chicago, 1992.
13. Frazer, Lang and McLennan are mentioned by Freud in the first chapter of *Totem and Taboo*.
14. Robert Ackerman, *J. G. Frazer: his Life and Work*, Canto edition, 1990, pp 255–6.
15. Robert Crawford, 'Frazer and Scottish Romanticism: Scott, Stevenson and *The Golden Bough*', in Robert Fraser, ed., *Sir James Frazer and the Literary Imagination*, London, 1990.
16. Robert Fraser, *The Making of the Golden Bough*, London, 1990, p. 212.
17. Alec R. Vidler, *The Church in an Age of Revolution: 1789 to the Present Day*, Harmondsworth, 1961, pp. 172–3.
18. Quoted in Ackerman, *op. cit.*, p. 60.
19. On Smith's influence on Durkheim, see Steven Lukes, *Durkheim*. George Davie, 'Scottish Philosophy and Robertson Smith', *Edinburgh Review*, no. 69, is a rare and fascinating essay, which ends by lamenting the astonishing neglect of nineteenth-century intellectual life in Scotland: 'the Scots perversely preoccupy themselves only with the side of their nineteenth-century history which shows their country to have been a failure', p. 96.
20. Edward Said, *Orientalism*, Harmondsworth, 1991, p. 235.
21. Stanley L. Jaki, *Lord Gifford and his Lectures*, Edinburgh, 1986.
22. MacIntyre, *op. cit.*, p. 225.
23. *Ibid.*, p. 117.
24. Bertrand Russell, *The Problems of Philosophy*, London, 1912.
25. MacIntyre, *op. cit.*, p.151.
26. *Ibid.*; pp 79–80.
27. *Ibid.*, p. 231.
28. *Ibid.*, pp 60–1.
29. *Ibid.*, p. 84.
30. *Ibid.*, p. 91.
31. *Ibid.*, p. 63.
32. Barry Barnes, 'Thomas Kuhn', in Quentin Skinner, ed., *The Return of Grand Theory in the Human Sciences*, Canto edition, 1990, p. 90.

33. MacIntyre, *op. cit.*, p. 102.
34. See for instance Alan Bloom, *The Closing of the American Mind*, Harmondsworth, 1987.
35. MacIntyre, *op. cit.*, pp 227–8.
36. *Ibid.*, pp. 229–30.
37. *Ibid.*, p. 222.
38. See for example Charles Martindale, 'Tradition and Modernity', in *History of the Human Sciences*, Vol. 5, No. 3, August 1992.

Chapter 9

1. Gilles Lipovetsky, *L'ère du vide*, Paris, 1983.
2. Colin Kirkwood, *Vulgar Eloquence: from Labour to Liberation*, Edinburgh, 1990.
3. Tom Nairn, *The Enchanted Glass: Britain and its Monarchy*, London, 1988.
4. For a discussion of Marcuse's view, see Alasdair MacIntyre, *Marcuse*, London, 1970, p. 92.
5. David Hume, *A Treatise of Human Nature*, Penguin Classics edition, Harmondsworth, 1984, p. 462.
6. M. F. Burnyeat,'Aristotle on learning to be good', reprinted in Ted Honderich, ed., *Philosophy through its Past*, Harmondsworth, 1984, p. 73.
7. Charles Guignon, 'Authenticity, moral values, and psychotherapy', in Guignon, ed., *The Cambridge Companion to Heidegger*, Cambridge, 1993, p. 223.
8. Charles Taylor, *Sources of the Self: the Making of the Modern Identity*, Cambridge, 1989, p. 47.
9. R. D. Laing, 'A Note to "The Politics of Experience"', *Edinburgh Review*, No. 84, 1990.
10. Alasdair MacIntyre, *Three Rival Versions of Moral Inquiry*, London, 1990, p. 140
11. Charles Taylor, *op. cit.*, p. 57.
12. Alasdair MacIntyre, *Three Rival Versions of Moral Inquiry*, pp. 235–6.
13. David McCrone, *Understanding Scotland: the Sociology of a Stateless Nation*, London, 1992, p. 4.
14. *Ibid.*, p. 4.
15. Adam Smith, *The Wealth of Nations*, Book 5, ch. 7.
16. Richard Bernstein, *The New Constellation*, Oxford, 1991, p. 335.
17. Alasdair MacIntyre, 'Philosophy, the "Other" Disciplines and their Histories: a Rejoinder to Richard Rorty', in *Soundings*, 1981, No. 135
18. McCrone, *op. cit.*, p. 32.
19. *Ibid.*, p. 30.
20. *Ibid.*, p. 30.
21. Alasdair MacIntyre, *After Virtue: a Study in Moral Theory*, 2nd edition, London, 1985, p. 222.
22. McCrone, op. cit.,p. 195.

23. Ernest Gellner, *The Psychoanalytic Movement: or the Coming of Unreason*, London, 1985, p. 14.
24. Alasdair MacIntyre, *Whose Justice? Which Rationality?*, London, 1988, p. 368.

Index